PUBLIC ORGANIZATION MANAGEMENT

PUBLIC ORGANIZATION MANAGEMENT

The Development of Theory and Process

Jamil E. Jreisat

Westport, Connecticut
London

The Library of Congress has cataloged the hardcover edition as follows:

Jreisat, Jamil E.
    Public organization management : the development of theory and
    process / Jamil E. Jreisat.
        p.   cm.
    Includes bibliographical references and index.
    ISBN 1–56720–121–0 (alk. paper)
    1. Public administration.   2. Public administration—History.
    I. Title.
    JF1351.J76   1997
    351—dc21   97–8853

British Library Cataloguing in Publication Data is available.

A hardcover edition of *Public Organization Management* is available from
Quorum Books, an imprint of Greenwood Publishing Group, Inc.
(ISBN 1–56720–121–0)

Library of Congress Catalog Card Number: 97–8853
ISBN: 0–275–96767–0 (pbk.)

First published in 1997

Praeger Publishers, 88 Post Road West, Westport, CT 06881
An imprint of Greenwood Publishing Group, Inc.
www.praeger.com

Printed in the United States of America

The paper used in this book complies with the
Permanent Paper Standard issued by the National
Information Standards Organization (Z39.48–1984).

P

Contents

Preface

Public management is reasoned, purposeful action in the context of a public organization. It is knowledge and skills, attitudes and commitment. A determining aspect of public management is the capacity to adapt to changing conditions in its environment, whether demographic, political, economic, technological, or social.

Over the years, scholars and practitioners have advanced myriad concepts and techniques on how to correctly manage organizations to best serve society's needs and demands. In this book, I seek to establish linkages and a sense of progression in the development of theory and practice of public management. The evaluations I provide are stimulated by considerations of utility and application of administrative knowledge. Because the highest objective of most tinkering with organizations is to improve their performance, the reader should find in this book many promising ideas for change and refinement of managerial processes.

For decades, I have been studying, researching, and teaching how to manage public organizations efficiently and effectively and how to change them deliberately and successfully. Ultimately, improvement of performance is measured in terms of increased output, reduced cost, improved quality, and elevated levels of satisfaction of employees and citizens. The profession of management, therefore, continues to be challenged to develop administrative institutions that work and to reform those that do not.

This volume is an expansion and update of my earlier work (*Managing Public Organizations*, 1992). The feedback on the 1992 book from students and colleagues has been most gratifying. The favorable responses encouraged me to pursue this project, which expands and refocuses the discussions in many areas, particularly those on leadership, the drive for quality management, the political environment, and the "reinvention" of government movement.

Finally, I shall not burden the reader with acknowledgments in a lengthy list of names of people in the management profession who influenced my thinking over the years, but I would like to single out students in the Public Administration Program at the University of South Florida, my permanent base, and at the Askew School of Public Administration and Policy, Florida State University, where I visited in 1996 and 1997. They gave me the opportunity to share with them my information and analysis and to receive from them enlightened and practical reactions.

Also, I express a profound appreciation for the professionalism of the editors at Greenwood's Quorum Books with whom I worked on this project. In particular, I am thankful to James Ice, Alan Sturmer, Catherine Lyons, and Ellen Dorosh.

1

Introduction

Organizations permeate contemporary societies and render essential services to both public and private functions. Governments, at all levels, depend on public organizations in formulation and in implementation of public policies. Public organizations deliver vital services to citizens, ranging from regulating traffic and providing education and health care to protection of the environment and defense of the country. Because of their indispensable roles to society, organizations have been the subject of study by scholars from various fields of knowledge. Over the years, notable conceptual and practical contributions originated in fields such as anthropology, sociology, psychology, political science, public administration, and law.

Consequently, theories of organization vary without being exclusive. These theories often converge, overlap, extend other theories, or force adaptation and rethinking of existing ones. For illustration, consider the following examples.

In a system perspective, the organizational pattern consists of a self-regulating social system that maintains certain essential consistency or repeated cycles of input, transformation, output, and renewed input (Katz & Kahn 1982, pp. 14–28). Emphasizing the social feature, organizations also are seen as small societies in which people create for themselves shared meanings, symbols, norms, and cognitive schemes that allow them to create and maintain meaningful interactions between themselves and in relation to the world beyond their small society (Argyris & Schon 1978, p. 327; Schein 1985, pp. 1–9). Thus, focusing on the individual and the small group is most relevant for understanding behavior in the organization and for explaining variables such as employee performance, satisfaction, motivation, absenteeism, and turnover.

Inquiries on the nature of organizations and how they function generated concepts that are compatible with a definition of the organization as a cooperative system. Thus perceived, the organization is regarded as an adaptive social structure, made up of interacting individuals, subgroups, and informal plus formal relationships in the tradition of Chester Barnard and Philip Selznick. This tradition, in fact, has been instrumental in stimulating and in profiling a new image of organizations since the 1940s. As a social, cooperative system, the organization also exhibits clear organic characteristics, autonomously interacting with its environment. As such, Gareth Morgan (1986, p. 40) notes that "organization theory has become a kind of biology in which the distinctions and relations among *molecules, cells, complex organisms, species,* and *ecology* are paralleled in those between *individuals, groups, organizations, populations (species) of organizations,* and their *social ecology.*"

Perhaps the most widely known characterization of the organization is its bureaucratic features, such as defined roles, hierarchically arranged lines of authority and control, rationally coordinated functions, and programs to maximize the benefits of specialization and division of labor. These constructed, bureaucratic organizations are considered most efficient and effective instruments to accomplish larger societal goals, beyond and above their impacts upon their members (Perrow 1984, p. 6). The organization as a bureaucracy is a classic theoretical formulation that has become a fountain of operational folklore based on popular stories of blunder and incompetent performance, real and imagined, but often augmented by mass media and political campaigns.

Yet another conception of the organization is as a polity and its leader as a "statesman"; this has special appeal to students of government. In this image, the organization is made up of contending parties and divided powers, applying processes of conflict resolution and vying for control of resources, and perpetually attempting to adapt and change its organizational forms and practices (Selznick 1957, pp. 4–5). This is congruent with frameworks that emphasize the legitimizing effects of structurally determined power in organizational decision making.

Each of these images of the organization — a system, a bureaucratic structure, a subculture, or a polity — offers distinctive properties, but none by itself offers a complete picture of organizational life. The multiplicity of theories and models and the lack of a unified theoretical view have inspired the phrase "management theory jungle." Nevertheless, by the end of the twentieth century, a remarkable accumulation of knowledge and experience has developed about organizational variables and their interactions. Actually, the process of revising and modifying knowledge of organizations seems incessant. It is important, however, to emphasize that contemporary organization theories do not convey sequential relationships in which one theory induces another. Rather, the theoretical evolution has been like a mosaic of particular concepts that somehow are connected to produce a larger view than any one detached piece could. Perhaps a useful way to conceive the variation, as Morgan (1986, p. 39) points out, is to "identify different species of organization in different kinds of environments."

Thus, professional management of public organizations requires constant analysis and evaluation of operations, policies, values, and contexts. Unlike the natural sciences, each with its core of proven axioms, students of public management continually search for conceptualizations of the organization that are realistic and practical. On the surface, the search offers public management a challenge to learn and to develop. In reality, this learning is most productive when the strategic mission of the organization is understood and when the professional ethics of its management are above reproach. If leadership is vital at the strategic organizational apex, overall capacity of management — applied through neutral competence and professional values — is indispensable for effectively directing dynamic impulses of change.

Actually, new management theories and innovative techniques regularly evolve, supplying fresh materials for teaching, publishing, and training. This situation often is creatively exploited by dedicated consultants who excel in packaging, advertising, and glamorizing management ideas far beyond their presumed practical benefits. Whether by design or not, this intellectual productivity often appears more of trendy tendencies than authentic creation of new knowledge. Irrespective of faith in market forces, practitioners and academicians have not been able to properly appraise and sift through the successive approaches to organizational management in a timely fashion. As a result, managers frequently express dismissive attitudes that inevitably risk disregarding some potentially valuable information.

Periodically, practitioners' frustration surfaces in various forms. As Jonathan Walters (1996, p. 49) points out, "the phenomenon of dueling management theories is hardly exclusive to government." However, Walters contends that the list of trends being embraced and discarded by state and local governments these days is long and growing. His evidence: hundreds of governments are getting into Total Quality Management, managing for results, benchmarking, reengineering, value engineering, privatizing, systems management, competitive contracting, and so forth, all with varying degrees of commitment, sophistication, and success. Hence, practitioners disagree with approaches that have been disparagingly branded "management by best-seller" or "management flavor of the month" (p. 49).

Although the true impact is hard to measure, the cost and time spent on consultants' assessments and in training programs in topics of doubtful benefits to operations can be quite onerous to public employees. In fact, popular magazines have reported a widespread manipulation of the market behind the ascendancy of certain management frameworks (Green 1995, p. 8). Specifically, books on the "reengineering revolution" were propelled to the bestseller lists through manipulation of large consultancy firms where the authors work. The headline in one magazine reads: "A scam over a 'best-selling' business book shows how obsessed management consultancies have become with producing the next big idea" (*The Economist* 1995, p. 57).

Despite conceptual variation or market manipulation of ideas, all organizations share common attributes. Organizations commonly are viewed as consciously coordinated activities of two or more people to accomplish defined goals. Thus, organizations have specific objectives, known boundaries and locations, explicit systems of communication and coordination, and fairly identifiable financial and human resources. At the same time, organizations may differ significantly in size, overall efficiency and effectiveness, and type of technology they employ as well as in levels of citizens' support and the nature of tasks they perform. The advantages are simply that, through organizations, societies are able to accomplish more and greater tasks than an individual alone could ever hope for. The most significant and lasting accomplishments of human civilizations have been largely through organizations. Whether building the great pyramids of Egypt or constructing the modern highways in the United States, manufacturing and distributing thousands of commodities, or landing on the surface of the moon, organizations have been the key to all such abilities.

Appropriately, the search is continuous to define the public organization as a unit of analysis and to understand the contextual influences that determine its behavior and performance. "The big questions facing public administration," Francis Neumann (1996, p. 412) points out, are to probe into the nature of the public organization and how it relates to its environment. Such endeavor is constant because it has been central to public administration education. This book aims to examine critical features of public organizations and their relationships with their contexts while focusing on what is significant in public organizational management.

PREMISE AND PLAN

The challenge for the study of organizational management is to realistically delineate salient and representative concepts and practices that have advanced knowledge or augmented the operational capacity of public organizations. At the outset, these important choices have been implicitly and explicitly defining this discussion and orienting the analysis throughout this project:

First, it is essential to recognize that public organizations have their own internal processes and dynamics and continually interact with an intrusive but crucial environment. These organizations encompass many elements — people, structure, technology, and material resources — all of which are coordinated in complex processes geared to accomplish certain goals.

Second, overall goals of a public organization usually are defined within the parameters of legitimate public policy. To ensure compliance, the political context applies a host of procedural and institutional mechanisms of control, inspection, audit, legislative oversight, and so forth.

Third, a system of coordination is essential to unify the various processes of work and to ensure continuity of managerial functions of decision making, evaluation, communication, and monitoring.

Fourth, because people are the most important resource of the organization, issues of motivation, inducement, and adaptation are central to managerial performance as well as to increasing employee satisfaction, cooperation, and cohesion.

Fifth, no other position in the organization has greater impact on its total performance than its leaders. Leaders represent the organization to its environment, define its mission, mobilize necessary resources, defend its interests, resolve its internal and external conflicts, and so forth.

Finally, organizational exchange across boundaries invites interaction and mutual influence with significant political, legal, economic, and cultural elements in the external environment. Public organizations cannot survive for too long as closed systems. They have permeable boundaries and regularly interact within their political context. They respond to economic conditions, accommodate citizens' views and preferences, and continually search for outside support.

Once an organization is created, it acquires a relative independence and stability in relation to individuals and society. Herbert Kaufman (1976) has examined the staying power of public bureaucracies and concluded that the death rate of government agencies during a 50-year period was less than half the annual number of failures of business organizations. Public agencies are comparatively stable social structures — as long as their exchanges with the external world are satisfactory. Also, all organizations have a sort of dual personality: formal and informal. The first relates to fairly established structures and formalized codes, laws, and roles. The second, clearly identified and articulated by Barnard (1962), is the aggregate of personal contacts and interactions of associated groupings of people without specific conscious joint purpose.

The conceptual diversity of organizations expanded the domain of analysis in significant ways. In fact, research on cognition, motivation, attitude formation, and individual hierarchy of needs is routinely harmonized and synthesized with contemporary analysis of organizations. Whether we deal with organizational design, change, decision making, or conflict resolution and goal setting, knowledge of individual and group behavior can only enrich our analysis. At the same time, the internal organizational processes, despite their importance, are not sufficient for understanding the operational dynamics. The context or the environment within which the organization operates is crucial. In fact, administrators themselves are actors in a political system that embraces a wide range of other actors, governmental and nongovernmental. Here, public managers learn the significance of relating their functions to those of the political order that surrounds them.

Public agencies implement laws determined by legislators, approved by chief executives, and, frequently, interpreted, reviewed, and adjudicated by courts. The special relationship between public bureaucracies and other segments of the government makes the bureaucracy a partner in the political process, rather than a disposable technical tool for implementation of public policy. The exchange between bureaucracy and legislators, for example, involves more than the statutory "authority to operate"; it includes information, expertise, advice, definition of public policy, and determination of societal needs.

Interactions between chief executives (president, governor, or mayor) and their administrative staffs are also complex and multifaceted. As with legislators, the traffic between the bureaucracy and offices of chief executives frequently takes place in both directions. Too, public bureaucracy interacts with other forces in the society that are outside the political structure but are tied to social and economic formations. Employment level in the economy, taxation policy, and educational opportunities, for example, evoke certain alternatives and bar others, as we often see reflected in personnel and budgetary decisions of public agencies. Indeed, one of the most crucial exchanges for public organizations is with citizens receiving public services. In fact, citizens, as voters and taxpayers, provide essential financial and human resources; their support is also a source of legitimacy to operations of public agencies.

Thus, the attempt here is to examine the multiplicity of managerial issues related to public organizations in a coherent, realistic, and uncluttered way. The specific plan of this book consists of the following components:

Chapter 1 introduces conceptual and definitional matters and defines the parameters of the book.

Chapter 2 outlines the formative years and the crucial forces that influenced the cumulative development of modern public administration in response to legal, political, and economic needs.

Chapter 3 discusses critical features and functions of theory and process of public organizations.

Chapter 4 examines how political, legal, economic, and cultural elements of the environment influence the management of public organizations.

Chapter 5 explains basic premises and practical effects of the classic approaches: scientific management, administrative management, and the bureaucratic model.

Chapter 6 defines human relations perspectives and criticisms against them.

Chapter 7 focuses on attempts to synthesize structuralist and humanist perspectives into more realistic and comprehensive frameworks, such as neobureaucratic and systems analysis.

Chapter 8 examines decision making and communication as major functional processes determining organizational performance.

Chapter 9 presents influential perspectives on organization leadership.

Chapter 10 deals with organizational culture and the growing recognition of its significance in managing modern organizations.

Chapter 11 considers recent campaigns for reforming management and for building the capacities of public organizations.

Chapter 12 expands the search for the ultimate purpose of all tinkering with organizational management: improving performance.

Chapter 13 draws some final managerial conclusions.

REFERENCES

Argyris, Chris and Donald A. Schon. 1978. *Organizational Learning: A Theory of Action Perspective*. Reading, MA: Addison-Wesley.

Barnard, Chester I. 1962. *The Functions of the Executive*. Cambridge, MA: Harvard University Press.

Green, Hardy. 1995. Reengineering Royalties. *Business Week*, June 12.

Katz, Daniel and Robert Kahn. 1982. *The Social Psychology of Organizations*, 3rd ed. New York: John Wiley.

Kaufman, Herbert. 1976. *Are Government Organizations Immortal?* Washington, DC: Brookings Institution.

Management Focus: Manufacturing Best-Sellers. 1995. *The Economist*, August 15.

Morgan, Gareth. 1986. *Images of Organization*. Beverly Hills, CA: Sage.

Neumann, Francis, Jr. 1996. What Makes Public Administration a Science, Or, Are Its "Big Questions" Really Big? *Public Administration Review*, 56, 5 (September-October).

Perrow, Charles. 1984. *Complex Organizations: A Critical Essay*, 3rd ed. Glenview, IL: Scott, Foresman.

Schein, Edgar H. 1985. *Organizational Culture and Leadership*. San Francisco, CA: Jossey-Bass.

Selznick, Philip. 1957. *Leadership and Administration*. New York: Harper & Row.

Walters, Jonathan. 1996. Management Fads. *Governing* 9 (September).

2

Public Administration:
A Developmental Perspective

As a field of study, public administration is more than the sum of its managerial techniques being fashionably applied at any period in modern history. I view administration of government affairs in a developmental perspective in order to accentuate important relationships and continuities in the evolution of the intellectual administrative legacy over time and place. Even if not tied in sequential relations, few significant concepts of modern organizational management are cut off totally from their forerunners. The justification for this approach is summarized in the following.

First, knowledge about social systems hardly is generated through sudden discoveries but rather evolves cumulatively, each stage of evolution being linked to the one before it. Thus, continuity is vital and must be underscored in any realistic portrayal of the development of administrative knowledge and skills. Moreover, recognizing this continuity helps to "stabilize, moderate, and give meaning to change" (Scott, Michell, & Birnbaum 1981, p. 4).

Second, public administration aspiration for a mature, professional, and multidisciplinary standing requires greater acceptance of its intellectual heritage. A review of critical theoretical and methodological milestones in the evolution of public organization management suggests valuable explanatory information about change over time. This way, we realize that frameworks of basic concepts remain as common grounds, even if challenged from time to time. So far, no organizational model has completely nullified or rejected the notion that the basis of organization is rational coordination among human efforts to accomplish a defined goal. How, then, do we choose among theories and models that may not have a rational reason beyond the fact that a large number of academicians, practitioners, and consultants have made the transition that made the new perspective (model, paradigm) dominant. Thus, change from one theoretical perspective to another rarely is accompanied by fundamental change of reality. Until we have reliable tools to evaluate each theory for its utility, students of management have to contend with intractable anomalies by relying first and foremost on their own experiences and the educated judgments of their peers.

Third, viewing management developmentally indicates that the apparent contradictions in public administration are not always intrinsic or "genetic" to the field. Public administration often serves states forged through historical accidents or by arbitrary decisions or based on inconsistent philosophies. Also, many concepts and applications of organization and management emerged without specific prior designs or plans but according to needs and demands forcing managerial actions. The early U.S. administrative experience, for example, is a vivid illustration of the dynamic surge of public administration, generated in response to political and economic imperatives of the new state and developed as a particularly U.S. system of organization and management. In one sense, the U.S. experience is not entirely dissimilar to experiences of many developing countries at the dawn of independence.

Thus, complete separation of administration from its societal setting is unrealistic. Public administration development is part of the total institutional development of the society in its philosophical, political, technological, and economic dimensions. To be sure, various stages of this evolution have yielded some inconsistencies, but the overall thrust displays more continuity and coherence among the elements than has been conveyed by most current relativistic conceptual creations.

THE FORMATIVE YEARS

Knowledge of the larger scope of administration is important for the additional reason of articulating links between managerial capabilities and the development of the society they serve. For better or worse, Gerald Nash observes, "civilization and organization have been mutually dependent" (1969, p. 23). In fact, superior (effective) organizational and managerial abilities are major attributes of powerful and dominant societies through history. In his seminal work on *The Rise and Fall of the*

Great Powers, Paul Kennedy (1987, p. xv) underlines such connection as follows: "The relative strengths of the leading nations in world affairs never remain constant, principally because of the uneven rate of growth among different societies and of the technological and organizational breakthroughs which bring a greater advantage to one society than to another."

In fact, national development is unattainable without creating appropriate administrative and institutional structures with essential capacities for action. In all societies, developed and developing alike, bureaucratic organizations have served as the main instruments for achieving national objectives. As Milton Esman (1991, p. 20) points out, what most distinguishes advanced societies and their governments is not their cultures, or their natural endowments, or the availability of capital, or the rationality of public policies, but precisely the capacities of their institutions and management.

The predicament is that students in current programs on administration, anxiously attending to immediate and utilitarian aspects of their profession, often tend to miss the fundamental forces and the broad view of their field. Even administrative curricula repeatedly fail to reflect nonparochial views or to consider a wide range of human administrative experiences and their contextual linkages. This is a different issue altogether from the important refinements of such knowledge that have resulted from self-examination and from what Frederick Mosher (1975, p. 5) calls the "thoughtful introspection about where we are, how we got here, and whither we are tending."

History and standing monuments convey that several ancient empires, such as the Roman, Greek, Persian, Arab, and Chinese, had utilized their own approaches and skills, which often required fairly refined and complex organizational concepts and processes to attain goals of the state and its leaders. Thus, management has been utilized universally for the achievement of great goals, and administration is an old subject that continually changes. Yet, Western literature has been highly selective among human experiences, and not because of objective considerations.

The earliest administrative practices can be traced back 6,000 years to the origin of organized social systems in the Middle East and other sites of ancient civilizations. For example, one divine king of Babylon named Hammurabi (2123–2081 B.C.) issued for his state (in Iraq today) a unique code of 282 laws that governed business dealings, personal behavior, interpersonal relations, wages, punishments, and a host of other societal matters (Wren 1979, p. 16). This is probably the precursor of all known written constitutions and public laws in the history of mankind.

A list of contributions to administrative knowledge, compiled by Jay Shafritz and J. Steven Ott (1996, pp. 11–13), illustrates greater continuity of administrative knowledge than has been acknowledged so far in Western scholarship. The following three examples, from different cultures (Greek, Arab, and Italian), challenge the intellectual "establishment" in organization theory to welcome new or contradictory ideas from other places (Clegg, Hardy, & Nord 1996, p. 7). We find no indication in the background information to acknowledge that Aristotle (360 B.C.), in *The Politics*, asserts that the specific nature of executive powers and functions cannot be the same for all states (organizations) but must reflect their specific cultural environment. There also is no significant reference to Ibn Khaldun (A.D. fourteenth century), who argues in *Al Muqaddimah: An Introduction to History* that organizational improvement can be developed through the science of culture. He specifically introduces concepts of formal and informal organization, organizations as natural organisms, and esprit de corps.

Perhaps Machiavelli (A.D. sixteenth century) has less of a problem of recognition in the West because of location as well as interests of the political science field. In *The Discourses*, Machiavelli counsels in favor of the principle of "unity of command." He acknowledges that "[I]t is better to confine any expedition to a single man of ordinary ability, rather than to two, even though they are of the highest merit, and both having equal ability."

Contemporary literature extends measured consideration to the European practices of the seventeenth century as precursors to the emergence of modern bureaucracies. The period of the seventeenth century and after is a foundation phase and an excellent source of information on administrative structures and the influences that shaped them. As E. N. Gladden (1972, p. 141) points out, early in the seventeenth century, power drew away from the provinces and localities of Europe and became concentrated in the central government, requiring the active aid and development of administration and finance. Those early changes resulted in strengthening the bureaucratic elements and improving the information services for governmental use. During this time, Germany led the West in "professionalizing" the public service. Government activities and services expanded, creating a need for appointees with particular knowledge and skills. Also, Gladden (1972, pp. 158, 163) indicates that Prussia had the distinction of being the first modern state to introduce and develop a system of entrance examinations for the public service. This system involved the central administration and the individual departments. It comprised both oral and written tests in subjects of a practical as well as academic nature. Reading, writing, arithmetic, and law were emphasized in these competency tests. Frederick William II of Prussia worked through a privy council, which deliberated and acted with him as a unifying and supreme authority. Beginning as a strictly advisory body, the council acquired definite executive powers. The administration became specialized into departments, some of whose chiefs sat on the council, where their specialized knowledge could aid in decision making.

The role of education and specialized training to attain necessary skills to manage government operations became quite obvious at an early phase. The German state took the initiative to ensure that suitable instruction was available at the universities. As early as 1727, Frederick William I established a chair in cameralism at two German universities to give instruction "in efficient administration and government of towns" (Gladden 1972, p. 162), among other subjects. The death of Frederick William II transformed the Prussian administration. By 1808, an aristocratic regulative bureaucracy had replaced the royal autocracy of king and council. The career bureaucrats invariably were selected from the intellectual elite of the nation by means of rigorous examinations. This created a sort of aristocracy of experts who purported to be true representatives of the general interest (Gladden 1972, p. 165).

REVOLUTION AND ADMINISTRATION

Between 1650 and 1850, the West experienced significant political and economic upheaval that resulted in reexamination and restructuring of its administrative systems. Historically, the West experienced revolutions against the status quo, but soon the consequences became far-reaching and universal. The English Revolution of 1688, the American Revolution of 1776, the French Revolution of 1789, and the industrial revolution extended over several decades to the beginning of the twentieth century. Their individual and their collective impacts have been profound: political, economic, and administrative changes first within a particular society and then far beyond.

The French Revolution was driven by hungry citizens who revolted against the whole slumping political and economic structure of privileges and monopolies granted by the king. This revolution made it the duty of government to provide for welfare of the people; it transformed the nature of politics (as well as administration) by the dramatic introduction of notions such as citizen, right, liberty, equality, and social and political justice.

The American Revolution, on the other hand, was managed differently by men of different outlooks and experiences. As the common wisdom had it, these men sought to reflect the Anglo-Saxon tradition, particularly the ideas of John Locke, David Hume, and Adam Smith. However, as discussed below, contemporary historians and researchers are finding evidence that the "story of how European immigrants to America shared ideas with native peoples goes much deeper" (Johansen 1990, p. 279). In all of this, the autonomy and will of the individual are paramount, no matter what final political and economic designs were to be forged.

By the middle of the nineteenth century, the feudalistic-economic order dissolved and commercialism emerged, followed by the industrial revolution. As commercialism expanded, new urban centers took shape. Power struggles intensified for seaways, colonization of other territories, and domination of world trade. Western imperialistic expansions affected almost every area of the known world, particularly Asia and Africa.

On the political level, many important philosophical and practical changes were in the making. In England, the birth of constitutionalism inhibited the arbitrary rule of the Crown and instituted the supremacy of the Parliament. In France, the attack on the excessive central authority set the stage for new centralized structures, such as those governing local authorities initiated during the Napoleonic period. In both France and England, the orientation and the structures of public institutions were dramatically altered. Managing the affairs of the state in the context of the new political and economic realities required different levels of skill, commitment, and values.

A revolution is the subversion and the renunciation of the status quo for the promise of a better alternative. Thus, these British, French, and American political revolutions ushered in more than dazzling political alternatives; they also laid the foundations of the "organizational society," as we know it, along with advancement of modern values such as reason, liberation, and justice for all. By official design as well as a result of new socioeconomic realities, formal organizations and professional management became indispensable for the new states. Organizations as newly invigorated social structures and professional management, which had gained more autonomy in practicing their specialized craft, both became the trusted enforcers of public decisions. These public decisions became bound to the public will rather than personal authoritarian commands. The style of public decisions finally was aimed at representation of societal interests rather than individual wants of the powerful, as in the past.

The industrial revolution, too, sharpened, refined, and rationalized the managerial concepts and practices in order to serve capitalist objectives, the maximization of capital returns on investments. The new organizational focus turned to rational theories that emphasized science, technology, and improved managerial practices. The organization became more confirmed as a sociotechnical instrument, essential for the attainment of great objectives envisioned by entrepreneurs as well as political leaders with expansionist views of the roles of their countries in the fast changing world order.

EARLY U.S. EXPERIENCES

Modern U.S. scholars of public administration are markedly reserved in recognizing the indebtedness of early U.S. public administration to the intellectual and vocational developments in other nations. Mosher (1975, p. 7) asserts: "It was for the most part an American invention, indigenous, and *sui generis*." However, as Michael Reed (1996, p. 33) points out, "[N]either the history of organization studies nor the way in which that history is told are neutral representations of past achievements." Indeed, interpretation of achievement and influence as well as their consequences always are open to disagreement and to refutation.

Links with European administrative and organizational thinking are difficult to ignore. Most conspicuously absent from the U.S. literature on government, however, is any reference or discussion of the impact, or lack of it, of the native (indigenous) systems of government in existence before the arrival of European settlers. Bruce Johansen (1990, p. 280) states, for example, that "[T]he Iroquois and other native confederacies that bordered the original thirteen colonies in the eighteenth century provided *a* model — one among many — that gave our founders raw material for their own unique, ideological constructs." In her research on native American governments, Sharon O'Brien (1989) depicts the rich heritage and the sophisticated democratic processes of government in operation when the Europeans discovered the New World. She points out that between 5 and 10 million people already were living in fairly complex political structures. Each system possessed its own language or dialect, its own set of traditions, and its own form of government (O'Brien 1989, p. 14).

The tribe was a basic unit for governing; each tribe was independent and sovereign with rights to structure itself, conduct foreign relations, trade with other nations, make its own laws, and regulate its own resources and property. O'Brien (1989, p. 16) describes this heritage as follows:

Indian governments in general were highly decentralized and democratic, based on rule by the people. Leaders lacked the power to dictate or to enforce their decisions. Their rule depended on their performance, their power of persuasion, and the respect they were accorded. . . . Tribes made decision based on consensus because their cultures stressed harmo ny of the whole. . . . Many tribal governments contained provisions for initiatives, referendums, and recall. The right of male and female suffrage was the norm among many tribes.

With some detail, O'Brien (1989, pp. 16–17) offers information about the daily operations of a general council, which discussed and decided on matters of general importance to native citizens. Deliberations of such a council indicate a deep sense of respect to the individual and to norms of participation. Leadership in such authority systems fell naturally to the elders, who were respected for their wisdom, and to individuals who exhibited fairness, bravery, or skills, depending on a community's needs. These leaders governed only by what we now call "consent of the governed."

It is difficult to establish, conclusively, links or to measure the extent of influence by the native American tradition of government on the early conception and design of the U.S. state system. Contemporary literature on U.S. government maintains almost a blackout on the rich indigenous heritage while chronicling every possible relationship and influence with European ideological patterns and, quite often, despotic practices.

Free from the dictatorial experiences that England, France, and other European systems were seeking to discard, the United States represented a different challenge. With independence in 1776, the 13 colonies had formed a confederation that left to each community its sovereignty and freedom. Their loose association was based more on the desire to break away from Britain than on a sense of nationhood. The task for the new leaders soon became one of forging a greater centralization of power — a necessity if the union was to survive.

The U.S. Constitution revitalized and reorganized the fundamental law that created three separate branches of government, sharing powers among them. This balancing act fashioned a new and uniquely U.S. political community, but also one without an administrative organization or function. Public administration was ignored or left unspecified in the Constitution and in the period following the drafting of it (Stillman 1990, p. 161; Mosher 1975, p. 8). This conclusion is only partially correct. Significant constitutional contributions to the administrative functioning of government were indirect and contextual, however. The Constitution determined the overall structural frame of the system, adapted norms and values of political discourse and behavior, and placed emphasis on checks and balances within a system of laws. True, no bureaucratic system was designed, and no specific organizational setting was assigned the tasks of enforcing policy decisions. This evolved later and gradually.

Other scholars focus almost exclusively on the U.S. domestic scene. Alice Stone and Donald Stone (1975) declare that public administration education in the United States was developed in response to national and local dissatisfaction with the performance of government. Rumblings of discontent were heard even before the turn of the century, during the corrupt period following the Civil War. Abundant illustrations of corruption include the excessive patronage system in appointments of public officials and malfeasance by high and low officials, contractors, lawyers, and pensioners. These conditions, the Stones conclude, led to the struggle for reform and the search for higher standards of morality and efficiency in public management.

Undoubtedly, the development of public administration in the United States is inextricably linked to the domestic concerns of the time. However, it is difficult to obscure the links of U.S. administration, however distant, with German cameralism, foreign military reforms, British fundamental law, French emphasis on justice and equality, and other theories and practices contemporary of the Founding Fathers. These early examples of administration should be properly acknowledged without exaggeration in order to register the full impact of European and native American traditions and the human experiences at large on the U.S. political and administrative innovations.

Important articulation of administrative issues in the United States came after nearly a century of independent rule. Intellectual pronouncements of managerial concerns began with Woodrow Wilson and Frank Goodnow. A few basic ideas may be distilled from *The Federalist*, of course, but *The Federalist* only indirectly addresses the actual administration of policy and does not represent a full-blown theory or a model capable of directing administrative decisions. The following excerpts from *The Federalist* are particularly relevant (quoted in Mosher 1981, pp. 17–28):

Federalist Paper No. 70 (Alexander Hamilton)
A feeble Executive implies a feeble execution of the government. A feeble execution is but another phrase for a bad execution; and a government ill executed, whatever it may be in theory, must be, in practice, a bad government.

Federalist Paper No. 76 (Alexander Hamilton)

It has been observed in a former paper, that "the true test of a good government is its aptitude and tendency to produce a good administration." . . . It is not easy to conceive a plan . . . to promote a judicious choice of men for filling the offices of the Union; and it will not need proof, that on this point must essentially depend the character of its administration.

The sole and undivided responsibility of one man will naturally beget a livelier sense of duty and a more exact regard to reputation.

Federalist Paper No. 51 (James Madison)

But what is government itself, but the greatest of all reflections of human nature? If men were angels, no government would be necessary. If angels were to govern men, neither external nor internal controls on government would be necessary. In framing a government which is to be administered by men over men, the great difficulty lies in this: you must first enable the government to control the governed; and in the next place oblige it to control itself. A dependence on the people is, no doubt, the primary control of the government; but experience has taught mankind the necessity of auxiliary precautions.

These ideas in *The Federalist* indicate that Hamilton believed a strong executive model of administration was essential for "good" implementation of governmental decisions and a "livelier sense of duty" by the administrator. "Of all the founding fathers," Richard Stillman (1996, p. 361) points out, "none displayed more interest in and enthusiasm for administration and organization than Alexander Hamilton." Hamilton, as the first Secretary of the Treasury, had the opportunity to influence the first cabinet and to demonstrate his knowledge and skills in defining the agency's mission and in building the administrative structure needed for achieving this mission. In fact, it has been argued that Hamilton may be considered the founder of the U.S. administrative state, because he was also the chief administrative officer during the first period of U.S. history (Van Riper 1987, p. 4).

Madison relied on "primary" and "auxiliary" means of control — the former dealing with popular control through voting, the latter presumably dealing with all the other measures created by government to control itself and maintain honesty in the execution of its policies. Madison's influence has been evident in the many checks and balances in the Constitution to prevent concentration of power and to mitigate factional politics that he foresaw emerging in future processes employed in making public policy. His advice in *Federalist 51* on the framing of a stable, enduring government was: "Ambition must be made to counteract ambition" (Stillman 1996, p. 363). What was missing in the design of the system, however,

was any specific consideration of administrative issues such as centralization, coordination, or other managerial processes.

In summary, *The Federalist* offers little help or guidance as to what the
Founding Fathers considered valuable and ideal in the administration of
the newly established state. Their statements do not represent an integrated conception or model of management. *The Federalist* falls short
when it comes to specific management tools and methods of implementation; the authors were seeking to achieve other objectives. Perhaps they
considered ensuring that rights and freedoms of citizens were protected
more significant than dealing with the issues of administration and organization of the state. It is also possible that administrative questions required
specific skills that the Founding Fathers lacked or generated disagreements that they sought to avoid.

True, the U.S. system may be different from any other system that
existed before it in some fundamental aspects. Nonetheless, as Stillman
(1990, p. 163) points out, "America was formed . . . with a hodgepodge of
assorted beliefs, doctrines, principles, myths, and postulates, often in
conflict with one another that make fitting them into a stable administrative state at a later date difficult." Some of these important influences are
outlined here to illustrate impact and to compare structural aspects of the
systems.

For example, certain provisions of the U.S. Constitution resemble those
of Locke's synthesis of the doctrines of natural right and social contract at
the end of the seventeenth century. Similarities with Locke's philosophy
could be found in the declaration of certain U.S. principles in 1776 such as
man's natural rights to life, liberty, and property. Man needed government
because he needed a legislature to define those rights and an executive to
enforce them, so he entered into a contract with his fellow humans to
establish government. The basic premise of such notion was that government rested on the consent of men, not upon the divine ordination of
kings.

According to Emmette Redford and colleagues (1968, p. 45), Locke
may have given the United States the concept of limited government,
restricted in its actions through known general rules. Although Thomas
Hobbes argued for the absolute power of kings and Rousseau for placing
absolute power in the will of the people, Locke combined the liberal
philosophy of rights and contract with the British tradition of rule of law.

A review of major influences on the U.S. constitutional system has to
include the works of Baron de Montesquieu, whose writing in 1748 modified Locke's listing of powers. Montesquieu defined the chief powers of
government as legislative, executive, and judicial as he pointed out the

need for separation of these powers. He argued that there could be no liberty if any two of the three powers were united in the same person or body (Redford, Truman, Hacker, Westin, & Wood 1968). More than any contemporary government, the United States faithfully maintains such separation among the three branches, with adequate powers in each branch to check the others. Also, the principle that no person shall occupy a position in more than one branch is meticulously observed by the U.S. system, unlike the practices of parliamentary democracies, in which a cabinet officer can concurrently occupy a seat in the legislature.

The principle of separation of powers in the U.S. Constitution evolved into a serious hindrance to the contemporary administrative state, seeking to blend many of the constitutionally separated powers into single public organizations. Because of this, John A. Rohr (1986, p. 5) points out, "the administrative state has never been at ease in our constitutional tradition," although it may be consistent with the framers' intent and a fulfillment of their constitutional design. Very few public institutions in modern society have faced the same intense questioning of their constitutional legitimacy as public organizations known as "regulatory agencies." Their mix of semilegislative and semijudicial functions as well as their executive-administrative roles have always encountered resistance not only from affected economic interests but also from those who adhere to strict interpretation of constitutional provisions.

Frederick Thayer[1] advances a modified view of these political principles and issues formulated from official practices of politics and administration. He points out that the principle of "separated powers" also has been called, quite often, "shared powers," and it is easy to argue that the concept of "shared" takes precedence. The administrators, Thayer contends, implement laws that have no basis except by legislative and executive agreement (a veto override constitutes a form of legal and official agreement).

Beyond these definitions of roles and powers, the radical political and economic changes experienced in the West during the period described above promised improvements through new types of institutions and policies. The implication to public bureaucracy was that adaptation to the new order was imperative. No doubt, local political, economic, and social conditions had varying degrees of influence, but all helped to usher in a new age of administrative introspection (professionalization) and search for rational methods. In the United States, other factors indirectly influenced changes in the public sector. Until the mid-nineteenth century, for example, the federal government was confined to a few basic functions. Most federal efforts were concentrated in areas such as defense, foreign affairs, postal services, taxes, tariffs, pensions, and law enforcement. However, overall federal influence on the economic life of the country was significant and increasing.

The post–Civil War period was one of great business expansion and rapid industrialization. The linking of both coasts of the country with railroads in 1869, along with successive discoveries such as petroleum, electricity, automobiles, and telephones, created conditions in the society that required new administrative competencies and values. A steady growth of urban centers accompanied the economic and technological changes and promoted a gradual countrywide shift from rural and agricultural to urban and industrial. The serious challenge to public service institutions became how to cope with these changes and to adapt operations accordingly. The magnitude of change is most clearly reflected in federal expenditures and federal employment. At the end of the first century of independence, the entire federal budget was $318 million. By the end of the second century, federal expenditures exceeded $1.5 trillion. In the employment area, according to U.S. Bureau of the Census statistics, the number of federal civilian employees stood at 19,000 by 1830, reached 230,000 by 1900, and now stands at about 2.7 million.

Clearly, the search for rational administration of public activities in the United States became quite noticeable in the latter part of the nineteenth century. On the practical level, civil service reform was a profound demonstration of the change. The writings of scholars such as Woodrow Wilson and Frank Goodnow provided the intellectual and conceptual authenticity necessary for the emergence of the new field of study.

The Civil Service Reform

During the first hundred years of U.S. independence, little attention was given to the problems and issues of managing the public service. The political leadership was concerned only minimally with effective, responsible, and professional public management. Administration was subordinated to politics or consumed by it. O. Glenn Stahl (1983, p. 37) describes the situation in the following way:

It was the progressive degradation and degeneration of public life under the spoils method that finally called forth a movement in the 1860s that demanded reform of the civil service in the name of government efficiency and public morals. The disastrous turnover, in which experience was systematically scrapped; the exaltation of inexperience and incompetence; the stagnation in administrative policies; the favoritism and partiality in the ordinary conduct of public business; and the taboo that grew up about the public service as a career — combined to make reform imperative.

Although Andrew Jackson's name has been associated most frequently with the spoils system, similar employment policies were practiced by the first six U.S. presidents. Government jobs were awarded for political services, and recruits were drawn from a narrow social base. Technical competence and equal opportunity — as understood today — were neither accepted nor practiced. Paul Van Riper (1987, p. 13) describes the Jacksonian regime: "Politically, the result was what many of the Founding Fathers had feared, the dominance of a demagogic majoritarianism that, driven by an intense concern for power, pandered to the nation's worst instincts through the spoils system and unbridled exploitation of natural resources.

Several factors provided the necessary impetus for reform and change. In 1881, a New York lawyer, Dorman B. Eaton, founded the Civil Service Reform League. Earlier in 1879, Eaton published a study of the civil service in Great Britain, a study made at the request of President Rutherford B. Hayes. Later, Eaton helped to draft the Pendleton Act of 1883 and became the first head of the U.S. Civil Service Commission (Van Riper 1987, p. 8). The civil service reformers were much influenced by the merit principle used by the British civil service system, particularly competitive entrance examinations, employment security, and prohibition of removal for political reasons instituted earlier. The assassination of President James Garfield at the hands of a disappointed job seeker provided an immediate reason for Congress to pass the reform legislation. Garfield's death mobilized sentiments for change that overcame the opposition and helped ensure the passage of the Pendleton Act in 1883.

The Pendleton Act created the Civil Service Commission to administer a public service system based on the competence and character of employees. Recruitment was to be governed by competitive examinations rather than by political connections. The adoption of the merit principle was followed by many extensions of its coverage, by statute and executive order, to include a larger and larger proportion of the employees in the federal service. State and city governments followed or acquiesced to the new reality (Nigro & Nigro 1980, p. 291).

In principle, civil service reform was a repudiation of the spoils system and its brazen application of the doctrine "to the victor belongs the spoils." However, more importantly, the Pendleton Act was a legislative milestone in the history of professionalization of the management of public functions. Before the end of the nineteenth century, the government took on new responsibilities for numerous public services ranging from banking to health and from education to public works. The expansion of service as well as the increasing demands for control and accountability rendered the old system inadequate.

In addition, the increasing technical character of public service and its growth required a continual process of change and adaptation — a process not limited to the federal civil service system. Similar adaptations took place in every state and every major city across the country in the following decades. Various techniques of federal interventions and inducements elevated both the merit system in employment and the principle of equal opportunity; both are now the dominant values and practices at all levels of public service.

The legislation of the merit system, along with the growing momentum of the administrative reform movement, has ushered in an era of greater awareness of the administrative process in the United States. This occurred with a growing realization that political dominance of administrative issues and questions has a stifling effect. The new civil service system came to symbolize the "administrative state." Civil service offered institutional protection and job security to employees, and it promised stability, proficiency, and uniformity of rules and regulations in managing public organizations. Today, at the dawn of the twenty-first century, these values are no longer sufficient. A variety of new ideas currently are challenging the common wisdom, as will be discussed in the next chapters.

Woodrow Wilson

The first comprehensive, articulate view of public administration comes from Wilson. In his seminal article "The Study of Administration" (1887), Wilson advanced many concepts and ideas that greatly influenced the development of public administration in the United States. In fact, his article frequently has been referred to as the birth of public administration as a field of study. Wilson pointed out that, before his time, political scientists had occupied themselves with legal and philosophical dimensions of government and neglected its operations and its visible actions, that is, administration. With clear perception, he declared that no political or constitutional debates were of more immediate practical moment than questions of administration. "It is getting to be harder to *run* a constitution than to frame one," he concluded.

Wilson (1887) viewed Europe as a model of public administration competence, efficiency, and honesty. He urged the United States to learn from Europe the "science of public administration," free it of the spirit of autocracy or absolutism, and put it to the service and benefit of democracy. He cautioned against a parochial orientation to the study of public administration that would limit looking anywhere but home for suggestions. He believed that nowhere else in the field of government could the historical, comparative method be used more safely than in administration. "If I see a murderous fellow sharpening a knife cleverly, I can borrow his way of sharpening the knife without borrowing his probable intention to commit murder with it," Wilson wrote.

Wilson (1887) regarded the civil service reform of the 1880s as "but a prelude to a fuller administrative reform." His demands were for reform outside congressional deliberations. He saw in congressional government a system of standing committees that was secretive, fiscally irresponsible, fragmented, and confused. He viewed the study of public administration as a possible method for correcting political abuses and building an efficient and prompt government.

Wilson recognized civil service reform as clearing the moral atmosphere of official life by establishing the sanctity of public office as a public trust and by making the service unpartisan. He applauded the civil service reformers for insisting that administration be kept outside the proper sphere of politics. It is not without reason to state that Wilson's ideas have been studied, analyzed, and evaluated during the past century probably more than any other works in public administration. Scholars, one may add, have not always agreed in their interpretations.

Vincent Ostrom (1973) considers Wilson's ideas congruent with Max Weber's theory of bureaucracy. Among the main elements of what Ostrom calls the "Wilsonian Paradigm" are the following propositions:

A single center of power in any system of government, rather than divided power; the more division of power, the more irresponsible the system becomes.

The field of politics sets the task for administration, but the field of administration lies outside the proper sphere of politics.

Efficient modern governments have strong similarities in their administrative structures and functions. This proposition indicates an assumption that there are common identifiable independent principles of administration.

Perfection in the hierarchical ordering of a professionally trained public service provides the structural conditions necessary for "good" administration. Also, hierarchical organization maximizes efficiency (least cost).

Improvement of administration in the direction outlined above is a necessary condition for modernity and advancement of human civilization and welfare.

Thus, the reformers (including Wilson) advocated not only a neutral administration but also administration by experts. Wilson never attempted to resolve the tension between experts and the democratic process (Meyer 1991, p. 182). He and the reformers articulated a model in which citizens control officials who, in turn, direct the administrative apparatus of the state. This model is similar to the practice of industry, in which shareholders exercise control over corporate managers who, in turn, direct daily business operations (Meyer 1991, p. 182). Rational administration then assumes a single and direct relationship between the preferences of the electorates and the elected officials. Consequently, the constancy of purpose in government is not a problem for the administrators.

Wilson's essay was a product of his values, vision, and his time. Students of public administration always are reminded of Wilson's exhortation that nonpolitical administrative techniques should be employed in government. Less often explained, however, is Wilson's belief that the separation of politics and administration would provide administrators the opportunity to wield large powers.

According to James Doig (1983, p. 292), Wilson's views of power are related to his concept of efficiency as "the simplest arrangements by which responsibility can be unmistakably fixed upon officials." Consequently, responsibility becomes a central concern; agencies must be organized so that "clear-cut responsibility" is assumed. The indispensable conditions of responsibility, Wilson believed, are large powers and unhampered discretion. There is no danger in power, if it is responsible. If power is "dealt out in shares to many, it is obscured; and if it be obscured, it is made irresponsible," Wilson (1887) asserts. Thus, it is assumed here that centralization of administrative power assures its monitoring and control.

Van Riper (1987, p. 4) offers a revisionist view of the presumed influence of Wilson's essay, denying any connection between Wilson's essay and the later development of the discipline. He points out that Wilson's work had no influence on the evolution of the theory or practice of public administration in the United States until well after 1950. One evidence Van Riper mentions is that, prior to World War II, only one of four published textbooks in public administration referred to Wilson's work (1987, p. 4). Despite the criticisms, Wilson's essay remains the best-known comprehensive statement on public administration available until the 1880s. Deserved of the honor or not, Wilson's analysis of the issues and articulation of the difficulties of public management overshadow all earlier contributions.

Public administration literature is replete with evaluations, dissections, and interpretations of Wilson's essay. Whatever position one may adopt toward his various proposals or reasons, the fact remains that management still is troubled by the same challenges and contradictions he exposed more than a hundred years ago (Fesler 1980, pp. 16, 17).

How to implement public laws more efficiently? How to improve the morality of the public service? How to protect administrative action against political intrusion? How to serve the public honestly, efficiently, and responsibly? Wilson's identification of the questions is no less valuable than the answers he provides. To a large extent, in Wilson's skill at articulating these problems lies his astonishing survivability.

Another important contribution came in 1893, when Frank J. Goodnow published his two volumes on *Comparative Administrative Law*. Stone and Stone describe this publication as "the first American treatise on public administration" (1975, p. 27). In 1900, Goodnow published his classic volume *Politics and Administration*, considered an extension and elaboration of Wilson's essay.

Goodnow is cited frequently in public administration textbooks as the author who spelled out the difference between administration and politics. Government has two distinct functions, Goodnow declared in 1900 (pp. 82, 83): "Politics has to do with policies or expressions of state will. Administration has to do with the execution of these policies."

Thus, U.S. public administration faced the twentieth century with some fundamental concerns of its own — independent of politics and law. These concerns were formulated in straightforward ideas that provided conceptual roots for the more elaborate classic models of management early in this century. The embryonic period, extending between U.S. independence and the end of the nineteenth century, witnessed activism in the theory and practice of public administration only in the final three or four decades. During these later years, public administration was recognized as distinct from politics and law — the two fields that always had dominated government thought and operation. Therefore, the search for efficient and effective managerial processes for implementing public policies was open and wide. In the meantime, many administrative principles became integral parts of succeeding perspectives. Some durable notions advanced by the administrative management model are a single source of power (unity of command), rule of hierarchy (definition of responsibility), emphasis on the technical content of the job (merit system), development of appropriate structures (organization), and need for reform and renewal (administrative development). These fundamental ideas and practices provided the basis for conceptual continuity in U.S. management. Some have endured numerous modifications and elaborations through research and application. Contemporary needs, however, require more flexible, more entrepreneurial, and more participatory concepts and practices of organizational management.

NOTE

1. Correspondence between the author and Frederick Thayer in 1989 and after.

REFERENCES

Clegg, Stewart, Cynthia Hardy, and Walter Nord, eds. 1996. *Handbook of Organization Studies*. Thousand Oaks, CA: Sage.

Doig, James W. 1983. "If I See a Murderous Fellow Sharpening a Knife Cleverly . . .": The Wilsonian Dichotomy and the Public Authority Tradition. *Public Administration Review*, 43, 4 (July-August).

Esman, Milton J. 1991. *Management Dimensions of Development: Perspectives and Strategies*. West Hartford, CT: Kumarian Press.

Fesler, James W. 1980. *Public Administration: Theory and Practice*. Englewood Cliffs, NJ: Prentice-Hall.

Gladden, E. N. 1972. *A History of Public Administration*, vol. II. London: Frank Cass.

Goodnow, Frank J. 1900. *Politics and Administration*. New York: Macmillan.

Johansen, Bruce E. 1990. Native American Societies and the Evolution of Democracy in America, 1600–1800. *Ethnohistory*, 37, 3 (Summer).

Kennedy, Paul. 1987. *The Rise and Fall of the Great Powers*. New York: Random House.

Meyer, Marshall W. 1991. The Concept of Rational Administration. In *Public Management*, edited by J. Steven Ott, Albert C. Hyde, and Jay M. Shafritz. Chicago, IL: Lyceum/Nelson-Hall.

Mosher, Frederick C., ed. 1981. *Basic Literature of American Public Administration (1787–1950)*. New York: Holmes & Meier.

____, ed. 1975. *American Public Administration: Past, Present, Future*. University: University of Alabama Press.

Nash, Gerald D. 1969. *Perspectives on Administration: The Vistas of History*. Berkeley: University of California, Institute of Governmental Studies.

Nigro, Felix A. and Lloyd G. Nigro. 1980. *Modern Public Administration*, 5th ed. New York: Harper & Row.

O'Brien, Sharon. 1989. *American Indian Tribal Governments*. Norman: University of Oklahoma Press.

Ostrom, Vincent. 1973. *The Intellectual Crisis in American Public Administration*. University: University of Alabama Press.

Redford, Emmette S., David Truman, Andrew Hacker, Alan Westin, and Robert Wood. 1968. *Politics and Government in the United States*, 2d ed. New York: Harcourt, Brace.

Reed, Michael. 1996. Organizational Theorizing: A History Contested Terrain. In *Handbook of Organization Studies*, edited by Stewart Clegg, Cynthia Hardy, and Walter Nord. Thousand Oaks, CA: Sage.

Rohr, John A. 1986. *To Run a Constitution: The Legitimacy of the Administrative State*. Lawrence: University Press of Kansas.

Scott, W. G., T. R. Michell, and P. H. Birnbaum. 1981. *Organization Theory*, 4th ed. Homewood, IL: Richard D. Irwin.

Shafritz, Jay M. and J. Steven Ott. 1996. *Classics of Organization Theory*, 5th ed. Belmont, CA: Wadsworth.

Stahl, O. Glenn. 1983. *Public Personnel Administration*, 8th ed. New York: Harper & Row.

Stillman, Richard J. II. 1996. *The American Bureaucracy*, 2d ed. Chicago, IL: Nelson-Hall.

____. 1990. The Peculiar "Stateless" Origins of American Public Administration and the Consequences of Government Today. *Public Administration Review*, 50, 2 (March-April).

Stone, Alice and Donald C. Stone. 1975. Early Development of Education in Public Administration. In *American Public Adminstration: Past, Present, Future*, edited by Frederick C. Mosher. University: University of Alabama Press.

Van Riper, Paul P. 1987. The American Administrative State: Wilson and the Founders. In *A Centennial History of the American Administrative State*, edited by R. C. Chandler. New York: Free Press.

Wilson, Woodrow. 1887. The Study of Administration. *Political Science Quarterly*, 2, 1 (June). Reproduced in Jay M. Shafritz and Albert C. Hyde, eds. 1992. *Classics of Public Administration*, 3rd ed. Pacific Grove, CA: Brooks/Cole

Wren, Daniel A. 1979. *The Evolution of Management Thought*, 2d. ed. New York: Wiley.

3

Issues in Organization Theory and Process

THE THEORY-PRACTICE CONNECTION

Public administration frequently is described as a "practical" field of knowledge with a strong rational bent to its prescriptive concepts. From the practitioner's point of view, an underlying assumption about inherent rational and ethical quality of public management continues in the commitment to action and to making a difference to the way the organization operates. Not surprising, then, that government officials tend to use the term "theoretical" to denote "not practical" and, thus, to assort management literature according to its proclivity to confront the action element in the theory-practice relationship.

Positing theory in contrast to practice, however, is the equivalent to removing theory from its action and empirical core. This is not to say that theory photocopies reality; all theory involves some degree of abstraction that disregards certain characteristics of its subject or reduces their importance (Kaplan 1964, p. 297). However, a sharp, mutually exclusive distinction between what is "practical" and what is "theoretical" inevitably leads to fundamental distortions in the subject.

Although the roots of public administration in political theory often have been neglected, usually in favor of more immediate technical concerns, some theorists have maintained an interest in the political theory of public organizations, as in the "new public administration" and in certain aspects of the recent emphasis on public policy (Denhardt 1993,

p. 14). Another significant theoretical thrust has been allied with the larger field of organization theory, drawing on research and findings from various disciplines such as sociology, psychology, economics, and even engineering.

Effective application of organization theory requires specification of conditions. The familiar criticism that a plan is "all right in theory but won't work in practice" may well be reasonable — but did the theory specify conditions that are not fulfilled in the particular case at hand? If so, then "all right in theory but won't work in practice" means that the solution works, but for a different problem (Kaplan 1964, p. 295). Theory has not failed here, but its application.

Theory may seem to fail to solve specific problems, or even aid in their resolution, simply because theory assumes conditions that cannot be met. Ideal-type theories or models (e.g., Max Weber's bureaucratic model) assume perfect conditions that cannot exist in reality. It is easy to make such theory a scapegoat when it is difficult to discern its true value. The strength of such theoretical models usually lies in their explanatory power, along with their capacity to generate propositions and generalizations applicable to concrete cases.

However, conditions surrounding public organizations have changed so dramatically over the past few decades that a description of spectacular is hardly a surrender to overstatement. At the global level, the list of changes can be very lengthy. A selection of a relevant few would include the end of colonialism and the consequent reshaping of world order, renunciation and abandonment of apartheid and the affirmation of human dignity and equal rights, dwindling of communism and the end of the Cold War, and the emergence of new modes of international economic and trade practices.

More directly affecting public organizations are changes within the society. Public policy affirmation of civil rights and legal protection to women and minorities has the effect of increased bureaucratization of human resources management (Clegg, Hardy, & Nord 1996, p. 4). The expanded government function of rule making to regulate, protect, and augment what citizens have been demanding in areas such as the environment, food, health, travel, and financial transactions has resulted in dissensions over the exercise of operational powers in the organization. Public management has been caught between two powerful but contradictory currents. From one side, the pressure is to downsize and to increase output; from the other side, it is the effect of declining economic rewards to employees on top of the uncertainty caused by constant declarations of reforming (reinventing or reengineering) public organizations. What is unfolding here is more than shattering the foundations of the conventional wisdom of public management. It actually is becoming very difficult to convince public employees of old claims of public employment such as security on the job or sensibility of the incentive system of government employment. With decreasing employment opportunities in government, at least in the short run, it is increasingly harder to entice new talents or to rekindle the aspirations of young people to join the "noble profession of public service."

Undeniably, earlier theories and processes of public organizational management, emphasizing coherence, cooperation, and symmetrical patterns of interaction in the midst of a certain and secure environment, are insufficient for today's needs. How well current managers are able to adapt to the new conditions is an empirical question. Next, one asks whether management theory and process will successfully adapt to a new world of turmoil, dissension, conflict, and rough competition for shrinking resources. What are the implications to public organizations in the new environment?

ADAPTIVE ADMINISTRATIVE THEORY

When a social theory loses its adaptability, it is transformed from a tool of dynamic analysis and inquiry into a set of static ideological beliefs, but administrative theories are continually revised, modified, and reformulated in light of new data or evidence. Change is a salient feature of public organization theory and practice, even when scholars are not in full agreement on what administrative theory is or ought to be. Theory interrelates concepts and associates them in specific patterns after such concepts have received an acceptable measure of evidence and support. It is important for students of public organizations to realize that theories are constantly disproved, modified, or rewritten. Still, despite this changeability, sound theories retain a measure of effectiveness as tools for organizing data, explaining actions, anticipating events, or speculating about relationships.

Broadly speaking, there are several ways for developing and accepting significant conceptual constructs. The preference for one theoretical model over another is a matter of consensus among experts (Dubin 1978, p. 13). Consensus rests on the judgment and agreement of a jury-like community of professionals and scholars who determine which theoretical model best provides understanding of the management of public organizations or some aspects of it. Means to promote consensus depend on strength of the logic employed in building the theory, the level of support from accessible evidence (e.g., comprehensive and reliable), and, yes, agreement of enough people to make the transition to accept dominance of the new theory.

However, to define administrative theory only as "publicly verifiable generalizations" and to assume that different researchers should reach the same conclusions in their investigations of the same variables and their relations is to unnecessarily confine theory, perhaps depriving it of critical elements. Implicit in such a definition, too, is a claim of exactitude and precision rarely attainable in the social sciences. If theoretical formulations are always publicly verifiable, then prediction should be no problem (as in the natural sciences, in which control of the environment is possible and the property of materials can be precisely determined). Two compelling criticisms to such a line of thinking are relevant:

The first is by Frederick Thayer,[1] who inquires if an administrator looks upon theory as "lawlike propositions," then the question she or he asks is "what *ought* I to do in this situation?" The answer is: "I *ought* to do what *other* administrators have done in similar situations that have led to positive decision outcomes." By definition, Thayer concludes, this leaves absolutely no room for such things as "innovation" or situations that appear to have never existed before.

Second, the literature has recognized both the contributions and the limitations of those attempts at exact conceptualizations (that usually are accompanied by ostensibly precise measurement techniques that use quantitative methods of verification of a hypothesis). Promises of such attempts — and their liability — have been highly publicized. Skeptics point out problems of transfer to the "real world" and object to selectivity of data and simplification of usually complex administrative relationships. As Lawrence Mayer (1972, p. 4) points out, "the popularity of newly acquired skills in statistical analysis and electronic data processing has led to an unhealthy preoccupation with methodological tools at the expense of analysis." As Robert Behn (1995, p. 315) correctly points out, "A reverence for methodology is not, however, what makes an endeavor scientific." Scientists do not start with data and methods, he notes. Scientists start with significant questions. The problem often is that emphasis on methodology and manipulation of data results in addressing trivial questions and issues of little epistemological value.

Explaining the complexity and variation of public organization theory inevitably points to three major factors: human behavior vicissitude, imprecise techniques of observation and measurement, and uncontrollable environmental forces (particularly at the economic and political levels). It should be no surprise that students of the social sciences (and of public administration in particular) often live through a "crisis of confidence" concerning the theoretical foundation as well as the utility of their subject of specialization. Increasingly, public administration activities and performance are determined not only by administrative needs and preferences but also by external and uncertain influences, namely, political, economic, and social forces impose significant empirical and normative constraints. In a broad context, these influences and interferences are indications that public organizations are too important to the success of the state in its various endeavors to be left exclusively to the free will of the managerial class.

Faced with numerous uncertainties and operating in an intrusive environment, theoretical perspectives on public organizations tend to rely on forms such as "under what conditions such-and-such is expected to happen" or the "if-then" formula. Other escape phrases frequently used are "other things being equal," assuming that no variables unspecified by the analysis will significantly alter the relationship, and "it all depends," assuming that environmental variables are so numerous and significant that establishing definite generalizations is neither feasible nor practicable.

Among the common methods of constructing theories of public organization are the inductive and the deductive modes. The inductive method draws on practical experience and knowledge, culminating in conceptual formulations. In arriving at theoretical generalizations, this approach relies heavily on descriptive data about actual situations and behavior. The movement is from the specific to the general. The deductive models take the form of complete equivalence where A always follows B, under given assumptions. Such statements may not correspond to real-world conditions, but they help to clarify logical relationships and, thus, help the investigator not only to understand the empirical coincidence of variables but also to derive logically related corollaries from relationships (Riggs & Weidner 1963, p. 12). In the deductive model, a particular fact is explained from a generalization, that is, the movement is from the general to the specific. It is possible to build deductive corollaries from propositions based on inductive models and evidence, but deductive models have been used far more in the natural sciences, while the inductive method is the mainstay of public organization theory.

Finally, no doubt, adaptation is central to organization theory, past and present. Indeed, within the current changing conditions, globally and within the society, adaptation has assumed greater urgency. The crucial questions remain of what elements to change and how to change them? Public management draws on a rich intellectual and practical heritage, extending from ancient times to the present. In the United States, since

Woodrow Wilson, some distinguishing high points of public administration tradition may be recognized, such as provisions for basic principles, ideological and theoretical orthodoxy, resistance to centripetal trends that threaten the coordination of activities, and strict adherence to enforcement and to operating rules.

On the other hand, there is what Michael Reed (1996, p. 32) calls "paradigm proliferation" through separate intellectual development that nurtures distinctive approaches within different domains, uncontaminated by contact with competing perspectives. Such new entrepreneurship sometimes transformed into calls for "revolution" that "challenges everything we thought we knew about managing, and challenges over a hundred years of American tradition" (Peters 1995, p. 9). This managerial "revolution" is proclaimed in the name of refocusing the organization on creativity, the only way for the organization to thrive. To generate creative ideas, accordingly, is to "attract creative people and then to give them the right environment to work in" (Kao 1996, p. 55). Obviously, it is the concern of the business company that is paramount in these considerations.

The problem is that the search for alternative concepts, with potential for helping public managers, so far had unearthed few relevant notions of what may be called "new" or "radical" thinking. One cannot consider restated themes such as "flexibility, adaptation and experimentation" (Peters 1995, p. 9) as anything resembling radical change. Nor are exhortations such as "proactive management," "Thriving on Chaos," or "The Pursuit of Wow!" adequate solutions to challenges of public organizational management. Public managers also cannot find much help in postmodern concepts still being defined and debated among intellectuals with a predilection for abstract thinking. The output of postmodernism so far has included discourse on structuralism, poststructuralism, deconstruction, postcapitalism, critical theory, and so forth, but in terms of organizational management, no drastically new perspectives have emerged. "If postmodernism is to provide a solid base for useful social analysis and if it is to contribute to the formulation of a new theory of organizations," concludes William Bergquist (1996, p. 578), "then it must move beyond the status of fad and find roots in the soil of history and precedent." Finally, there is the "reinvention" of government movement, a different genre of proposed change (discussed later) that also has been a mixed bag of exaggerations and "old wines in new bottles" themes. The tenacity of its advocates, as well as their connections to high offices, are largely credited for its measured popularity in the public sector.

Structures of formal organizations, as Philip Selznick (1996, p. 127) points out, "represent rationally ordered instruments for the achievement of stated goals." We know that structures vary in complexity, degree of formalization, functions they serve, and several other aspects, but in government, organizational structure has greater staying power than in a business corporation and, thus, exhibits different dynamism and distinct connection to performance. The point is that few managers would thrive on "chaos" or on management relativism in implementing public policy, and fewer still would risk possible violation of laws that decree such policies. Although "high-tech," speculative industries may benefit by proposed revolutionary managerial techniques (if they do not fade away in the process), public organizations, in comparison, apply different rules of conduct, abide by different ethics, and serve different expectations.

Between the rigidities of the traditional approaches and the uncertainties of speculative relativism, the need, perhaps, is for legitimating approaches that provide a synthesis of these drastic trends. Such approaches, as Reed (1996, pp. 32–33) points out, "question both a return to fundamentals and unrestrained celebration of discontinuity and diversity: neither intellectual surfing or free riding on the rising tide of relativism, nor retreating into the cave of orthodoxy, are attractive futures for the study of organization." Whatever the final features of future managerial perspectives, they need to address the practical and theoretical concerns, maintaining continuity in the midst of diversity and minimizing the frustrations of students of public management facing unnecessarily embellished conditions of chaos and confusion. It is in the direction toward balance that this book is pointed.

THE STUDY OF ORGANIZATION THEORY

As stated earlier, organizations pervade all aspects of contemporary life and are the dominant form of institutions in society (Robbins 1990, p. 8). It is not surprising, then, that there is a widespread interest in understanding organizations, how they are structured, and how they normally act. In teaching and in training, theoretical frameworks play significant roles in the development and application of administrative knowledge. Teaching and research, in fact, sustain their intellectual integrity through sound conceptualization of public management and its problems. In the absence of theory, university classrooms would become workshops for vocational training; the field itself would be relegated to a collection of low-level techniques of dubious validity and applicability. Recognizing that some of these functions remain aspirations more than reality, administrative theory usually serves these particular functions:

Theory provides a systematic view of our existing knowledge and helps to organize scattered insights gained through research and application. As Robert Denhardt (1993, p. 11) points out, "most agree that the purpose of theory generally is to provide a more coherent and integrated understanding of our world than we might otherwise hold." In effect, the more basic function of theory is "to make sense of what would otherwise be inscrutable or unmeaning empirical findings" (Kaplan 1964, p. 302).

Theory serves as a guide for research by discerning gaps in existing knowledge and ongoing research. By directing research efforts to areas where they are most needed, theory expands the frontiers of knowledge, draws together facts, helps in interpreting information, and suggests other generalizations of equal validity.

Theory offers criteria of relevance to the questions under investigation. It disciplines the process of information gathering and restrains individual bias and perception. Practitioners benefit greatly by replacing intuitive concepts of organizations with theories that have been reliably and systematically derived.

Administrative theory aspires to become a guide to administrative action and behavior. It provides practitioners a measure of performance evaluation as it offers academicians a balanced perspective in areas of curriculum development for teaching and training.

Theory leads to better analysis and understanding of administrative problems, an essential step in the development or identification of problem-solving techniques. By providing the conceptual tools for study and analysis of the administrative unit, both the analyst and the practicing administrator are in a better position to recommend solutions. Therefore, relevant theory helps to improve practice.

In social science literature, the terms "theory" and "model" often are used interchangeably. Such is the definition offered by Dwight Waldo. A model, he says, "is a conscious attempt to develop and define concepts, or clusters of related concepts, useful in classifying data, describing reality, and (or) hypothesizing about it" (Waldo 1980, p. 2).

As an extension of the earlier analysis, we must indicate that, since the turn of the century, public administration has accumulated a wealth of speculative thought, common-sense generalizations, axioms, paradigms, premises, models, frameworks, and concepts about administrative action and behavior. One can argue that very little of this heritage can be elevated to the level of scientific theory, defined as a "system of logically related, empirically testable, lawlike propositions" (Rapoport 1958, p. 973). Methodologists argue that all of the above are a prelude to the process of theory building — the highest level in the evolution of thought and knowledge. For public management, and perhaps mostly because of the nature of the field, such ideal is dismissed as more of a mental bombast than as valuable insights, practical or abstract.

Scholars of various persuasions criticize the current state of conceptual affairs, and many have proposed alternative theories or strategies for reaching a theory that unifies, integrates, or better represents the field. In this orientation, public organization theory is only a part of the larger field of organization theory. In contrast, however, a widely supported argument describes public administration as a professional field (much like medicine, law, or engineering) that draws on various theoretical perspectives to achieve its objectives and to produce practical impacts. Consequently, from this position, as Denhardt (1993, p. 14) points out, "a theory of public organization is both unattainable and undesirable."

GENERIC OR DIFFERENTIATED THEORY AND PRACTICE

Almost four decades ago, Edward Litchfield (1956) introduced *Administrative Science Quarterly* with a call for a general theory of administration. Litchfield identified three major inadequacies in the growth of administration as a science. First, the confusion of terminology makes it difficult to communicate accurately within one field and across cultures. Second, administration fails to achieve a level of generalization enabling it to systematize and explain administrative phenomena that occur in related fields: there may be business, hospital, and public administration and military, hotel, and school administration, but is there administration without adjective? Third, if current thought fails to generalize the constants or articulate the universals of administration, it may then be criticized for its failure to accord a broad range to the variables in the administrative process.

Litchfield's call for a general theory of administration follows a strong tradition of initiatives with a similar purpose. In the United States, an earnest search for generic principles of management (applied cross-culturally) spans over two centuries. In the 1880s, Wilson proclaimed public administration to be a separate field of study with its own rules and principles, but it was the publication of *Papers on the Science of Administration* in 1937, edited by Luther Gulick and L. Urwick, that popularized the principles approach and deepened its impact on the study and operation of U.S. public administration.

Actually, one of the earliest articulate efforts to define and apply a principles approach to management goes back to the fourteenth century. An Arab Muslim, Ibn-Taymiya, wrote *As-Siyasah Ash-Shareeyah* (Principles of Politics), in which he used scientific method to outline the principles of administration within the framework of the Islamic state, including principles such as the right man in the right job, patronage, and the spoils system (Shafritz and Ott 1996, p. 12). Although the precise year of publication is unavailable, we know that Ibn-Taymiya died in Damascus on September 26, 1328 (Ahmad 1982, p. 8).

In 1916, a Frenchman, Henri Fayol (1996, p. 52) wrote that the "soundness and good working order of the body corporate depend on a certain number of conditions termed indiscriminately principles, laws, rules." He made certain to disassociate these "principles" from any suggestion of "rigidity," "for there is nothing rigid or absolute in management affairs" (Fayol 1996, p. 52).

Still, U.S. public administration was fully propelled in the generic perspective through the classic schools of management and continued the search for the discovery of applied rules and principles to the present. Certainly, establishing patterns and defining general administrative principles that apply cross-culturally have been central themes in the mission of the comparative administration movement. Perhaps, debates on the issue of generic versus differentiated theoretical development of the field may never be resolved in a final, lasting form.

One particular aspect of the above question, however, is related to differences and similarities between "public" and "business" administration. With varying degrees of emphasis, "general theory" advocates challenge the "dual development" of private and public management. Michael A. Murray (1975, p. 364) writes, "For perhaps two generations, scholars and practitioners have realized that management can be viewed as a generic process, with universal implications and application in any institutional setting — whether a private firm or a public agency." Murray argues that the view of the private management model, with its criterion of economic efficiency, and the political public management model, with its criteria of consensus and compromise, are obviously idealized types and, consequently, tend to accentuate inherent conflicts.

Regardless, the generic approach has not attained consensus among scholars, nor has it earned acceptance within the educational establishments of either public administration or business administration schools. Graham Allison (1992, p. 472), calling the disputants "assimilators" and "differentiators," likens their disagreement to the old argument over whether the glass is half empty or half full. He concludes that public and private management are at least as different as they are similar and that the differences are more important than the similarities.

Apparently, comparisons of public and private organizations indicate agreement on a number of important distinctions, however. Although the literature does not reveal unqualified endorsement of the concept of a generic management, we find definitions of categories of factors describing the significance of the differences between public and private organizations. As J. L. Perry and H. G. Rainey (1988, p. 191) report, an increasing accumulation of findings on the relationship of the public-private dimension points to a number of dependent variables such as work-related attitudes of employees, management roles, structural variations, managerial perception of external control, strategic decision processes, and performance norms and outcomes.

The absence of clear distinctions and the changing nature of the connection underline the need for a flexible conceptualization. It should allow for various depictions of organizations across the public-private continuum. Organizations have been classified on the basis of ownership and funding (Wamsley & Zald 1973). The distinct attributes of public organizations have been perceived as a logical consequence of the absence of the market mechanism (Perry & Rainey 1988; Downs 1967; Warwick 1975); as a result of being an intimate, integral part of a constitutional legal system (Gortner, Mahler, & Nicholson 1987, p. 19); because of the political context and the imperatives of the political process within which public organizations operate (Lynn 1981); or by recognizing that "all organizations are public" and, thus, should be distinguished only as "more or less public or private" (Bozeman 1987, p. 5). Also, many of the practical aspects of the distinctions between public and private management have been articulated by executives who experienced both.[2]

Overall, literature comparing public and private organizations appears to position the differentiation argument on three broad sets of factors (Rainey, Backoff, & Levine 1976; Allison 1992):

1. *Environmental factors*. These relate to the degree of market exposure as well as legal and political constraints. As a source of revenues and resources, the market enforces relatively automatic penalties and rewards, providing incentives for reducing costs, operating efficiently, and performing effectively. Organizations that obtain resources through political appropriations processes are less subject to such influences.

Public organizations also face unique legal and formal constraints, especially in terms of autonomy and flexibility. Private organizations need only obey laws and public regulations. Most governmental bodies are far more regimented. Their purposes, methods, and spheres of operation often are defined by law and governed by a proliferation of formal specifications by statute, court rulings, or dicta from hierarchical superiors. Public agencies are subject to political influences as well, through political appointments, interest-group demands, legislative interference, and mass media exposure that sometimes influences or shapes decision making.

2. *The nature of public service*. Interactions between the organization and its environment underline several important distinctions between public and private organizations. Public organizations practice coercion, as in arresting and incarcerating violators of the law. They monopolize regulating and setting standards for numerous public needs ranging from traffic control to maintaining safety of food, water, and air. Many activities of public organizations are of the "unavoidable" type, such as licensing and tax collection. None of these distinctions is exactly applicable to activities of business organizations, in which choice of the individual and ability to pay determine the relationship.

In executing public policy, public organizations exercise broad and potentially enormous impact on society. Consequently, greater scrutiny of public officials and their actions is employed, through various mechanisms of oversight and accountability. Public expectations from civil servants usually are high in terms of demonstrating integrity, fairness, responsiveness, and openness when managing public programs. In fact, public service has been notable in its drive for providing equal employment opportunities and for eliminating all sorts of biases from its previous practices. As taxpayers, citizens demand that goods and services produced by the public sector maintain certain quality and be offered to them at cost or below cost, rather than according to market mechanisms.

3. *Internal structures and processes*. Public organizations have greater multiplicity and diversity. Their objectives are more vague; their goals are more likely to conflict (resulting in more trade-offs). Managers of public organizations generally have less authority and less flexibility in decision making than their corporate counterparts. Complementing these many distinctions are other differences, including incentive systems, political exposure, mass media attention, recruitment practices, innovation, and work satisfaction.

In summary, distinctions in public management as related to public and private, theory and practice, or simply in defining the characteristics of administrative theory with some finality are not the only subjects of controversy in management literature. Too often, one encounters the usual reference to a presumed "crisis of identity" in public administration. The assumed cause of this crisis is the absence of a "basic theoretical paradigm or framework in which a community of scholars shares common theoretical assumptions, and a common language defining essential terms and relationships" (Ostrom 1973, p. 13). The insufficiency of the paradigm inherent in the traditional theories of public administration attracted a variety of alternative suggestions. One such framework that attracted some attention as a contrast to the theory of bureaucracy is the theory of "public choice," offered as an alternative form of organization for producing goods and services by a multiplicity of enterprises transcending the limits of particular governmental jurisdictions (Ostrom 1973, p. 20).

The end result of the search for a unifying framework may be futile and fundamentally unattainable. New frameworks have not erased old doubts or resolved the problem of continually seeking to uphold and maximize incompatible values. As David Rosenbloom (1983, p. 219) contends, the central problem of contemporary public administration theory is that it derives from three disparate approaches to the basic question of what public administration is. Each approach has a respected intellectual tradition, emphasizes different values, promotes different types of organizational structures, and views individuals in markedly distinct terms. The managerial approach promotes values of efficiency, effectiveness, and economy. The political approach stresses the values of representation, political responsiveness, and accountability. The legal approach embodies values of procedural due process, individual substantive rights, and equity. Like the separation of powers under the Constitution, each approach may be more or less relevant to different agencies of administrative issues and is unlikely to be synthesized without violating some basic values.

Consequently, it is reasonable to conclude that no common theoretical assumptions exist, nor does a basic theoretical framework enjoy the consensus of the community of scholars and practitioners of public administration. This leaves the managers in an obvious predicament of searching for a valid, integrative conceptual understanding of their organizations. Equally perplexed are the academicians seeking skills and instruments to define critical characteristics of the organizational entity and its managerial processes.

What follows is a state of acquiescence to a condition of theoretical segmentalism in which various theories and models concurrently exist, each dealing with certain aspects of the administrative system. Moving to a stage of unification of administrative theories and models, although desirable, is not imperative to the health and prosperity of a field with unambiguous interdisciplinary concerns. Unification may not even be possible because of the widespread, changing, and multifarious nature of the administrative process.

Under such conditions, it is not surprising that the contingency approach has been gaining attention as a useful tool of administration. The contingency approach implies that there are no absolutely "good" or "bad" organizational designs or managerial styles. Rather, managers are required to analyze problems and to devise tactics to meet them based on evidence. This approach offers management flexibility and pragmatism in serving the aims and objectives of the organization (Scott, Mitchell, & Birnbaum 1981, p. 67). The contingency perspective is a powerful development in the opposite direction of the "unified" or "general" theory of administration. However, to avoid theoretical confusion, criteria of relevance have to materialize and tendencies for conceptual convergence be encouraged. Convergence is crucial to the cumulative effect of knowledge and to establishment of the consensus essential for theoretical reliability, particularly when administrative theories tend to be self-contained and independent of each other. Also, convergence need not mean "integration" or "unification," precursor to the establishment of a general theory, nor does it require agreement on a basic theoretical paradigm. Instead, convergence is an essential reconciliation of theories. It allows for refutation or modification of poor or erroneous ones. Essential to the advancement of knowledge, convergence is possible only if researchers take account of the achievements of predecessors. Without convergence, theories and models develop in parallel form, perpetuating the current state of doubt, confusion, and intellectual insularity.

LEVELS OF ANALYSIS

A major factor in the ostensible fragmentation of management concepts is lack of deliberate distinction between levels and units of analysis in public administration literature (Jreisat 1991, p. 16). Authors move freely from one level of generalization to the other without recognizing the change in scope and function of the administrative aspect under discussion.

Three major units of analysis have a strong tradition of research and inquiry with definite disciplinary foundations.

First is the individual administrator as the unit of analysis. This perspective purports to discover patterns of administrative behavior and explain causes and influences. Implicit in this microadministration approach is the presupposition that we must understand small-scale phenomena, such as the human personality, before we attempt to understand what happens in the larger ones, such as complex organizations or society.

Chris Argyris (1957) separates the individual and the formal organization as the two major components of social organizations. The properties of each component must be known to determine the impact of their simultaneous interaction; consequently, this orientation usually begins with a discussion of human personality in an effort to discern why people behave the way they do in organizations. Relevant research on individuals and factors influencing their behaviors and characteristics (particularly contributions from psychology) has been exploring the following areas (Szilagyi & Wallace 1983, pp. 22–26):

Motives consist of internal factors that influence observable acts or work behavior. They are not directly observable, but their presence usually can be inferred from observed behavior. Motives can be physiological (e.g., need for food) or psychological (e.g., need for affiliation) in nature.

Personality is the sum of the many facets and characteristics that make up each individual. Personality variables include aptitude, interests, values, beliefs, and state of mental health.

Perception is the selective processing of information that results in short-term behavior — how individuals attend to incoming stimuli and translate them into responses.

Learning is a cognitive or experiential process that results in long-term, permanent adjustment of behavior.

Job satisfaction is attitudes that each individual forms toward his or her job.

Herbert Simon, whose recent work focuses on the human information processing that enables people to perform complex intellectual tasks, claims that the "Thinking Man is capable of expressing his cognitive skills in a wide range of task domains: learning and remembering, problem solving, inducing rules and attaining concepts, perceiving and recognizing stimuli, understanding natural language, and others" (Simon 1979, p. x).

Second is the formal organization as a unit of analysis. The formal organization is the most meaningful (definable) unit of analysis for understanding administrative action. The pervasive influence of formal organizations in contemporary society is widely recognized as affecting not only individual and group behavior but also societal aspects of political, economic, social, educational, and even religious life. Organizations unite people around common goals and values and provide them with the working environments in which they spend a major portion of their lives.

From an analytical perspective, the formal organization has convenient assets and practical characteristics that facilitate focused and rigorous investigation, namely, formal organizations exhibit these significant features:

Specific communications channels are followed and exhibit a high degree of specificity with respect to content (March & Simon, 1958, p. 3).

Roles in organizations, in contrast to many other individual roles, tend to be highly elaborate, relatively stable, and defined to a considerable extent in explicit (often written) rules and procedures.

The high specificity of structure and coordination within organizations differentiates them from the diffuse and variable relations of unorganized individuals and groups. The individual organization, as a sociological unit, is comparable to the individual organism in biology (March & Simon 1958, p. 4; Thompson 1967, p. 6; Morgan 1986, p. 40). Almost organically, it grows, changes, matures, contracts, and, sometimes, dies.

Organizations possess limited, achievable objectives, relatively distinct boundaries, and identifiable patterns of interaction with their larger environments. Organizations may differ in technology, product, age, and tradition, but they are often similar in form, procedure, and the claims they make upon their members for loyalty and consistency (Presthus 1978, p. 19).

The public organization, entrusted with the implementation of legitimate public policy, shares these characteristics of specific structure, central coordination, defined communication patterns, concrete goals, and determinable boundaries. The formal organization is the unit most relied on in this analysis for these reasons and because the most meaningful administrative functions also take place within the organizational context.

Third, the national administrative system as a unit of analysis is the macro level that focuses on the national bureaucratic system and its interactions with the environment (particularly the political authority). In the context of Third World countries, studies taking such a tack often steer into examinations of bureaucracy's performance and influence on issues of national economic, political, and social development (Heady 1996).

In the United States, the study of national administration remains heavily weighted in the legal and constitutional aspects, the reconciliation of policy and administration, and the development and management of systems of regulation. The U.S. bureaucracy has been repeatedly examined from perspectives of its constitutional foundations, its relations with the other branches of government, its nature and development, and competition for sharing responsibilities in areas that traditionally have been thought properly reserved for Congress, the president, and the judiciary. The common conclusion of this type of work is that bureaucracy is deeply involved in the political process (Woll 1977; Rohr 1986; Rourke 1984; Ripley & Franklin 1984). Political science has been the mainstay of studying national systems, just as psychological research has been the major impetus to personality and behavior studies and sociology to the formal organization. The disciplinary interests of these fields in each of the three levels of analysis are longstanding and deeply rooted. However, a firm, growing trend is toward a multidisciplinary (interdisciplinary) investigation and evaluation of administrative theory and practice that expand the range of options and choices beyond narrow, traditional disciplinary concerns.

In conclusion, this discussion indicates that many controversies over the nature of administrative theory and process may not be settled in a final, universally accepted solution. However, what emerges, hopefully, is a better and deeper understanding of public organizations and their performance. Indeed, today's conceptualizations of organizations and their management indicate greater flexibility and adaptability, even when convergence remains more of an aspiration than a reality.

NOTES

1. Correspondence by Frederick Thayer with the author in 1989 and afterward.

2. See, for example, Michael Blumenthal. January 29, 1979. Candid Reflections of a Businessman in Washington. *Fortune Magazine.*

REFERENCES

Ahmad, Khurshid. 1982. Introduction. *Public Duties in Islam* by Ibn Taymiya. London: Islamic Foundation.

Allison, Graham T., Jr. 1992. Public and Private Management: Are They Fundamentally Alike in All Unimportant Respects? In *Classics of Public Administration*, 3rd ed., edited by Jay M. Shafritz and Albert C. Hyde. Pacific Grove, CA: Brooks/Cole.

Argyris, Chris. 1957. *Personality and Organization.* New York: Harper & Row.

Behn, Robert D. 1995. The Big Questions of Public Administration. *Public Administration Review*, 55, 4 (July-August).

Bergquist, William. 1996. Postmodern thought in a Nutshell: Where Art and Science Come Together. In *Classics of Organization Theory*, 4th ed., edited by Jay M. Shafritz and J. Steven Ott. New York: Wadsworth.

Bozeman, Barry. 1987. *All Organizations Are Public*. San Francisco, CA: Jossey-Bass.

Clegg, Stewart, Cynthia Hardy, and Walter Nord, eds. 1996. *Handbook of Organization Studies*. Thousand Oaks, CA: Sage.

Denhardt, Robert B. 1993. *Theories of Public Organization*. Belmont, CA: Wadsworth.

Downs, Anthony. 1967. *Inside Bureaucracy*. Boston, MA: Little, Brown.

Dubin, Robert. 1978. *Theory Building*, rev. ed. New York: Free Press.

Fayol, Henri (1916). 1996. General Principles of Management. In *Classics of Organization Theory*, 4th ed., edited by Jay M. Shafritz and J. Steven Ott. New York: Wadsworth.

Gortner, H. F., J. Mahler, and J. B. Nicholson. 1987. *Organization Theory: A Public Perspective*. Chicago, IL: Dorsey Press.

Heady, Ferrel. 1996. *Public Administration: A Comparative Perspective*, 5th. ed. New York: Marcel Dekker.

Jreisat, Jamil E. 1991. The Organizational Perspective in Comparative and Development Administration. In *Handbook of Comparative and Development Public Administration*, edited by A. Farazmand. New York: Marcel Dekker.

Kao, John. 1996, August 17. (Quoted in "Face Value: Mr. Creativity.") *The Economist*, p. 55.

Kaplan, Abraham. 1964. *The Conduct of Inquiry*. San Francisco, CA: Chandler.

Litchfield, Edward H. 1956. Notes on a General Theory of Administration. *Administrative Science Quarterly*, 1, 1 (June).

Lynn, Laurence E. 1981. *Managing the Public Business*. New York: Basic Books.

March, James G. and Herbert A. Simon. 1958. *Organizations*. New York: John Wiley.

Mayer, Lawrence C. 1972. *Comparative Political Inquiry*. Homewood, IL: Dorsey Press.

Morgan, Gareth. 1986. *Images of Organization*. Beverly Hills, CA: Sage.

Murray, Michael A. 1975. Comparing Public and Private Management. *Public Administration Review*, 4 (July-August).

Ostrom, Vincent. 1973. *The Intellectual Crisis in American Public Administration*. University: University of Alabama Press.

Perry, J. L. and H. G. Rainey. 1988. The Public-Private Distinction in Organization Theory. *The Academy of Management Review*, 13, 2 (April).

Peters, Tom. 1995. *Thriving on Chaos*. New York: Wings Books.

Presthus, Robert. 1978. *The Organizational Society*, rev. ed. New York: St. Martin's Press.

Rainey, H. G., R. W. Backoff, and C. H. Levine. 1976. Comparing Public and Private Organizations. *Public Administration Review*, 2 (March-April).

Rapoport, Anatol. 1958. Various Meanings of Theory. *American Political Science Review*, 52 (December).

Reed, Michael. 1996. Organizational Theorizing: A Historically Contested Terrain. In *Handbook of Organization Studies*, edited by Stewart Clegg, Cynthia Hardy, and Walter Nord. Thousand Oaks, CA: Sage.

Riggs, Fred W. and Edward W. Weidner. 1963. *Models and Priorities in the Comparative Study of Public Administration*. Washington, DC: American Society for Public Administration.

Ripley, Randall B. and Grace A. Franklin. 1984. *Congress, the Bureaucracy, and Public Policy*, 3rd ed. Homewood, IL: Dorsey Press.

Robbins, Stephen P. 1990. *Organization Theory: Structure, Design, and Applications*, 3rd ed. Englewood Cliffs, NJ: Prentice-Hall.

Rohr, John A. 1986. *To Run a Constitution*. Lawrence: University Press of Kansas.

Rosenbloom, David H. 1983. Public Administration Theory and the Separation of Powers. *Public Administration Review*, 43 (May-June).

Rourke, Francis E. 1984. *Bureaucracy, Politics, and Public Policy*, 3rd ed. Boston, MA: Little Brown.

Scott, William, T. Mitchell, and P. Birnbaum. 1981. *Organization Theory*, 4th ed. Homewood, IL: Richard D. Irwin.

Selznick, Philip. 1996. Foundations of the Theory of Organization. In *Classics of Organization Theory*, 4th ed., edited by Jay M. Shafritz and J. Steven Ott. Belmont, CA: Wadsworth.

Shafritz, Jay M. and J. Steven Ott, eds. 1996. *Classics of Organization Theory*, 4th ed. Belmont, CA: Wadsworth.

Simon, Herbert A. 1979. *Models of Thought*. New Haven, CT: Yale University Press.

Szilagyi, A. D., Jr. and M. J. Wallace, Jr. 1983. *Organizational Behavior and Performance*, 3rd ed. Glenview, IL: Scott, Foresman.

Thompson, James D. 1967. *Organizations in Action*. New York: McGraw-Hill.

Waldo, Dwight. 1980. *The Enterprise of Public Administration*. Novato, CA: Chandler and Sharp.

Wamsley, G., and M. N. Zald. 1973. *The Political Economy of Public Organizations*. Lexington, MA: Heath.

Warwick, Donald. 1975. *A Theory of Public Bureaucracy*. Cambridge, MA: Harvard University Press.

Woll, Peter. 1977. *American Bureaucracy*, 2d ed. New York: W. W. Norton.

4

Environment of Public
Organizations

The environment of public organizations consists of various elements that exert different levels of influence on the organization and on its operations. The environment legitimizes goals, supplies resources, consumes products and services, influences structures, and restricts behaviors of public organizations. The common elements that constitute this environment are political, legal, and economic as well as social, pertaining to citizens' expectations and demands.

Traditional organization theories simply assumed the existence of external environmental influences but treated them as a given, mostly applying closed-systems analysis. Current analysis does not accept anymore the separation of the organization from its environment, often the major source of change and variation in performance.

To borrow a metaphor from Ferrel Heady (1996, p. 94), the environment of public organizations is viewed as "concentric circles," with public organizations at the center. "The smallest circle generally has the most decisive influence, and the larger circles represent a descending order of importance as far as the bureaucracy is concerned." As such, the larger circle represents the society as a whole, with its cultural norms and social traditions. The next circle represents economic conditions, followed perhaps by the judicial one. The inner circle is the political system, so closely associated with organization and management that the separation often is in analytical terms rather than in material ones.

THE POLITICAL CONTEXT

The political context defines many aspects of public management. Typically, the existence of public organizations, their overall budgets, their personnel practices, and their purposes are all prescribed by and amended through the political process, in the form of public laws.

The U.S. Constitution does not provide many administrative details, for example, but it sets a framework and constructs numerous restraints on the operations of public agencies. Consider the effects of requirements such as: no public money shall be spent, but in accordance with the law, all bills for raising revenue shall originate in the House of Representatives, and Congress shall have the power to make binding rules for the government. These provisions create boundaries for public authority and regulate the process of its use.

In modern democratic societies, the legislative influence on administrative performance is manifested in several ways, ranging from approval of financial spending and staffing practices to enactment of a variety of public laws that legitimize and sanction administrative actions. Congress enjoys particularly broad and varied methods of intervention in the administrative function, together called "oversight." Through such mechanisms, Congress is given the power to oversee executive and administrative performance. The most significant tools of legislative oversight are:

authorization of policies to be administered by executive departments (this entails passage, amendment, and repeal of the enabling legislation that establishes the functions of a department);

appropriation of funds through approval of the public budget;

investigation of political or administrative misconduct;

contacting agencies directly for whatever reason (casework for constituents);

confirmation of top executive appointments by the Senate;

reorganization of the federal government, through approval or veto of executive plans of reorganization;

auditing administrative agencies (by the General Accounting Office) to ensure accountability in spending of public funds;

employing sunset legislation that stipulates self-termination of a program after a limited period unless the management of the agency or program can convince the legislators that the program is essential and successful; and

use of the veto power in various forms to require an administrative agency to submit its final rules or decisions to Congress or to a particular committee for approval.

Just as the legislative veto approach was gathering speed, the Supreme Court dealt it a fatal blow in 1983 by nullifying Congressional veto of administrative decisions on constitutional grounds. The Supreme Court decision in *Immigration and Naturalization Service v. Chadha* (462 U.S. 919, 1983) declared, in effect, legislative veto to be unconstitutional. For years, the constitutionality of such legislative vetoes had been disputed by presidents and administrative agencies. The court's position was that, once Congress passed a law, it could not constitutionally share in its administration. Congress may express displeasure with administrative action or amend or repeal the law, all of which are proper exercises of legislative power (Nigro & Nigro 1989, p. 5).

The specifics of *Immigration and Naturalization Service v. Chadha* are these: Under the Immigration and Nationality Act, a decision by the attorney general suspending deportation of an alien could be nullified by veto of either house of Congress. When the House of Representatives exercised this power in Chadha's case, Chadha brought suit. The Supreme Court held that this "one-house veto" scheme violated Art. I, 7, of the Constitution. Under that section, no legislation can be valid unless it is passed by both houses of Congress and signed by the president. The House's veto should be presumed to be an exercise of legislative power, the court explained, and, thus, the Art. I, 7, requirements applied (Gellhorn & Levin 1990, p. 40).

Consequently, public organizations invest considerable energies gauging their political environment and adjusting to it. They also seek to modify and influence the actions of the political system and do not simply act like obedient soldiers who unquestioningly carry out their leaders' wishes. Public organizations are autonomous structures; they are protective of their domains and their prerogatives.

Public organizations generally are proactive in the formulation as well as in the implementation of public policy. They possess certain qualifications and resources such as knowledge and expertise; they are buttressed by accumulation of information and continuous focus on specialized functions and policies. Many of these organizations also succeed in building viable connections with citizens benefiting from public services. The constituent groups often become loyal supporters who defend the organization and lobby for enhancement of its resources. Veterans, farmers, educators, business people, professional groups of lawyers and physicians, and many others all have favorite programs and public policies and lobby legislators and other elected officials for support. The association of public organizations and their constituents improves chances of influencing public policy outcomes on terms acceptable to administrative units, not only the direction of policy but also its budgetary allocations.

However, the relationship of public organizations to their political contexts is crucial for a variety of reasons. The most important one is grounded in the ideals of the democratic process in which elected persons, deriving their legitimacy from being elected to represent citizens, enact laws that prescribe public policies. Thus, elected officials ultimately are accountable and responsible to the public for formulating public policies. Management, in turn, implements those policies with expertise and in accordance with norms of the profession of management. Analytically, a dichotomy of policy-administration separates the two functions, but as Jack Rabin (1996, p. 149) comments on Norton Long's famous article on public policy and administration: "The doctrine of political supremacy of the elected over the nonelected branch of the government has inspired the delusion that to be politically supreme the legislature must not only make final decisions on policy but must also have primacy in the whole process of policy formulation — that the bureaucracy should be an instrument rather than a brain."

Over the years, this conceptual distinction has been subject to criticism, modification, rejection, and support. The literature does not seem to conclusively accept or reject such a notion for the simple reason that the dichotomy theory is "partially accurate in describing the relationship between the elected officials and administrators" (Savara 1995, p. 3). In reality, although the separation endures for maintaining democratic control over matters of the state, an accepted practice has emerged that rejects the notion of absolute dichotomy. Management influences policy-making in many ways, and political leaders shape management through a variety of direct and indirect means. The broad statement of policy contained in legislation, executive order, ordinance of a city government, or a decision by an elected official hardly provides detailed instructions on enforcement. In the meantime, such policies are inconsequential until translated into activities with concrete results. As Long argued in the 1950s, administrative organizations, too, should reflect the needs of society and, thus, engage in both policymaking and administration.

Thus, the current view of the relationship between policy and administration is not a separation but a blend, a combination, of processes in which elected officials and administrative staff share each others' role without abdicating ultimate responsibility for their own traditional functions. Elected officials retain final responsibility for policymaking, and administrators remain the definitive authority on carrying out such policies, even when the formulation and the implementation are dependently joined.

Clearly, the political context has a defining influence because it is a source of many incongruities in operational management. True, taxpayers fund public organizations and provide their staffs and programs with a sense of security and continuity. At the same time, such funding is authorized by individuals who are removed from operations and, frequently, have goals and values inconsistent with those of management. This variance repeatedly tests organizational endurance and proficiency. In the final analysis, not recognizing the capacity of administrative units to think on their own and to independently propose possible ranges of policies that politicians will find it judicious to espouse will only weaken the task of formulating rational and responsible public policy (Rabin 1996, p. 149).

Certainly, most public organizations have their own interests and are not without powers to represent such interests throughout the complex processes of policy formulation and implementation. Actually, a widely used practice by federal agencies in dealing with the legislative branch is to establish a "legislative liaison" to focus on communication and interaction with Congress. Activities of the liaison office include more than objective public policy concerns and may involve personal services and privileges extended to influential members of Congress to receive and sustain their good will and positive dispositions toward an agency.

At the local level of government, the political environment of administrative units inevitably includes needs and demands of citizens in the community being served. Because of size and proximity, citizens' attitudes are more noticeable and often have more impact on actions of administrative units than at the state or federal levels. In fact, cities and counties periodically conduct surveys to assess degrees of citizens' satisfaction with public services. These governments also hold open hearings on tax rates and annual allocations of funds to various services and programs. They often use various citizens' advisory boards to provide feedback on different municipal services such as police, fire protection, budgets, and community relations. At the same time, local governments are subjects of confining restraints imposed by state governments. Even those local governments granted charters by the state find considerable limitations imposed on their powers of action by state laws and regulations.

Public administration, therefore, is in the midst of a political environment shaped by larger forces with high stakes in policy processes. These forces consist of legislators, interest groups, mass media, political parties, and political appointees. Interactions between them and public managers often are strained by incongruities of managerial and political values. Management of public organizations is not neutral to the process or to the outcome of policymaking. When professional concerns are frustrated by political actions, ensuing tensions affect not only the immediate operations of public organizations but also long-range managerial factors of morale, confidence, and focus on matters of public interest.

The predicament for public managers is how to truly serve professional ethics, efficiency, effectiveness, and equity in public service within a turbulent and often erratic political environment. True, the political process is entrusted with functions of citizens' representation, but frequently, the process produces impaired decisions. It is not unusual to find decisions poorly developed, serving narrow but powerful interest groups, prematurely authorized, vaguely stated, and lacking consensus and support. Legislators and other elected officials, beholden to lobbyists and interest group financiers, habitually blame the "bureaucrats" for failures of policy. Thus, public service becomes a convenient scapegoat for bad public policies, and public managers in turn retrench into safer terrains of inaction and practicing survival techniques.

Politically corruptive influences, in fact, are not new in the U.S. policymaking process. The spoils system, predating the civil service reform of 1883, has not disappeared altogether. Pork-barrel financing and raids on the treasury by political leaders preceded budgetary reforms of 1921 and still are prevalent in current public budgeting decisions at all levels of government. Local party leaders remain a significant force influencing decisions in county and city governments. Investigations and trials of corruption among state and local elected officials are more numerous across the country than commonly realized or acknowledged.

Ineffectiveness of the Congress and the unethical conduct of many of its members are almost daily news. Congress is not working so well anymore. It is paralyzed by its own bloated bureaucracy and numbed by the cynicism of its members. Partisan sniping and issue ducking are so pervasive that such basic congressional functions as budget approval have become hard to manage. Conditions have not improved, and sentiments of delusion are commonly expressed. The actual federal budget deficit, for example, has not disappeared, despite more than a decade of bipartisan bickering. The total deficit of the federal budget between 1981 and 1991 reached $1,979 billion. At the beginning of the second Clinton administration, total federal debt was $5.280 trillion ($19,800 for every American).

The gap also is growing between citizens and their government for broken promises by politicians as well as for failed policies. Increasingly, government appears to be controlled by special interests, and public officials are viewed as living in a world of privilege and power. Long-range problems do not get full attention from political leaders, preoccupied with immediate concerns of their own personal agendas. Obtusely, political leaders find ways and means to receive huge sums of money from special interests seeking favors at the expense of public interests.

The ever-rising cost of campaigns has made the pursuit of contributions an all-consuming passion for most members of Congress. For several years, citizens' groups accorded top priority to programs of reforming campaign financing and limiting contributions to legislative elections by interest groups but to no avail. "Today, unless you're wealthy, or willing to accept the largesse of wealthy corporations, you will not be elected to the U.S. Senate or Congress" (Garvey 1997, p. 8). The high cost of 1996 campaigns revived public protests and revealed again the magnitude of funds collected and spent. In a "Follow the Money" (Zaldivar 1997, p. A1) report from the Knight-Ridder Washington Bureau, the chasing of campaign money was described in the following:

It works out to about $21 a voter. That's what you get if you take the estimated $2 billion raised and spent in the 1996 presidential and congressional campaigns and divide by the 97 million Americans who showed up to vote on Election Day. But campaign finance is not simple arithmetic. Money is a powerful catalyst in politics, and contributors and candidates know it. . . . Twenty-year old federal laws meant to temper the influence of money all but collapsed, undermined by widening loopholes and the aggressive ingenuity of fundraisers and contributors.

According to the Federal Election Commission, a record was set by all candidates for congressional races of money collected and spent in 1996 (*New York Times* 1997, p. 8A). Moreover, the published numbers do not include costs in kind by organized groups or express the newly uncovered money from foreign sources. In a comment on "Democracy vs. Free Speech?" Garvey wrote: "Never has the power of money in politics been more obvious. A 1992 poll showed that 74 percent of American voters thought 'congress is largely owned by the special-interest groups,' and 84 percent agreed that 'special-interest money buys the loyalty of candidates.' In the last four years, things have only gotten worse. In the 1996 campaign, Senate candidates spent between $5 million and $30 million to win their seats. And the Presidential campaign was the most expensive in history, running up a tab of $800 million" (1997, p. 8).

The impact of these negative influences on professional public management has not been adequately articulated in the literature. There are few exceptions, such as the works of Laurence Lynn (1987), Charles Goodsell (1983), and Frederick Thayer (1990). Despite the view that "the bulk of policymaking is based on cooperation" between the legislators and the administrative agencies (Ripley & Franklin 1984, p. 15), the negative political influences remain considerable.

Consequently, public managers are constricted by the political environment; perhaps, they cannot be significantly more effective than they are. The "legislative response to the growth of public administration," David Rosenbloom concludes (1986, p. 61), "is somewhat cynical and perverse." Promotion of their own incumbency and self-interest and the fact that it is becoming increasingly difficult to unseat them in elections are among the reasons for such negative assessments. As Lynn (1987, p. 3) concludes, focusing on the potential for administrative reform and on the criticisms of individual managers' administrative performance, instead of on the process and structures of government, is misdirected.

Policymaking requires a wide range of skills by individuals and institutions, but only those with expertise, access to information, and continuity of focus can provide necessary proficiency. This is true for the federal as well as for state and local authorities. Actually, the problem of having adequate skills is frequently very acute at the local level, where basic knowledge by elected officials is lacking. How to define a problem, to conduct public meetings, and to agree on policy direction are difficult propositions for many elected local leaders. Too often, local officials seem eager to compete, not to do something to solve a problem but to say something about it. Voters who attend or watch proceedings cannot help but conclude that their elected leaders lack either discipline or a basic grasp of issues or both. Such is the political environment within which public organizations and public managers work.

The connections of public organizations to their political contexts, therefore, remain decisive for the survival of programs and for the well-being of the organization itself. Unavoidably, the political system relies on complex bureaucratic organizations in formulating and implementing public policy but without ignoring critical issues such as responsiveness, representativeness, and accountability. Elected officials as well as mass media and interest groups have always found information, however episodic or infrequent, that portrays pictures of inefficiency of management in the public sector. An unintended consequence is that the separation of politics and administration has facilitated mutual scapegoating, where management blames policy and politicians for failures and politicians, in turn, blame the bureaucrats. This familiar scene in U.S. politics contributes to many rigidities in managing programs, diffuses accountability, and underscores other negative effects, such as low motivation and a host of customary charges of bureaucratic pathologies or dysfunctions.

Opposition to government, antibureaucratic sentiment in particular, has been a global phenomenon since the 1970s. Failures of national socioeconomic development plans in Third World countries and the collapse of communism in Russia and East Europe have stimulated waves of disappointment and even anger directed at the central authority of the nation-state. In the United States, the negative sentiment was manifested in downsizing and cutbacks of financial allocations to public sector functions. This trend continued in the "reinvention of government" movement that called for moving away from traditional managerial approaches and for the adoption of entrepreneurial management judged by customer satisfaction (Osborne & Gaebler 1992).

As Hal Rainey (1997, p. 7) explains, negative views of government and bureaucracy around the world are reflections of two central premises: "First, that governmental activities differ from those controlled by private actors and organizations, and, second, that governmental activities are performed less effectively and efficiently." What is new here, perhaps, is not the premises themselves as much as the self-serving exaggeration and manipulation of negative information about government, no matter what level of proficiency it demonstrates in performing its functions.

THE JUDICIAL CONTEXT

The proliferation of laws in modern society has been translated into greater power for public organizations, which already command significant power of expertise and functional specialization. Certain public agencies and commissions performing regulatory functions also have delegated powers that allow them to perform semilegislative and semijudicial roles. As a result of these large accumulated administrative powers, judicial review has become an important safeguard against arbitrary use of such administrative authority. Courts review administrative decisions and interpret existing laws to ensure protection of constitutional rights and liberties granted to individuals and groups. Over the years, the judicial impact has increased through implementation of defined operational standards in public agencies, as required by administrative procedures acts, at the federal and the state levels.

A judicial review provides relief to an individual who is harmed by a particular agency decision. In contrast, political oversight controls generally influence entire programs or policies. Also, judicial review differs from political controls, according to Ernest Gellhorn and Ronald Levin (1990, p. 73), "in that it attempts to foster reasoned decisionmaking, by requiring the agencies to produce supporting facts and rational explanations." In essence, judicial review provides an independent check on the validity of administrative decisions.

Despite these generalizations, judicial review is limited by factors of institutional competence; the court may decline to intervene and review an administrative decision under certain conditions. Specifically, the court declines review if the administrative process has not been exhausted, if the statute precludes the decision from judicial review, or if the decision is beyond the competence of the court. The latter situation is exemplified by decisions with scientific or technical core beyond the knowledge capability of a judge trained in law. Although, traditionally, only a small percentage of administrative decisions are ever reviewed by courts, judicial review generally is available in cases that deal with questions of law and constitutional rights, statutory jurisdiction, use of required procedures, abuse of administrative discretion, or actions taken that may not be in accordance with the law (Gellhorn & Levin 1990, pp. 75–77).

A significant development in the 1970s that underlines the changing legal environment of public administration is the Supreme Court abandonment of the notion of absolute immunity of public officials, which had provided protection from civil suits for damages. By ruling for qualified immunity, rather than an absolute one, the court has forced public administrators to scrupulously avoid any violation of individual constitutional rights and has made them personally responsible for paying damages to the injured party. Under the current standard for determining the scope of qualified immunity, "the public administrator is very likely to be personally liable if he or she knew or reasonably should have known that the official actions taken violated someone's constitutional or legal rights" (Rosenbloom 1986, p. 66).

The legal constraints on public administration from strengthening protection of individual rights, applying the doctrine of qualified immunity, and the stricter observance of the procedural due process mean that public administrators are under greater pressure to justify their decisions and to demonstrate their legal validity. In public personnel administration, judicial decisions have had significant impact on public employment. In several employee lawsuits brought against governments during the 1970s and 1980s, court decisions affirmed public employees' basic constitutional rights (freedom of speech, freedom of association, political activity, and equal protection). Court decisions rejected the traditional notion of public employment as a "privilege" and extended to public employees the procedural due process protection (Jaegal & Cayer 1988, p. 212).

The Administrative Procedures Act (APA) of 1946 is Congress' response to the growing powers of regulatory agencies in modern society and to the constitutional dilemma of combining executive, legislative, and judicial functions in administrative units. The APA establishes minimal procedural standards for federal agencies and does not supersede stricter procedural requirements imposed on agencies by their enabling legislation. Through APA, Congress has been providing procedural guidance to proliferating administrative agencies since the New Deal and World War II. As Florence Heffron and Neil McFeeley (1983, p. 86) point out, the APA as finally passed was largely an outcome of the struggle among Congress, President Franklin Roosevelt, and the American Bar Association to establish supremacy over the administrative process. The substance of the argument by the advocates of the APA, particularly the legal profession, is the desire to afford protection to individuals and groups against encroachment by administrative agencies.

Moreover, the APA establishes public access to agency information by stipulating that an agency must publish in the *Federal Register* descriptions of its organization, rules, and methods of making decisions. Procedures are established for informal rule making, adjudication, conduct of hearings, imposing sanctions, agency review, and so forth. About half of the states have adopted administrative procedures acts of their own based on the APA of 1946. The other states have accepted modified or watered-down provisions. Considerable variation still exists, despite narrowing of differences as a result of the influence of federal statutes.

Critics of the growing legal restrictions on administrative behavior in contemporary society consider such a development as a continuation of numerous deliberate initiatives to weaken the administrative process. A significant impetus in this direction comes from unrelenting conservative campaigns against government powers in society. Marshall E. Dimock (1980, p. 3) points out that the passage of the APA in 1946 was a climax of such conservative campaigns against government. Subsequently, most public agencies "began to judicialize, which made them progressively tentative, formalistic, and bureaucratic." Nevertheless, any weakening of administrative powers caused by the APA restrictions wanes in comparison with the ideological onslaught of conservative politics against administrative agencies in the 1980s, during the Reagan administration.

The efforts to limit administrative powers and discretion received support from many quarters. The legal profession probably is the most instrumental in bringing Congress and the courts into action to restrict administrative authority. "What was represented as an attempt to strengthen private rights and due process of law became, by gradual extension and in actual operation, a progressive slowing down and confusion of the administrative process" (Dimock 1980, p. 3).

In conclusion, the legal environment is an important aspect of contemporary public administration. Laws determine a great deal about the mission, structure, resources, and general power of public agencies as well as their practices in managing their own personnel. Also, laws specify standards of operation as well as methods of challenging arbitrary and capricious decisions made by these administrative units. With the expansion of public responsibilities in society beyond the traditional functions of government, the need is dramatized for protection of individual rights and strengthening the political oversight and the judicial review. Government today is not limited to levying taxes, defense, foreign policy, and the like. Government assumes many fairly new roles in a changing society, such as protection of consumers, health care, protection of the environment, work safety, and regulation of brokerage firms, broadcasting, advertising, and so forth. Industrialization and urbanization and their by-products such as pollution, social strife, issues of law and order, and demands for various policy outcomes have changed government by expanding the role and power of administration. Indeed, the growing powers of administrative agencies justify the view that currently we live in an "administrative state."

In sum, judicial review provides a vital and essential check on the exercise of administrative power. Agencies constantly must maintain vigilance against abuse of individual rights and due process as well as being able to verify and explain the basis of their decisions. Also, delivery of services at any level of government underlines once more the issue of public accountability. Public employees operate in the open; their records, decisions, meetings, and deliberations are subject to public disclosure and scrutiny unless secrecy is required for specific reasons, such as national security. The courts have been a major force upholding such principles at the risk of undermining administrative discretion and stimulating bureaucratic resistance.

THE ECONOMIC LINKAGE

The economic environment creates limitations and opportunities for public management. In times of recession or depression, the impact of economics is unmistakable. General economic conditions affect returns of state revenues, which, in turn, influence decisions on allocation of resources, employment, incentive systems, and many other internal organizational processes. At the national level, bad economic conditions place special responsibility on government to direct resources through the budget and other instruments of public policy in order to realize policy objectives in the areas of employment, economic growth, and stability of wages and prices.

During the 1990s, public managers are particularly aware of the economic constraints surrounding public organizations at all levels of government because debates all around them are focusing on cutback, retrenchment, downsizing, fiscal stress, efficiency, and productivity improvement. As expected, the adjustments of public organizations are not always smooth or ending in happy experiences. Apparently, easing the pain is possible only if such financial pressures provide the means of instilling discipline into public decision making and forcing greater rationality into the various spheres of policy deliberations (Bell 1985).

Economic constraints first affect employment in the public sector. Economic stress makes reduction of government jobs unavoidable. Public managers, particularly at the local level, are constantly challenged in their effort to reduce taxes, balance the budget, and stimulate economic growth. The less dramatic target seems to be elimination of positions and work force reductions as the road to surviving shortfall of revenues and weak economic conditions, particularly in many state and local governments.

However, high unemployment means less tax revenues and greater pressures to increase public expenditures to stimulate the economy and improve the employment level. Although such economic consequences may be felt directly at the federal revenue side, their impact is just as crucial, though indirect, at the state and local levels. The opposite situation of employment is also problematic. Low unemployment or full employment directly affects the personnel practices of government (the largest employer in the society) by forcing competition with the private sector for the best talents. Consequently, government has to improve its pay scale and adjust to general economic conditions in order to have comparable standards of pay in the market place.

Supply-side economists argue for a reduced government role in the economy by producing less regulation, lowering taxes, and limiting spending. The basic concept is that governmental intervention in the economy is less efficient than free market competition in allocating goods and services, directing investments, and generating economic growth. Such economic thinking influenced public policy in general and budget recommendations in particular during the 1980s. Also, this approach is quite

different from the Keynesian economic theory that oriented the administration of the federal government since Roosevelt in public spending as
well as in stimulating the economy. Keynesian economics support a
proactive role of government in steering the economy and reaching desirable goals of fiscal policy: acceptable levels of employment, wage and
price increases, and economic growth. These goals, according to this
economic thinking, are attainable mainly through considered regulatory
and budgetary measures.

In fact, federal spending has become so massive that whole segments of
the private sector are dependent on it, and drastic reduction could result in
serious negative economic consequences. State and local spending also
experienced high growth, with their governments often being major
employers and consumers in the local economy. Perhaps the impact of the
government on the economy is most pronounced in the area of public
debt. The huge deficits of the federal budget have affected many
economic indicators, such as interest rates, levels of saving, business
investment, and consumer confidence. Also, state and local governments
often borrow money to finance various capital improvement projects.

Overall, government functions are linked to economic factors, and no
aspect of government can be truly separated from considerations of its
economic environment. Government, and public administration in particular, influences and is influenced by economic factors through imposition
of taxes and fees, spending and borrowing, producing goods and services,
and regulating private individuals and groups in their economic pursuits.
As all those working for the public sector know too well, public employment, benefits, annual raises, recruitment practices, and so forth are
governed fundamentally by general economic conditions and are sensitive
to changes in the revenue side of the public budget.

NATIONAL CULTURE

Culture is an all-embracing constellation of norms, traits, and patterns
that identify a society and distinguish its people. Some of these cultural
dimensions are unique to certain societies, although others are universal.
Almost always, culture is inferred from statements and behaviors more
than directly observed or measured. There is no profound disagreement in
the literature over the existence of cultural influence on organization and
individual behaviors. The problem, however, is in how to specify,
measure, and interpret such influence in order to steer it in positive directions, such as to improve performance. Apparently, research in this area
has to contend first with the issue of specification of cultural determinants

as a prerequisite for gauging the impact on administration. Another vital inquiry in this delineation of influences is the degree of association, if any, between culture and form of government.

Research in developmental psychology, sociology, and anthropology shows that there are major differences among the cognitive processes of people from different cultures (Adler, Doktor, & Redding 1986, p. 295). Contributions from this research have served training efforts in cross-cultural management for business purposes. Comparing organizations and individual behavior cross-culturally became important for managers who seek to understand and improve their effectiveness in interacting with their counterparts from other cultures. Global economics and multinational corporations further enhanced interests in cross-cultural research and promoted training in cross-cultural management (Harris & Moran 1987).

A motivating factor for comparative public administration is the search for discovering regularities in administrative processes and behaviors throughout the human experience, irrespective of place and time. Early research in comparative administration also sought to explain and analyze the relationship between management and culture (Riggs 1961, 1964). Thus, comparative public administration devoted considerable attention to identification of environmental factors that affect the performance and the operation of bureaucracy. A significant body of literature has been produced on various aspects of management in various cultures of the world and cannot be adequately reviewed here. However, despite the long, sustained interest in the cultural component of the environment, organization theory has not been successful in overcoming certain confirming biases to Western-style rationalism in concept and in methods. The fields of comparative and cross-cultural management, according to Nancy Adler, Robert Doktor, and Gordon Redding (1986, p. 297), are still asking the following questions: does organizational behavior vary across cultures, and if so, how much of the observed difference can be attributed to cultural determinants?

Efforts to study variance of organizational behavior worldwide produced two different, but not mutually exclusive, motivating concerns. One is a utilitarian motivation that seeks to understand how organizations can manage cultural diversity competently in order to compete in international markets. The second is a social science concern that seeks explanation and interpretation of relations and influences of various objectives; in this area are the professional interests of public administration best served.

Certainly, universal principles of administration evolve mainly through cross-cultural studies. Recognizing the trend toward globalization, Fred Riggs (1991, p. 473) points out that public administration must be comparative in order to compel us to rethink the context of what we call "public administration." Thus, Riggs (1991, p. 473) states that "we need to develop frameworks and theories for the study of public administration that are truly universal in scope — they will be based on a comprehensive ecological understanding of the place of public administration in all governments, historical as well as contemporary." Such a framework will focus on explanatory theories that account for the continuously changing properties and problems faced by governments as they seek to implement public policies. Riggs calls this "nomothetic," and distinguishes it from idiographic frameworks, which consist only of descriptive information and case studies. A closer examination, however, indicates that the "old" comparative approach resulted in broad-gauged applications that often lacked relevance and coherence (Jreisat 1975, pp. 666–667). Riggs seeks to anchor the normative guidelines of comparative administration in empirical knowledge of the institutions and dynamics of society. The expected advantage of this is the increasing use of comparative methods to understand U.S. public administration in a global framework and to find better solutions for its problems. Also, by understanding U.S. administration, Riggs (1991, p. 473) hopes that "we become less ethnocentric, and this will also help us acquire a more penetrating understanding of the administrative problems faced by other countries."

In recent years, few notable efforts have been made to define and measure the effects of culture on administrative practices. To operationalize culture by differentiating its effects from those of other environmental elements or by isolating its dimensions are notable advancements. Geert Hofstede (1993, p. 89) operationalized culture in terms of four dimensions, which he uses to describe and classify countries:

1. Power distance defines the degree of inequality among people whom the population of a country considers normal.

2. Collectivism-individualism measures the degree to which people in a country prefer to act as individuals rather than as members of groups.

3. Masculinity-femininity determines the degree to which values of assertiveness, performance, success, and competition, associated with men, prevail over tender values of quality of life, maintaining warm personal relationships, service, care for the weak, and solidarity, associated with women, occur in nearly all societies.

4. Uncertainty avoidance defines the degree to which people in a country prefer structured over unstructured situations. A scale measuring responses to issues dealing with the four dimensions was constructed based on data from a survey of 116,000 people in 50 countries.

Hofstede's conclusions include, first, that culture is "the collective mental programming of the mind which distinguishes one group or category of people from another" and, second, that "there are no such things as universal management theories" (1993, p. 89). Hofstede proceeds to assert that the validity of theories stops at the national borders. Consequently, under such cultural determinism, managerial actions and decisions become the inevitable consequence of their cultural antecedents (Jreisat 1991, p. 667).

There are at least three potential problems with analysis that subject organizations to a sort of cultural captivity. First, restrictive cultural conceptualization ultimately reduces the differences in managerial practices to consequences of ethnocentricity. Thus, for example, definitions of quality of life, managerial decisions, and efficient and effective organizations are all products of cultural relativity. Such conception leads to a sort of cultural determinism in which managerial decisions are the inevitable consequences of their cultural antecedents. Furthermore, because culture is difficult to change, administrative reform is consigned to failure unless it is in the image of existing cultural patterns of the society (Jreisat 1991, p. 667).

Second, and paradoxically, although consistency with fundamental societal values is important, organizations are regularly being used as instruments for modifying social norms and cultural beliefs of a society, such as by educational institutions. In the context of Third World countries, the notion of mutual influence between the organization and its environment is crucial in dealing with the task of socioeconomic development. If the organization is a captive of its culture, "the collective mental programming," in Hofstede terms, then the prospects of change and reform of bureaucratic performance are really bleak. Moreover, cultures vary within each society, and "cultural diversity" is a realistic concept, although we often deal with dominant patterns and rarely with all relevant patterns. Even such dominant cultural patterns, despite almost universal recognition of their impact on administrative behavior, specific information on elements, and degrees of the relationships, remain in a relatively primitive phase. The notion of what constitutes culture is still arguable. A review of 22 studies of comparative management that employed culture as an independent variable to explain differences in management practices among nations found that in most of these studies, culture was used as a pseudonym for nation (Nath 1988, p. 7).

Third, societies consist of individuals who interact according to patterns shaped by cultural factors, standardized and sanctioned by the society. Through socialization, sanctions, and other forms of influence, these patterns become significant contributory elements to personality configurations. Such notions are foundation concepts in anthropology and psychology. However, to assume that individuals are "programmed" by their culture is to deny the dynamic characteristics of personality and the processes of development, growth, and change. Individuals have the ability to learn, form new habits, forget old habits, recognize new situations, and develop new behaviors to deal with them (Linton 1945, p. 5). Even in the most integrated cultures, individuals retain distinctive characteristics and capacities for independent thought and feeling. Without such verifiable conceptual basis, administrative change would not be possible; training and development by outside technical assistance would be a futile effort. The theory that each culture develops its own administrative and organizational norms and processes and, therefore, that the transfer of knowledge and practices across boundaries is not possible is rejected here as defeatist and groundless.

Certainly, socioeconomic transformation of traditional societies cannot be achieved by destroying or emasculating their identifying cultures and traditions. Transformation has to be a synthesis, somewhat similar to what Gabriel A. Almond and Sidney Verba (1965, p. 6) refer to as an emergent "third culture, neither traditional nor modern but partaking of both." However, this is another matter altogether.

In the United States, the common depiction of public bureaucracy is particularly negative. Academics as well as mass media often regard public bureaucracy as overstaffed, inflexible, unresponsive, and power hungry. With few exceptions, Goodsell (1983, p. 6) points out, academic analyses of bureaucracy are pessimistic and condemnatory. Their criticisms may be organized in various ways, but at least three negative descriptions of bureaucracy are perceived as paramount: poor performance, manipulation of political power, and oppression of the individual.

A major source of antipathy to public bureaucracy also comes from the market-oriented economists. They are hostile to government bureaucracy on the grounds that competitive markets and profit-based incentive systems are the only feasible means to attain economic efficiency (Goodsell 1983, p. 6). The policy analysis community seems to have little or no faith in public bureaucracy as well. The failures of public policies frequently and conveniently are explained or identified with public bureaucracy not doing its part in carrying out policy. The powerful business sector, along with the influential legal profession often induced by conservative political and social ideologies, has placed public service on the defensive, particularly during the 1980s. The anti–public bureaucracy sentiments have been an element of the campaigns by most national politicians. "Businesslike" is the slogan frequently advanced by politicians, lawyers, and business executives for managing government programs, even when the business sector is ravaged by scandals, bankruptcies, embezzlements, and numerous unethical practices. The mass media often echo the need for public management to be run like business, even though the news headlines are replete with scandals by savings and loan associations, costing taxpayers hundreds of billions of dollars. Unethical manipulations on Wall Street, netting huge profits to white-collar criminals, have not caused reexamination of the often-assumed efficiency and effectiveness of U.S. corporations.

Finally, it is a mistake to attribute organizational dynamics in the United States to perceived inherent properties of culture, almost to the exclusion of other factors. In the final analysis, cultural norms themselves are not static. In so many basic ways, cultural values regularly adapt and change, as in general compliance with the law or the consequence of universal education. Other factors, too, foster cultural adaptation, such as open communication, technological advancements, and innovative managerial reforms. Thus (as in Chapter 10), we examine organizational culture as the norms and values espoused by an organization in dealing with its employees, customers, and operations, but here, the focus is on the societal cultural traits that condition bureaucratic patterns of action and determine interdependence. Clearly, organizational culture may be a creature or a consequence of societal culture, but it is not necessarily a mirror or a clone of it.

CONCLUSION

The relations between public organizations and their environments are intricate, interactional processes that often produce profound mutual influences. Public organizations enter such a state of interdependency with their larger environments that survival and stability of the organization become goals in themselves. The uncertainty created by such a relationship forces organizations to continually probe the environment in a search for appropriate survival tactics and for more acceptable alternatives in the operational side. This interaction is essentially an exchange in an open system that allows the organization to sort out from its numerous activities those essential for its survival and for achieving the acceptance of its environment. At the same time, organizational management strives to have this exchange not obscure but further differentiate the organization from its environment in order to retain its identity, define its responsibilities (territory), and maintain an orderly balance among its functional components and the environment.

Again, political, economic, legal, and cultural elements of the environment present challenges, provide resources, and impose restrictions on the performance of public organizations, which, in turn, provide essential services. Holistic analysis of public organizations has to accommodate the interdependence with the environment and deal with it as a central element and not an appendage to this reality.

The political context sets the framework for government, allocates resources, authorizes policies, and controls administrative actions in order to maintain equilibrium of power in the society. The judicial context deals with the increasing importance of administrative decisions on the lives of citizens, compelling greater safeguards against arbitrary use of administrative authority. In essence, judicial review protects individuals from such misuse of power, fosters reasoned administrative decision making, and ensures due process in the making of those administrative decisions. The cultural traits provide overall patterns of behavior and shape the underlying values and norms that influence organizational actions. Public administration has benefited by cross-cultural comparisons throughout its history. From the time of Woodrow Wilson to the present, public administration broke national boundaries to learn from other cultures, adapt its own national practices, and transfer its technical know-how to be applied outside the culture of origin.

It is within these environmental constraints, exchanges, interventions, and influences that today's public manager seeks to perform a balancing act. With power of expert knowledge, possession of vital information, and considerable resources (material, organizational, and political), modern management is facing greater and shifting expectations. Public administration is judged increasingly by its ability to develop professional management with the capacity to respond and to adapt to larger needs and to global norms. These new emphases boil down to greater commitment to excellence and professional ethics in performing public duties.

REFERENCES

Adler, Nancy, Robert Doktor, and Gordon Redding. 1986. From the Atlantic to the Pacific Century: Cross-Cultural Management Reviewed. *Journal of*

Management, 12, 2.

Almond, Gabriel A. and Sidney Verba. 1965. *The Civil Culture*. Boston, MA: Little, Brown.

Bell, Robert. 1985. *The Culture of Policy Deliberation*. New Brunswick, NJ: Rutgers University Press.

Dimock, Marshall E. 1980. *Law and Dynamic Administration*. New York: Praeger.

Follow the Money. January 12, 1997. *Tallahassee Democrat*.

Garvey, Ed. January 8, 1997. Democracy vs. Free Speech. *The Progressive*.

Gellhorn, Ernest and Ronald M. Levin. 1990. *Administrative Law and Process*, 3rd ed. St. Paul, MN: West Publishing.

Goodsell, Charles T. 1983. *The Case for Bureaucracy*. Chatham, NJ: Chatham House.

Harris, Philip R. and Robert T. Moran. 1987. *Managing Cultural Differences*. Houston, TX: Gulf Publishing.

Heady, Ferrel. 1996. *Public Administration: A Comparative Perspective*, 5th ed. New York: Marcel Dekker.

Heffron, Florence and Neil McFeeley. 1983. *The Administrative Regulatory Process*. New York: Longman.

Hofstede, Geert. 1993. Cultural Constraints in Management Theories. *Academy of Management Executive*, 7, 1.

Jaegal, Don and N. Joseph Cayer. 1988. Public Personnel Administration by Lawsuit: The Impact of Supreme Court Decisions on Public Employee Litigiousness. *Public Administration Review*, 51, 3 (May-June).

Jreisat, Jamil E. 1991. Bureaucratization of the Arab World. In *Handbook of Comparative and Development Public Administration*, edited by A. Farazmand. New York: Marcel Dekker.

_____. 1975. Synthesis and Relevance in Comparative Public Administration. *Public Administration Review*, 35, 6 (November-December).

Linton, Ralph. 1945. *The Cultural Background of Personality*. New York: Appleton-Century-Crofts.

Lynn, Laurence E., Jr. 1987. *Managing Public Policy*. Boston, MA: Little, Brown.

Nath, Raghu, ed. 1988. *Comparative Management*. New York: Ballinger.

New York Times. January 3, 1997.

Nigro, Felix A. and Lloyd G. Nigro. 1989. *Modern Public Administration*, 7th ed. New York: Harper & Row.

Osborne, David and Ted Gaebler. 1992. *Reinventing Government: How the Entrepreneurial Spirit Is Transforming the Public Sector from Schoolhouse to State House, City Hall to Pentagon*. Reading, MA: Addison-Wesley.

Rabin, Jack. 1996. In Retrospect: Public Policy and Administration. *Public Administration Review*, 56, 2 (March-April).

Rainey, Hal G. 1997. *Understanding and Managing Public Organizations*, 2d ed. San Francisco, CA: Jossey-Bass.

Riggs, Fred W. 1991. Public Administration: A Comparativist Framework. *Public Administration Review*, 51, 6 (November-December).

_____. 1964. *Administration in Developing Countries*. Boston, MA: Houghton Mifflin.

_____. 1961. *The Ecology of Public Administration*. New York: Asia Publishing House.

Ripley, Randall B. and Grace A. Franklin. 1984. *Congress, the Bureaucracy, and Public policy*, 3rd ed. Homewood, IL: Dorsey Press.

Rosenbloom, David H. 1986. *Public Administration: Understanding Management, Politics, and Law in the Public Sector*. New York: Random House.

Savara, James H. 1995. Dichotomy and Duality: Reconceptualizing Relationship between Policy and Administration. In *Ideal & Practice in Council-Manager Government*, edited by H. G. Frederickson. Washington, D.C.: ICMA.

Thayer, Frederick C. 1990. The Field of PA Is Professional not Political. *PA Times*, 13, 9 (September 1).

Zaldivar, R. A. 1997, January 12. Follow the Money. *Tallahassee Democrat*.

5

Classic Organization Rationality

Over several decades, and despite continuous challenges and criticisms, basic managerial concepts proved unusual durability. Such have been classic, traditional, or machine models, whatever the designation used in reference to three powerful and widely debated administrative approaches: scientific management or Taylorism, administrative management or the "principles" school, and the bureaucratic model by Max Weber. In this discussion, the aim is to provide a balanced perspective in studying each model and its contribution to knowledge of managerial techniques. Because of the significance of these frameworks to the evolution of public administration theory and practice, they are discussed methodically, according to a defined and connected set of questions:

What are the critical elements and attributes of each classic approach and how are they manifested?

What influence do these models have on theory and practice of public administration?

What failures and shortcomings are attributed to these models?

What contextual conditions have influenced the development of classic perspectives or were influenced by them?

The evaluation of each of the classic schools is governed by specific criteria that consist of several components: First, we do not relate each theorist to a preconceived model of organization that would bias the selection of information and predispose views on what is being studied. Instead, the initial step is to present a concise, accurate summary of each approach before judging, accepting, or rejecting it or some of its elements. Second, an important element of evaluation and analysis is to explain limitations as well as contributions, without violating the intent of the author or forcing the concepts into totally distinctive contexts. Certainly, our understanding of these perspectives will be incomplete, unless deliberate efforts are made to relate theory to practice and to establish continuity or lack of it in their evolution. Such linkages constitute critical elements in the accurate portrayal of public administration in its developmental mode and for recognizing its intellectual dynamics over time. Third, apparently, the assessment of the theoretical and practical values of these perspectives cannot totally avoid facing, even implicitly, basic defining ideas about the nature of man, of organization, and of the managerial environment.

SCIENTIFIC MANAGEMENT

Scientific management in the United States emerged at the beginning of this century. Its most widely acknowledged promoter is Frederick W. Taylor. Taylor's career offered him technical and managerial insights that proved extremely valuable in experimentation and analysis of task performance by the workers. He began his career as an apprentice machinist and rose rapidly to important posts in steel companies, including consulting engineer and general manager (Mosher 1981, pp. 98–99).

Taylor published *Shop Management* in 1903, *The Principles of Scientific Management* in 1911, and *The Testimony Before the Special House Committee* in 1912. His most influential ideas are incorporated in *The Principles of Scientific Management.*

Taylor's diagnosis of the basic social problem of his time, in the industrial firm and in society at large, was inefficiency. Thus, he pioneered the search for techniques and methods to increase and improve organizational productivity. In essence, Taylor attempted to replace the old, inefficient methods of production with a more scientifically based approach.

As Brian Fry (1989, p. 53) points out, Taylor blamed both management and the worker for inefficiency but reserved his sternest criticism for management. According to Fry, Taylor charged that management was deficient in terms of knowledge of the work and indifferent to proper managerial practices. Workers were hired without selectivity, assigned jobs without training, and supervised with authoritarianism and physical compulsion. Taylor referred to the process as "systematic soldiering" or purposeful and organized restriction of output.

The main techniques of scientific management are deceptively simple and rational. For example, a technique was devised to analyze the mechanical motions made during work in order to eliminate awkward or unnecessary motions. Another strategy was to discover or elaborate the correct method, "the best way" of doing a job. Taylor advocated thorough research to establish the best methods for carrying out every single element of the production. Once this has been done, the company's management must ensure a maximum standardization of each activity within the firm.

Taylor's recipe for increased labor productivity, therefore, provides concrete measures for rational utilization of the workers' energies as well as the other tools of production. Techniques include strict accounting of workers' time, control over use of material and equipment, analysis of work processes (by dividing them into their elementary components), and measuring (with a stopwatch) the time consumed in the implementation of each segment of the process. The use of these specific measures, Taylor suggested, is the "substitution of a science for the individual judgment of the workman" (quoted in Mosher 1981, p. 99).

The success of scientific management is dependent on other elements as well. One is "the scientific selection and development of the workman, after each man has been studied, taught, and trained, and one may say experimented with, instead of allowing the workmen to select themselves and develop in a haphazard way" (Mosher 1981, p. 99). Taylorism also demands the complete cooperation of the management with the workers so that, together, they may implement the scientifically developed laws.

Taylor attached major importance to the correct selection and training of workers and believed in choosing "the right person for the right job." He developed a pay-oriented inducement system based on the differential wage method.

However, Taylor warned against identifying scientific management by its mechanisms (such as time and motion studies) and their implements without recognizing the underlying philosophy. Scientific management, he explained, must not be viewed as merely a group of "efficiency devices," a new system of "figuring costs," a new scheme of wages, a "time study," or a "motion study." "Scientific Management," he declared, "involves a complete mental revolution" (Waldo 1948, p. 50). Ironically, scientific management continues to be discussed as essentially an array of mechanisms and techniques designed to enhance efficiency.

The following principles of scientific management summarize major elements in the model published in 1913:

science replaces rule of thumb,

systematic problem solving approach,

employee selection and development according to set criteria,

training of supervisors,

development of work measurement and work standards,

utilizing time and motion studies in work measurement,

advanced work planning,

order at work,

improvement of individual productivity, and

revolution in supervision and employee work.

Impact

In assessing the impact of scientific management on the theory and practice of public administration, we must realize that the pioneers in this area "never actually became involved in the abstract exercises of theory building" (Scott, Michell, & Birnbaum 1981, p. 11). Nevertheless, the impact of scientific management on the development of public adminis-tration is widely recognized. "Both arose concurrently," writes Dwight Waldo (1948, p. 47), "and were stimulated by the same circumstances." In addition, Waldo points out, scientific management made considerable technical and philosophical contributions to public administration.

At the local government level, Alice and Donald Stone report certain specific influences that scientific management has had on public organiza-tions. In fact, the Stones (1975, p. 24) indicate that the principles of scien-tific management, as developed by Taylor and others associated with the movement, "were ultimately commingled with the concepts initiated by the New York Bureau of Municipal Research and other contributors to the governmental research movement." Thus, Taylor's home city, Philadelphia, was not the only example of enthusiastic support of the new principles of management, when "a director of Public Works was appointed to institute Scientific Management procedures" (Fry 1989, p. 66). The federal military arsenals also successfully utilized some of Taylor's philosophy and methods of management between 1906 and 1908, paving the way for extensive application to new agencies in the 1930s.

During the second decade of this century, the federal budgetary system developed as a means of allocating resources to attain program results. In 1912, President Taft instituted the Taft Commission on Economy and Efficiency to study and suggest administrative reforms at the federal level. In a special message to Congress, Taft said: "We want economy and efficiency; we want savings, and saving for a purpose. We want to save money to enable the Government to go into some of the beneficial projects we are debarred from taking up now because we cannot increase our expenditures" (Lee & Johnson 1983, p. 66). It is not surprising, therefore, to note the strong emphasis placed on results, productivity, and efficiency by the Taft Commission. The administrator, the commission reported, "must be able to measure quality and quantity of results by units of cost and units of efficiency" (p. 67). Taylor himself probably would not say it differently. It is difficult to determine precisely the impact of scientific management on the "economy and efficiency" drive in the federal government in the years that followed publication of Taylor's work. However, the similarity of objectives, methods, and reasoning cannot be overlooked.

Taylorism primarily concerned itself with the managerial and productivity problems of the business sector, so it is appropriate to examine its impact in these areas. Reportedly, Taylor's techniques achieved improvements in productivity in the range of 200 percent. The most frequently cited example of his approach is the pig-iron experiment. The average output of each man, loading 92-pound blocks of iron onto rail cars, was 12.5 tons per day. Taylor, figuring that the number should be closer to 48 tons per day, made a detailed study of the job. By instructing the workers how to lift with the correct tools and equipment, having the workers follow their supervisors' instructions exactly, and motivating the workers through economic incentives, he was able to reach his 48-ton objective (Robbins 1981, p. 37).

Others who utilized Taylor's techniques also reported impressive improvements in productivity. Frank Gilbreth, for example, who gave up his career in contracting to study scientific management, reported in one study a 300-percent productivity improvement. He was able to reduce the number of motions in bricklaying from 18 to 4.5 per brick laid. Gilbreth specialized in work arrangements, eliminating wasteful hand and body motions, and designing and using the right tools and equipment for optimizing work performance (Robbins 1981, p. 36).

It is worth noting here that the scientific management movement extended its influence beyond the borders of the United States. It gained widespread recognition in Germany, England, France, Sweden, the Soviet

Union, and other countries. Initially, attention was focused exclusively on production and related business problems but later shifted to management principles of wider organizational and managerial application. In the former Soviet Union, the reaction was a mixture of reserved judgment and admiration. V. I. Lenin's statement exemplifies this attitude: "like all capitalist progress, [scientific management] is a combination of the refined brutality of bourgeois exploitation and a number of the greatest scientific achievements in the field of analyzing mechanical motions during work" (Gvishiani 1972, p. 175).

Context

The total range of meanings in scientific management cannot be appreciated in separation from the social, economic, and political conditions of the time. Many aspects of the era during which scientific management emerged are relevant to our understanding and evaluation.

First, scientific management emerged just as the Industrial Revolution was introducing a new social reality to the United States. At the turn of the century, labor unions gained strength and pressured corporate management for improvements in pay and work conditions. Management, unwilling to comply with labor demands, claimed factors of cost and profitability as obstacles. A period of strife and tension ensued, dampening hopes for a fundamental reconciliation. Taylor proffered scientific management as a means to solve the problems of the society and achieve the good life.

As discussed earlier, improved organizational productivity was the main objective of scientific management. With "larger and better results," it was assumed, industry would increase its profit and could afford to pay higher wages. Consequently, Taylorism and its adherents purveyed scientific management not as a collection of new techniques but as a revolutionary philosophy designed to deal with perennial problems engulfing the whole social order.

Second, the industrial revolution forced the society to adapt its value system to new realities. As Waldo (1948, p. 19) points out, science and machines brought to the forefront concerns with efficiency, measurement, utilitarianism, and rationality. The elevation of these attributes and values fueled the growth syndrome that had continued to permeate U.S. society. "Efficiency is a natural ideal for a relatively immature and extrovert culture, but presumably its high development and wide acceptance are due to the fact that ours has been, par excellence, a machine civilization."

Taylor responded to the management needs of his era and sought to promote his positivist, analytical approach to supplant intuitive or rule of thumb management techniques. His ideas evolved during a period of adjustment by U.S. traditional institutions and values to the emerging machine technology. His thinking coincided with the utilitarian, positivist, engineering-oriented tendencies of his era. The excesses of his techniques, however, clashed with the rising interests of certain other groups in the society, particularly organized labor. Consequently, despite Taylor's obvious desire to classify his contribution as revolutionary and philosophical, it is his techniques that have survived — flourished at times — and immortalized him.

Finally, of special importance during the period in which scientific management appeared was the search for new managerial knowledge and techniques. Equally significant was the growing movement for reform, against corruption, and for streamlining the managerial process.

By 1894, 84 citizens' associations and groups attacked specific abuses or campaigned for reform. These groups organized the first national conference for good city government that same year (Stone & Stone 1975, p. 19). From this meeting emerged the National Municipal League, which served as a strategy center for many reform ideas at the municipal level. Related to this, newspapers and national journals played an educational role, exposing deficiencies and corruption in city government and generating public awareness of municipal mismanagement. The reform groups, the press, urban growth, and a growing need for cities to provide essential services created a force for change.

The state of management skills and administrative knowledge was inadequate to provide needed help and guidance to administrative reform efforts. Therefore, it was considered a milestone when, in 1906, the New York Bureau of Municipal Research was established. Waldo (1948, pp. 31–32) refers to this as "an event of such great importance for later developments that not even the briefest sketch of the history of public administration could fail to note its significance." The Stones, too, consider it a "turning point" (Stone & Stone 1975, p. 19).

Reformists and business leaders joined in creating and supporting the bureau, which provided staff, research, training, and support for the professional administration of public agencies in the cities. The "bureau movement" played a central role in professionalizing public administration in the United States and helped to usher in a progressive and reform-minded era. The movement put a simple trust in the discovery of facts as the way to develop a science that would be sufficient for the solution of human problems (Waldo 1948, p. 32). Therefore, the resulting research movement shared similarities in philosophy and methods with scientific management, overlapping in ways that were more than coincidental.

Criticisms

Numerous criticisms were leveled against scientific management in the United States and abroad, both during Taylor's life and afterward. Few other approaches to management have been so widely acclaimed and, at the same time, so vehemently denounced. General criticisms directed against the three classical approaches will be discussed later; however, Taylorism in particular incited some specific objections.

First, U.S. labor unions bitterly resisted Taylorism, regarding it as a new means of intensifying the exploitation of working people. A resolution by the American Federation of Labor called Taylorism "a diabolical scheme for the reduction of the human being to the conditions of a mere machine" (Gvishiani 1972, p. 182). Laborites and other critics perceived Taylorism as ignoring certain social and ethical aspects of labor and characterizing the worker "essentially as a work horse" (p. 179).

Second, the U.S. House of Representatives empowered a special commission for the study of Taylorism in 1912. Testifying before the commission, Taylor defended scientific management: "The first great advantage . . . is that . . . the initiative of the workmen — that is, their hard work, their good will, their ingenuity — is obtained practically with absolute regularity" (Taylor 1987, p. 30). Remarkably, in 1915, Congress adopted an amendment to the law on the allocation of funds to the army, prohibiting time studies and the payment of bonuses in military arsenals. The law remained in force right up to World War II.

Third, big industry, Wall Street, and corporate management also gave Taylorism a cool reception. An investigation by Robert Hoxie (1920) for the U.S. Commission on Industrial Relations reported that Taylorism concentrated on the mechanical rather than the human side of the worker. The study pointed out, however, that scientific management had gained widespread recognition on an international scale.

Finally, the literature on organization theory and process criticizes Taylorism on several grounds. One of the most important criticisms is the confinement of the organization's incentive system to material rewards. A more general criticism refers to the manipulation of workers for the benefit of production, an argument that often has been pushed to extreme positions, accepting Taylorism as a dehumanizing managerial theory. More recent interpretations of Taylor's writings, however, dispute such conclusions and blame the interpreters and implementors of his ideas for the distortion. Hindy Schachter (1989) points out that the denigration of Taylor's ideas focuses on a narrow range of quotations and misrepresentations by people he repudiated. She claims that Taylor actually originated many of the human relations insights that public administration literature attributes to Elton Mayo, A. H. Maslow, and Douglas M. McGregor. As to motivation, Schachter (1989) indicates that Taylor's work is clearly tridimensional, centering on higher wages, improved communications, and opportunities for advancement.

Fry also seems to agree that scientific management suggested the importance of cooperation in the workplace and called for an end to the arbitrary exercise of managerial authority. "Taylor was hardly a humanist, but he did recognize the interests of the workers, at least to the extent that they shared with management a stake in higher productivity. Thus suspicion and mutual distrust were to be replaced by a joint pursuit of shared objectives" (Fry 1989, p. 68). This explanation of Taylor's perspective on the role of workers and their motivation is in contrast to the common view found in the literature, which still ascribes to Taylor a single-minded conception of the workers and their contributions, namely, that the workers are induced to join the workplace and to contribute only through bigger and bigger checks. Perhaps, the most lasting legacy of classic scientific management is the interest in measurement of output. In the final decade of the twentieth century, governments at all levels and various regions of the world are struggling to develop techniques and methods to measure and to improve results of public services.

ADMINISTRATIVE MANAGEMENT

This approach is often referred to as the "principles" school, though scientific management, too, sought to establish principles of management applicable to the entire organization. Administrative management is best represented in the works of Henri Fayol, Luther Gulick, Lyndall Urwick, James Mooney, and Alan Reiley, among others.

Fayol, a French engineer and executive, published his book *General and Industrial Management* in 1916 as an effort to explore various aspects of management theory. A major contribution of Fayol's work is his functional breakdown of administrative activities into elements of planning, organizing, command, coordination, and control. It has been noted that there is hardly a modern "principles of management" textbook that does not rely upon this or some variation of this system of classification (Scott, Michell, & Birnbaum 1981, p. 7).

Gulick and Urwick published their renowned volume *Papers on the Science of Administration* in 1937. With this contribution, public administration reached a stage of maturation and legitimacy that could not have been claimed two decades earlier. Although Gulick and Urwick's work is the most famous product of the principles school, it is not the only one. In 1926, Leonard D. White published *Introduction to the Study of Public Administration*, regarded as the first textbook in the field. In 1927, W. F. Willoughby published *Principles of Public Administration*. In 1931, Mooney and Reiley published *Onward Industry*, which became *The Principles of Organization* after Mooney revised it in 1947.

The existence of general principles of management that could be applied anywhere is a core assumption of administrative management. According to Mooney, organizational forms "will vary according to the nature of the aim; it is only through the finding of certain features essential to all forms that we can justify the claim that we have found a principle" (Mooney 1947, p. 1). Among the widely claimed principles of management (mostly those of Gulick [1937]) are the following.

First, the theory of organization in Gulick's prescriptions has to do with the structure of coordination imposed upon the work division units of the enterprise. It is not possible to determine how an activity is to be organized without, at the same time, considering how the work in question is to be divided. Work division is the foundation of organization and the reason for it. Management coordinates the structure of the organization and ensures that people are appropriately fitted to the structure. "Coordination . . . is the orderly arrangement of group effort, to provide unity of action in the pursuit of a common purpose" (Mooney 1947, p. 5). The organization chart is a major tool for monitoring and controlling the process of coordination.

Second, the structure of the organization may be classified in terms of one or more of four basic criteria: purposes served (education, defense), process used (accounting, recruitment, purchasing), clientele (veterans, children, the aged), and place (Boston, Florida, Africa).

Third, organization requires a system of authority whereby the central purpose or objective is translated into reality through the combined efforts of many specialists working in their fields at particular times and places. There needs to be a single authority at the center, however. This authority, through effective communication and control, coordinates the subdivisions of work and sees that the objective is realized. Authority and responsibility should be commensurate throughout the organization.

Fourth, unity of command should be maintained in the organization. Multiple commands and supervisions create confusion and conflict.

Fifth, the effective span of control in the organization should be limited (the narrow span is favored).

Sixth, technical efficiency of the group working together is directly related to the homogeneity of the work performed, the process utilized, and the purpose that activated them.

Naturally, there are variations in emphasis among the early contributors to the principles approach. Nevertheless, the common elements carry great weight and depth. For Mooney and Reiley, the four main principles of organization are the principle of coordination based on authority, the scalar principle (hierarchical structure), the functional principle (division of labor), and the staff-line principle (Mooney 1947).

Consistent with these notions are the functions of management described by Gulick (1937, pp. 4–10) in answer to what does the administrator (executive) do. The answer is POSDCORB: planning, organizing, staffing, directing, coordinating, reporting, and budgeting. These functions in POSDCORB are widely recognized in the literature.

planning — broadly outlines things to be done and the methods for accomplishing them,

organizing — establishes the structure of authority through which work is arranged,

staffing — maintains personnel functions: recruitment, training, good work conditions, and so on,

directing — makes decisions and embodies them in orders and instructions,

coordinating — relates the various parts of work,

reporting — keeps organizational members informed, and includes keeping records, conducting research, and carrying out inspections, and

budgeting — includes fiscal planning, accounting, and control.

Gulick perceives the implicit power of administrative action in modern society, but he remains convinced that the democratic process produces restrictions that balance the process and its outcomes. Thus, he describes the administrator's role as to understand and coordinate public policy and interpret policy directives to the operating services, but with loyalty to the decisions of elected officials (Fry 1989, p. 81). Nevertheless, Gulick allows administration broad scope in the sphere of government. Administration involves the determination of policy, development of programs, organization, staffing, allocation of resources (budgeting), coordinating of activities and functions, control, audit, and all other necessary actions to fulfill the administrative role efficiently and effectively.

The influence of administrative management on the theory and practice of public administration is profound. Public administration benefited by the availability of a set of principles for the study and analysis of organizations at a time when useful managerial tools were scarce. The new management principles offered a comprehensive, rational, practical, and seemingly consistent approach to effective and efficient administration. Even now, very few administration textbooks can realistically ignore administrative management and its contributions.

The most significant impact of administrative management, however, was in the area of application. It "spoke" to the practitioner in direct, understandable language, preaching the virtues of planning, the importance of organizational structuring, and the significance of coordination. The theory's appeal lay in its simplicity and common-sense approach, with its unity-of-command principles and its requirements that authority and responsibility be equalized.

Administrative management served very well the values and public policies of its time. The advocacy of a strong executive model provided the necessary arguments for the ascending powers of the president during the 1920s and 1930s. The president's role was dramatically enhanced in managing the federal bureaucracy and coordinating national public policies after the passage of the Budget and Accounting Act of 1921. The creation of the Bureau of the Budget and, later, the Executive Office (to provide essential services to the chief executive) also contributed to presidential powers and leadership. These changes in the structure of the national government were both consistent with the precepts of administrative management and supported by its advocates.

Rowland Egger describes how public administration began to incorporate and make operative its secular trends in the value-free philosophy of management science quite alien to the essentially moral thrust of the "Roosevelt revolution." Egger (1975, p. 50) writes: "Public administration, far from remaining modestly in its customary rear pew in the cathedral of the great transformation, became an element of prime importance in the entire undertaking" of the two New Deals.[1] In 1935, Franklin D. Roosevelt appointed the President's Committee on Administrative Management; its report has been described as "the first comprehensive reconsideration of the Presidency since 1887, and is probably the most important constitutional document of our time" (Egger 1975, pp. 70–71). Gulick made the case for centralization on grounds of effective managerial needs such as elimination of overlapping, conflict reduction, increased specialization, economies of scale, and planning processes.

One must not conclude that the impact of administrative management (or public administration in general) was felt only at the national level. Important institutions and programs for reform operated at the state and local levels as well. Such organizations as the National Municipal League and the National Civil Service Reform League long had directed their reformist activities at state and municipal government. Administrative management offered a pragmatic orientation to solving the problems of municipal management.

Also, administrative management has not escaped criticism. The most widely cited in the literature are shortcomings such as narrow perspective, contradictory "principles," tendency toward excessive centralization, rational bias, and ambivalence to organizational environment. However, Herbert Simon's fierce attack on this school of management remains the most interesting and most remembered (discussed later in this chapter).

THE BUREAUCRATIC MODEL

Classical bureaucratic theory is as identified with Weber as scientific management is with Taylor. Weber, a German social scientist, devoted his studies not just to bureaucracy but also to many other subjects. However, his brief discussion of bureaucracy as the form of administration functioning in a legal-rational system of authority (Western systems) became the most widely recognized statement on the subject. Weber (translated by Gerth & Mills 1946) outlines the characteristics of bureaucracy in the following:

Fixed and official jurisdictional areas generally are ordered by rules, laws, and regulations.

The principles of office hierarchy and of levels of graded authority mean a firmly ordered system of super- and subordination in which higher officers supervise the lower ones.

Management of the modern office is based upon written documents (files).

Management usually presupposes thorough and expert training.

Official activity demands the full working capacity of officials.

Management follows general rules, which are more or less stable and more or less exhaustive and can be learned.

Weber's core concepts, therefore, are division of labor, centralization of authority, rules, written records, and a personnel system that selects applicants on the basis of the qualifications for the job and their education, training, and skills in performing the task. The bureaucratic model proved to be a paradox to administrative theory and practice in many ways. Michel Crozier (1964, p. 175) points out that Weber had furnished a brilliant description of the "ideal type" of a bureaucratic organization and a suggestive analysis of its historical development that apparently paved the way for a positive, value-free sociological analysis, "yet the discussion about bureaucracy is still, to a large extent, the domain of the myths and pathos of ideology."

In addition to the legal and rational system of authority within which bureaucracy operates, two other patterns of political order in the world were recognized by Weber (Diamant 1962, pp. 69–70).

First, in the traditional authority system, legitimacy is based on the "sanctity of order" and obedience not to enacted rules but to persons who govern by tradition. The administrative staff is recruited from among the favorites of the chief and those tied to him by purely personal loyalties. Kinship, wealth, and family origin play an important role in the selection of staff. Consequently, the staff of traditional administrative systems lacks defined spheres of competence, rational ordering of offices, and technical training as a regular requirement.

Second, the charismatic authority system is legitimized by the superhuman qualities of the leader in power. Followers do not elect this leader; their duty is to recognize the charisma and respond to it. The administrative staff consists of followers and disciples chosen not in accordance with rules but on the basis of political loyalties. To be more than transitory, a system built on the charisma of its leader must routinize the line of succession.

Weber realized that, in the "real world," a mixture of the three patterns of authority may exist. However, usually one of the three designations — traditional, charismatic, or legal-rational — predominates.

It is difficult to assess the intellectual and practical influences of the classical bureaucratic model before the 1940s. Until that time, the interest of social science in the issues surrounding bureaucracy was not well-developed, and it was only in the 1940s that Weber's German writings were translated to English. During the period between the two world wars — the period of the Great Depression and the New Deal — the growing needs of public administration and business administration for practical managerial knowledge and skills became clear. However, managers were influenced more by other, more practically oriented administrative writings. Classical works by authors such as Fayol (French), Urwick (English), and Taylor and Gulick (American) were more favored in the first half of the century (at least in the United States) than

Weber's research on bureaucracy. Scientific management and administrative management addressed real and pressing problems facing
managers.

Weber's work, however, has attracted extraordinary attention by social
scientists in the United States and Europe in the past four decades. U.S.
scholars such as C. Wright Mills, Philip Selznick, Robert Merton,
Reinhard Bendix, Peter Blau, Alvin Gouldner, Talcott Parsons, and others
invested significant energies in interpreting, evaluating, extending, and
examining what Weber said and meant. Weber's impact on U.S. sociology
is deep and lasting. U.S. sociologists generally regard Weber as "the
founder" and the "fountainhead" for much theoretical and empirical
inquiry into bureaucracy.

To examine Weber's bureaucratic model only as an instrument of
managerial efficiency and effectiveness is to lose sight of its larger significance. Weber's "particular genius," Fry (1989, p. 42) notes, "was to place
administration in a broad historical context and to associate the processes
of bureaucratization with the processes of rationalization in the Western
world." The bureaucratic model was to emphasize technical skills,
knowledge, merit, justice, due process, and all those values inherent to
modern professional management. Nevertheless, persistent negative
images of bureaucracy continue at the popular level, often equating
bureaucracy with the "dysfunctions" or the "unanticipated consequence"
of its applications.

Perhaps the greatest tribute to Weber's model is that, in today's world,
the bureaucratic model is the dominant form of organization in the society.
It is true that Weber constructed an "ideal type" model designed to be logically precise and consistent and never to be found in concrete reality
(Mouzelis 1967, p. 82). However, it is difficult to find any large-scale
organization — public, private, or voluntary — that does not manifest
some characteristic of the legal-rational model of bureaucracy. "The ratio-
nal-legal form of bureaucracy," writes Charles Perrow (1984, p. 5), "is the
most efficient form of administration known." He regards the bureaucratic
model as "superior to all others we know or can hope to afford in the near
and middle future."

The fact remains that few administrative models excite as much debate
and controversy as the subject of bureaucracy. One can dedicate the rest of
this book to the subject without exhausting all salient issues.
Consequently, only selected issues are discussed to represent general
concerns about the role of bureaucracy in modern society.

One common theme in contemporary literature on bureaucracy is the
concern with power. Big government is equated with big and rigid

bureaucracy that wields excessive powers, potentially threatening citizens' free living. Instead of being the instrument of public policy implementation, the critics argue, bureaucracy is becoming the master dictating the policy. The central question becomes who has the power of control, or of "domination" as Mouzelis (1967, p. 16) refers to it, and on what grounds. Weber's formulation consists of the three types of authority system presented earlier. In the traditional system, legitimate power comes from the tradition and the inherited status of family and wealth. In the charismatic system, the legitimacy of power is tied to the exceptional qualities of the leader. In the legal-rational system, legitimacy of power emanates from the belief in the rightness of the law and the respect for it (Gerth & Mills 1946). Americans, for example, habitually describe their political order as a system of laws, and they like to justify many public decisions with the ultimate defense of pointing out that it is the law.

If bureaucracy were neutral in its values, obedient to the elected superiors and limiting its activities to enforcement of public laws and rules, then most controversies surrounding bureaucracy would melt away. However, the size of bureaucracy, its continuity in office, its expert knowledge, and its effective channels of communication with the public tipped the balance of power structure in the society in favor of bureaucracy. Hence, the question of whether bureaucracy is an impediment to democracy is salient, even if often molded in an exaggerated form.

The fears of bureaucratic despotism in democratic societies are radically magnified for ideological and political reasons. Two sets of factors should mollify the effects of bureaucratic power. First, the power of oversight in the hands of elected officials is versatile, if appropriately and competently employed. Numerous mechanisms are available to elected officials to check, monitor, approve, and evaluate bureaucratic performance. The failure of the political system to perform its responsibilities is often the source of the problem, rather than a surmised bureaucratic tendency for excess. Second, one assumes that bureaucracy is representative of the society in all its economic and social strata and not some novel or strange implant in the body politic of a society. Thus, bureaucratic values and preferences usually are not totally disharmonious with those of citizens. Charles Goodsell (1985) attempts to explain the sources of antibureaucratic sentiments and the numerous myths and distortions surrounding the subject. So many of these negative images have been internalized in the U.S. culture as well as in the literature that balanced consideration of the issues is hard to reach.

Finally, the issue of change and innovation in the bureaucratic system remains unresolved. Conventional wisdom has it that bureaucracy is

conformist, seeks standardization and routinization of work, and, therefore, causes inflexibility and unchanging organizations. Training in
administrative skills considered appropriate under certain conditions may
result in serious maladjustments when these conditions are altered
because of rigidities in the application of skills. In a bureaucratic system,
change must be universalistic, encompassing the entire organization
(Crozier 1964, p. 196). In fact, change even may lead to further centralization and further safeguarding of impersonality of the system. As
Crozier (1964, p. 196) argues, "Because of the necessary long delays,
because of the amplitude of the scope it must attain, and because of the
resistance it must overcome, change in bureaucratic organizations is a
deeply felt crisis."

At the end of the twentieth century, the charge of bureaucratic rigidity
and overconformance to rules and regulations rather than responsiveness
to community needs and to policy objectives takes a different shape and
assumes different motives. First, known bureaucratic structure is the
opposite of what a free-form organizational setting promises or a relativist
entrepreneurial leader searches for. Indeed, it is the destruction of the
bureaucratic edifice being envisioned or assumed by those seeking the
answers in managerial team building, Total Quality Management, reinvention, reengineering, and the like. These are the necessary conditions
for reform and rebuilding of modern organizations. Second, there is the
political motive, searching for escape from the responsibility for budget
deficits and huge public debts and retreating on the social welfare policies. These attitudes find the bureaucracy an irresistible target. Big
government is the explanation for this camp, even when the ratio of public
employees to citizens is at the lowest ever.

In summary, despite a notable variation in the literature on basic characteristics of bureaucracy, a consensus exists on central features, such as
hierarchy, specialization, and technical competence. Bureaucratic
attributes, however, are more than structural qualities. They are also
behavioral, although there is no full agreement on exactly what these are.
Ferrel Heady (1996, p. 75) recognizes three tendencies.

First, is the normal, desirable, functional traits associated with attainment of objectives of bureaucratic organizations, such as objectivity,
consistency, merit, discretion, balance, and qualities that make bureaucracy an efficient and effective system of management.

Second, is the more common emphasis on dysfunctions and pathologies of bureaucracy that defeat or frustrate the accomplishment of organizational objectives. Some of the negative aspects may be unintended
consequences of bureaucratic over-compliance with rules, rigidities,

undue control, and excessive depersonalization of operations. Cozier (1964, pp. 145–150) extends this explanation by introducing the problem of power. The paralyzing structures and virtually irresistible mechanisms of routine seem to develop for expanding power and control. These often exaggerated inadequacies cause the common equation of bureaucracy with its dysfunctions.

Third, is the definition of bureaucracy in terms of achievement of purpose. Heady (1996, p. 76) relies on Peter Blau's explanation, which does not accept the view that all behavior that deviates from the formal expectation or seems irrational is, in fact, dysfunctional. Blau (1956, p. 60) uses the term "irrational but purposeful," which should be judged by results rather than by reference to a preconceived set of behavioral traits assumed to accompany the structural components of bureaucracy (Heady 1996, p. 76). This perspective is useful for promoting essential value-neutral analysis of the bureaucratic system.

CLASSICS ON THE SCALE

Management literature is replete with criticisms of the classic theories of organization and management. Some critical views gained popularity in the 1950s and 1960s and became much more familiar to students of the field than the theories being criticized. This is particularly true of Simon's famous critique in *Administrative Behavior*, first published in 1945. Simon wrote: "It is a fatal defect of the current principles of administration that, like proverbs, they occur in pairs" (Simon 1961, p. 20). For almost every principle advanced by the classics, Simon concludes, one can find an equally plausible and acceptable contradictory principle.

Classical theory is most often criticized, however, for its assumptions about human motivation in the organization. These "incomplete and consequently inaccurate" (March & Simon 1958, p. 33) assumptions recognize the economic part to the exclusion of all other needs. Contemporary organization theory considers factors associated with the content of the work to be significant motivators: "achievement, recognition, responsibility, and opportunity for advancement" (Greiner, Hatry, Koss, Miller, & Woodward 1981, p. 5). For example, the need hierarchy theory of Abraham Maslow postulates a five-level pyramid of needs whose satisfaction governs human behavior: in order of importance, physical survival, safety and security, love and social belonging, self-esteem, and self-actualization.

Classical theory failed to see the inherent contradictions in every organization that lead to conflict. Differing values, goals, and interests in the organization fragment the system and encourage individuals and groups to attempt to gain advantages over others. Intraorganizational conflict of interests is an anathema to classic theory, which operates under assumptions of clear lines of authority, rules, and definitions of responsibility.

Another area in which classical theory is inconsistent with reality is in the application of rules. In the formal organization, impersonal rules control arbitrary behavior, define functions, determine career patterns, and protect employees from abuse by superiors (or subordinates). However, people frequently seek to get around rules, forcing management to make new rules to control the "deviant" behavior. The cycle repeats, inhibiting efficiency and resulting in a rule-heavy bureaucracy. Because the system is never so tight in practice as assumed in theory, individuals with deviant behavior will always discover loopholes and ambiguities to penetrate when self-interest is involved.

On the other hand, overconformance to rules can have negative consequences. In his classic study on bureaucratic structure and personality, Robert Merton (1987, pp. 107–113) argued that an effective bureaucracy demands reliability of response and strict compliance with regulations. However, Merton indicates that exaggerated adherence to rules leads to the transforming of means into ends. This results in the familiar process of "displacement of goals," whereby "an instrumental value becomes a terminal value." However, devotion to rules interferes with ready adaptation to circumstances not envisioned by those who drew up the rules. The very elements that encourage efficiency can sometimes produce inefficiency.

Classical management's emphasis on rules — especially in the bureaucratic model — has drawn a great deal of attention, helping to shape the negative public image of "bureaucracy" as slow-moving, fond of procedure and routine, lusting for power, rigid, and costly. The emphasis on "dysfunctions" of rules and structure diverted attention from the intended role of rules in the organization. Rules protect those who are subject to them and preserve the group's autonomy and freedom (Perrow 1984, p. 30). The classical theories could not have aspired to reach a high degree of discipline, prudence, and rationality without establishing rules that developed from past adjustments and sought to stabilize current operations. Here lies the paradox for the classical approach that is abundantly described in the literature: its inconsistency.

The classical models rely on a closed-system analysis that precludes consideration of environmental influences and, therefore, neglects the interrelations and interdependencies between the technical and the social aspects of organizations. Exchanges with the environment are numerous, ranging from providing the input necessary for organizational survival to utilizing or disposing of its output. The feedback mechanism processes and communicates information about conditions in the organizational environment and the state of internal operations — keeping the organization responsible, accountable, and responsive. Closing the feedback process threatens such values.

It is important to point out that not all organization theorists accept the above criticisms. Classical theory was derided for presenting "principles" that were really only "proverbs," writes Perrow, but all the resources of organizational research and theory today have not created better principles (or proverbs) than those ridiculed. Furthermore, Perrow asserts, classical management served the practitioner well in times when concepts such as planning or delegation of responsibility were rarely known or practiced. "These principles have worked and are still working, for they addressed themselves to very real problems of management, problems more pressing than those advanced by social science" (Perrow 1984, p. 61).

CONCLUSION

The evolution of administrative knowledge during the 60-year period following the 1880s demonstrates tremendous continuity and consistency. Woodrow Wilson, Taylor, Gulick, Weber, and others offered constructs that are surprisingly harmonious and, to a large extent, complementary. The organization presented by classical management accommodates only rational behavior by its members. It offers superior technical efficiency and administers rational rules of conduct to control human failures and predispositions. It is hierarchically structured, with authority and responsibility clearly defined. The organization accepts neither confusion nor ambiguity on the question of "who is in charge?" Unity of command is observed and graphically portrayed in the organization chart. Individual values, goals, and preferences are recognized only when they enhance organizational goals.

Attaining the benefits of specialization to the organization is crucial, as is balancing the centrifugal forces of specialization (through coordination exercised at higher levels of authority). The classical organization is isolated from the turbulence of its environment. It serves efficiently and effectively the authoritative masters at the top who set goals and objectives for the system. Thus, it is insulated from the troublesome exterior and oriented toward an orderly and manageable interior. The consequences of this conceptualization were discussed earlier; the coming chapter presents an attempt to break away from this tradition of administration.

NOTE

1.   One of the most important undertakings of Gulick's career was his work on the President's Committee on Administrative Management from 1936 to 1938. Serving on this committee with him were Louis Brownlow and Charles Marriam, together with a staff of specialists in government. The committee's report became the basis of President Roosevelt's reorganization of the administration of the federal government, including such recommendations as expansion of the White House staff, strengthening of the managerial agencies of the government, and establishment of accountability of the executive branch to Congress.

REFERENCES

Blau, Peter. 1956. *Bureaucracy in Modern Society*. New York: Random House.

Crozier, Michel. 1964. *The Bureaucratic Phenomenon*. Chicago, IL: University of Chicago Press.

Diamant, Alfred. 1962. The Bureaucratic Model: Max Weber Rejected, Rediscovered, Reformed. In *Papers in Comparative Public Administration*, edited by F. Heady and S. L. Stokes. Ann Arbor: University of Michigan, Institute of Public Administration.

Egger, Rowland. 1975. The Period of Crisis: 1933-1945. In *American Public Administration: Past, Present, Future*, edited by Frederick C. Mosher. University: University of Alabama Press.

Fry, Brian R. 1989. *Mastering Public Administration: From Max Weber to Dwight Waldo*. Chatham, NJ: Chatham House.

Gerth, H. H. and C. Wright Mills. 1946. *From Max Weber: Essays in Sociology*. New York: Oxford University Press.

Goodsell, Charles T. 1985. *The Case for Bureaucracy: A Public Administration Polemic*, 2d. ed. Chatham, NJ: Chatham House.

Greiner, John M., Harry P. Hatry, Margo P. Koss, Anne P. Miller, and Jane P. Woodward. 1981. *Productivity and Motivation*. Washington, DC: Urban Institute Press.

Gulick, Luther. 1937. Notes on the Theory of Organization. In *Papers on the Science of Administration*, edited by L. Gulick and L. Urwick. New York: Institute of Public Administration.

Gvishiani, D. 1972. *Organization and Management*. Moscow: Progress Publishers.

Heady, Ferrel. 1996. *Public Administration: A Comparative Perspective*, 5th ed. New York: Marcel Dekker.

Hoxie, Robert F. 1920. *Scientific Management and Labor*. New York: U.S. Commission on Industrial Relations.

Lee, Robert D., Jr. and Ronald W. Johnson. 1983. *Public Budgeting System*, 3rd ed. Baltimore, MD: University Park Press.

March, James G. and Herbert A. Simon. 1958. *Organizations*. New York: John Wiley.

Merton, Robert K. 1987. Bureaucratic Structure and Personality. In *Classics of Public Administration*, edited by Jay M. Shafritz and Albert C. Hyde. New York: Dorsey Press.

Mooney, James D. 1947. *The Principles of Organization*, rev. ed. New York: Harper & Row.

Mosher, Frederick C. 1981. *Basic Literature of American Public Administration (1787–1950)*. New York: Holmes & Meier.

Mouzelis, Nicos P. 1967. *Organization and Bureaucracy*. Chicago, IL: Aldine Publishing.

Perrow, Charles. 1984. *Complex Organizations: A Critical Essay*, 3rd ed. Glenview, IL: Scott, Foresman.

Robbins, Stephen P. 1981. *The Administrative Process*. Englewood Cliffs, NJ: Prentice-Hall.

Schachter, Hindy Lauer. 1989. *Frederick Taylor and the Public Administration Community: A Reevaluation*. Albany: State University of New York Press.

Scott, William G., T. R. Michell, and P. H. Birnbaum. 1981. *Organization Theory*, 4th ed. Homewood, IL: Richard D. Irwin.

Simon, Herbert A. 1961. *Administrative Behavior*, 2d ed. New York: Macmillan.

Stone, Alice and Donald C. Stone. 1975. Early Development of Education in Public Administration. In *American Public Administration: Past, Present, Future*, edited by Frederick C. Mosher. University: University of Alabama Press.

Taylor, Frederick W. 1987. Scientific Management. In *Classics of Public Administration*, edited by Jay M. Shafritz and Albert C. Hyde. New York: Dorsey Press.

Waldo, Dwight. 1948. *The Administrative State*. New York: Ronald Press.

6

Human Relations:
Focus on People

CHALLENGING TRADITIONAL MANAGEMENT

Like all tinkering with organizational variables over the past century, human relationists also have been searching for methods to enhance organizational productivity. The human relations perspective, however, departs from the classical conclusions in several important elements. Elton Mayo (1933), along with a string of converts and disciples who have interpreted, expanded, and popularized the theory of human relations, assumes a greater complexity of human behavior. People have personal needs, aspirations, and values and are influenced by peers. Their sociological, psychological, and physiological characteristics are better observed and understood in the context of the informal organization.

Advocates of the human relations approach (also called "organization humanists" or "industrial democrats") believe in the perfectibility of man; consequently, organizational interests and individual interests should be compatible. Several concepts from the human relations theory have profound presence or have become an important component within other major organization theories. Specifically, the behavioralist movement and Chester Barnard's articulations of organization and management converge with those of human relations in several attributes. The following is a discussion of critical elements in each of these connected perspectives.

The Hawthorne Study

The human relations approach to organizational management began with the Hawthorne study in 1927 (carried out at a Western Electric Company plant in Illinois). This research project, conducted by principal investigators F. J. Roethlisberger and W. J. Dixon, produced a perspective on organization that is different from anything the classical theories had produced. As a result of the new focus brought about by the Hawthorne experimentation, "human data and human tools" became essential for eliciting human solutions to human problems (Roethlisberger 1978, p. 68). In one experiment of the Hawthorne research, which lasted several years, the test group worked under different intensities of illumination while researchers observed any change in productivity. Another experiment segregated a group of workers, subjecting them to varying working conditions (changes in temperature, humidity, hours of sleep, amount of food consumed, and so forth). Records were kept concerning the quality and quantity of output as well as the physical conditions of the workers. Describing the massive data accumulated over a period of five years, Roethlisberger (p. 70) said: "Probably nowhere in the world has so much material been collected about a small group of workers for such a long period of time."

The far-reaching results of the Hawthorne research (Roethlisberger 1978, pp. 74–75) may be summarized as the following:

1. The attempt to relate changes in physical circumstances to variations in output did not result in a single correlation of sufficient statistical significance to be recognized as having any meaning.

2. The research dramatically demonstrated the importance of employee attitudes and sentiments. Clearly, the responses of workers to what was happening around them were dependent upon the significance the workers attached to these events. In most work situations, the meaning of a change is likely to be as important, if not more important, than the change itself.

3. Gradually, in the light of evidence, the experimenters were forced to abandon the notion of the "economic man" — a man motivated primarily by economic interest. The behaviors of workers could not be understood apart from a wide range of feelings and opinions. These emotional variables (such as loyalty, integrity, expectations, and solidarity) were difficult to recognize. Sentiments, the researchers found, could be disguised easily. To comprehend the "why" of a person's feelings, the experimenters had to explore a wide range of phenomena; two especially relevant factors were social conditioning and values. The second includes the kind of satisfaction the person

derives from social participation with other workers, supervisors, and work groups.

As a result of the Hawthorne experiments, greater attention was given to the informal work groups that tend to form within a formal organization but are not likely to be reflected in its organization chart. The study illustrated that output is a form of social behavior and that group sentiments (expressed in various ways) established norms of conduct, any deviation from which was punished. Workers, for example, resisted "rate busters," who produced too much; "chiselers," who produced too little; and "squealers," who criticized fellow workers to a supervisor.

The important findings emanating from the Hawthorne studies represent the beginning of some fundamental ideas about humans in the organization, underlining the importance of preconditions for effective cooperation. The employee-worker is not an unrelated entity but is a social being and member of a group. Therefore, legal definitions or contracts are not of primary importance in attaining cooperation unless the employee is an integral part of the social situation.

As the human relations perspective evolved, it competed with the "orthodoxy" of administration that enjoyed its greater influence in the 1930s and early 1940s. A conceptual dichotomy was unfolding with the concurrent publication of important works in both human relations and the classical approach. In 1937, Luther Gulick and L. Urwick published their renowned *Papers on the Science of Administration* just one year before Chester Barnard published his seminal work *The Functions of the Executive* and two years before Roethlisberger and Dixon published *Management and the Worker*. Over the following decades, this conceptual dualism, or some form of it, persisted with fervor in important organization theory literature.

Chester Barnard

One of the most influential works in social science to be published in the United States since the 1930s, Barnard's *The Functions of the Executive* (1938) pioneered many of the now-widely accepted ideas about organization and management. An insightful observer, Barnard "linked classical organization theory, Fayol's functional approach, and technical rationality to modern complex organizations and the need for the people who work in them to cooperate" (Scott 1982, p. 197). He described his book as consisting of two treatises: one an exposition of a theory of cooperation and organization, the second a study of the functions and the methods of operation of executives in formal organizations.

Barnard's (1962, p. 13) analysis of the economy of incentives has been the archetype for the behavioral approach to management. He recognized the noneconomic motives, interests, and processes, as well as the economic, as fundamental elements of behavior at all levels in the organization. The specific inducements that may be offered, according to Barnard, are of several types: material inducements, personal nonmaterial opportunities, desirable physical conditions, and ideal benefactions. General incentives also are created in making the association with the organization attractive, in adaptation of conditions to habitual methods and attitudes, in enlarging opportunities for the participation, and in the condition of communion.

Individuals possess certain characteristics important to Barnard's theoretical formulations: activities or behavior, arising from psychological factors, to which are added the limited power of choice, which results in purpose. The individual chooses to be part of a cooperative system; the choice is made on the basis of purposes, desires, impulses of the moment, and the alternatives external to the individual.

Cooperation, according to Barnard (1938, pp. 17–23), justifies itself as a means of overcoming the limitations of what individuals can do — limitations meaning biological faculties and physical factors of the environment. Cooperation exists when two conditions are met: accomplishment of the cooperative purpose and satisfaction of individual motives. Consistent with the above, Barnard's (p. 73) definition of formal organization is "a system of consciously coordinated activities or forces of two or more persons." A cooperative system "is incessantly dynamic, a process of continual readjustment to physical, biological, and social environments as a whole" (p. 59). Therefore, in such systems, among the functions of the executive is to secure the effective adaptation of these processes.

Barnard's analysis of organizations would be incomplete without pointing out his unique conception of authority. Authority for Barnard (1938, p. 163) is "the character of communication (order) in a formal organization." This means that authority does not reside in the person issuing orders but in the subjective judgment of the person accepting the communication as authoritative. The conditions that determine acceptability of orders vary: communication that cannot be understood can have no authority; communication incompatible with the purpose of the organization could not be accepted; if communication is believed to involve a burden that destroys the net advantage for the individual from being connected with the organization, there is no longer the inducement to comply with an order. Therefore, orders should not be issued that cannot be obeyed. Actually, orders received usually can be arranged reasonably according to their acceptability to the person affected. Some may fall in a neutral margin, that is, barely acceptable or barely unacceptable. Others are in the unquestionably acceptable domain. This last group lies within the "zone of indifference," within which orders are accepted without conscious questioning. Why is this significant? Barnard points out that the efficacy of organization is affected by the degree to which individuals assent to order (pp. 163–169). This view profoundly challenges the conventional wisdom (the classics) and the legalistic conception of organizational authority.

The human relations approach did not provide a comprehensive theory of organization or management but, nevertheless, made possible the questioning of conventional wisdom of existing management theories and processes of the 1930s and 1940s. Indeed, it offered a fundamental challenge to the rationale of the classical theory. As Michel Crozier (1964, p. 178) observed: "Interest in the dysfunctions of bureaucracy evolved with the discovery of the human factor and the wide development of the human relations approach in industry." As do James March and Herbert Simon (1958), Crozier finds a logical link between the rationale of human relations theories and the theory of bureaucratic dysfunctions.

However, it was Barnard who offered an original alternative conceptualization to the classical models that is comprehensive, coherent, and integrated. Barnard's thinking shares common ground with that of the human relations approach. Both questioned the notion of economic incentive as the sole motivator of employees. Both emphasized the role of the informal organization as a source of group formation and norms generation. Both recognized the relevance of outside influences on individuals and groups in performing their tasks. Barnard incorporated these concepts (rooted in the Hawthorne research), expanded them, connected them, and harmonized them with his theory of cooperation and executive management.

The Behavioral Movement

The behavioral movement in management begins with assumptions grounded in the Hawthorne research and advanced during the following three decades by scholars representing various fields in social sciences. The realization that man is not a cog in the wheel of modern organization but an independent being with values, needs, and motives of his own created new conditions for management as researchers sought to understand why people in the organization behaved as they did. The systematic study of behavior meant the development of a behavioral science movement embracing many schools of thought and several academic disciplines, including psychology, sociology, and political science. "The field has consistency only in terms of its unifying concern: the study of behavior in social or cultural settings" (Rush 1978, p. 32). In fact, the term "behavioral science" has been used to encompass all facets of the study of behavior, including those affected or caused by biological processes.

Interactions of individuals and organizations shape the behaviors of each side and affect various managerial processes, such as communication, participation, and feedback. However, the motivation factors have been at the center of attention by the behavioral theory not only for explaining complex interactions between employees and the organization but also to stimulate employees to do better and work harder at their jobs. Thus, the question of motivation is of prime interest to managers in most organizations, who see a connection between performance and human factors.

In 1943, Abraham Maslow published the most widely acclaimed theory of human motivation, setting forth the famous "hierarchy of needs." The main premises of Maslow's framework are based on the notion that people have needs that dictate their motivation; a satisfied level of needs is no longer a motivator, because a higher order need takes over as the motivating influence. This "hierarchy of needs" consists of these self-explanatory stages: physical survival, safety and security, love and social belonging, self-esteem, and self-actualization (the full utilization of an individual's talents, capacities, and potential).

Extensive and varied approaches to motivation gained prominence after Maslow's theory on motivation. Although space does not permit review of all these approaches, Herzberg's (1978, pp. 217–221) framework is particularly interesting for its practicality and effect. He explains that satisfaction and dissatisfaction of the worker are not necessarily opposites. Certain job benefits may minimize dissatisfaction but may not serve to increase satisfaction. For example, providing convenient parking to employees may add to their satisfaction, but a lack of good parking may not create dissatisfaction. Herzberg explains that providing fringe benefits serves to minimize dissatisfaction and keep people in the organization; it does not lead to more work or better performance.

According to Herzberg, job characteristics can be classified as creating either satisfaction or dissatisfaction. Dissatisfiers are called "hygiene" factors. These include such factors as technical supervision, interpersonal relationships with peers, salary, working conditions, company policy, job security, and interpersonal relations with superiors. The absence of a certain job factor in this category, such as good relations with peers or salary, creates dissatisfaction. Satisfiers are "motivators" because they are related to high satisfaction and willingness to work harder. These may induce more efforts and if absent will not produce dissatisfaction in most people. Such motivational factors encompass responsibility, achievement, advancement, the work itself, recognition, the possibility of growth, and a challenging job. A person is likely to be satisfied and motivated to perform better if, for example, a job is challenging. The lack of a challenging job does not create dissatisfaction, merely the absence of satisfaction. The manager, then, must work harder on the motivators by making the job more challenging, providing a sense of achievement, recognition, and increase in pay and responsibility. Today, techniques and applications of motivation are constantly evolving and increasingly occupying a central theme in management literature.

The behavioral approach advanced in different directions and resulted in a contemporary behavioral science movement in industry that is synonymous with none of its predecessor movements (Rush 1978, p. 36). For example, the behavioral movement is related to but differentiated from the human relations approach that generated much criticism to some of its tenets: The behavioral perspective is an applied one; it addresses issues and problems applicable to the work situation. It has a developmental bias that seeks to bring about change in a predetermined direction. It categorizes groups as social units and emphasizes their impact on organizational objectives (Rush 1978, p. 37; Eddy 1981, pp. 32–33).

In organization and management studies, the behavioral perspective denotes both a method and a point of view. Robert Presthus (1965, pp. 17–19) believes that a certain methodological commitment is the major differentiating characteristic of behavioralism. As the scientific study of human behavior, he points out, behavioralism is properly identified with empiricism, which means a temperamental and methodological affinity for aggregate factual data and field research.

The behavioral movement, it must be explained, is distinct from behaviorism in psychology. Impressed by the advancements made in contemporary natural science, behaviorists insisted that psychology, too, should use the experimental method and concentrate on behavior that could be observed, analyzed, and classified. Laboratory study of animal behavior and the use of the stimulus-response mechanisms became hallmarks of the new field. Behavioralism and behaviorism are similar in their emphasis on observation and measurement, but each deals with different materials and concerns (Presthus 1965, p. 23).

IMPACT OF HUMAN RELATIONS

No doubt, the human relations theory (and those perspectives that share some of its foundation concepts) has had lasting and significant intellectual and practical influences on the field of organization and management. As stated earlier, this research not only instigated important criticisms of the classical models but also questioned some of their fundamental assumptions about man and organization. The humanists, disenchanted with classic managerial precepts, formulated a litany of objections to what they view as hopeless bureaucratic anomalies. These include the charge that the bureaucratic approach does not allow personal growth and development and does not take into account the informal organization. Furthermore, the humanists argue, the bureaucratic model and the classics are more interested in authority and control without possessing adequate means for resolving intraorganizational differences and conflicts or assimilating the influx of new technology (Bennis 1970, pp. 3–4).

The human relations management contributed to the development of the behavioral movement and inspired extensive research seeking to determine causes and consequences of group and individual behavior. Humanist scholars sought an organization that is sufficiently flexible and adaptable while concerned with employee needs, job satisfaction, and self-actualization. To maximize these values, organizations have to be managed in a democratic way, which is another designation for participatory management. On the whole, the human relations approach offered a major departure from classical organizational views, a radically different alternative.

Although students of human relations are numerous, certain individuals — Douglas McGregor, Chris Argyris, and Rensis Likert, for example — are widely recognized for their advancement of the fundamental precepts of this school.

McGregor is credited with "popularizing" the human relations perspective by underlining the basic differences — and the assumptions behind them — in the polar systems of U.S. management spectrum (the hierarchical and the interactional). The result was two prototype models that became widely known as Theory X and Theory Y (McGregor 1960). These theories accentuate critical features of the two schools of management and their application in real organizations. However, it should be understood that McGregor's theories are not identical to the traditional or the humanist perspectives discussed earlier.

Theory X approximates an extreme implementation of the bureaucratic model in a closed system. McGregor introduces Theory X with three major propositions:

1. Management is responsible for organizing the elements of productive enterprise — money, materials, equipment, people — in the interest of economic ends.

2. Management directs people, motivates them, controls their actions, and modifies their behavior to fit the needs of the organization.

3. People would be passive and resistant to organizational needs in the face of such active intervention by management; management must, therefore, persuade, reward, punish, and control.

McGregor concludes that the conventional theory portrays a negative image of people in the organization. It assumes that the average person lacks ambition, dislikes responsibility, and prefers to be led. People, therefore, are lazy, noncreative, and motivated only by fear of punishment. (Although there is no denial that some of these characteristics of management may be found in the "real world," it is doubtful that this depiction constitutes a norm or represents the general application of classical theories.)

Theory Y, according to McGregor, is the contrast; a new theory of management based on more adequate assumptions about human nature and motivation. Theory Y recognizes many rewards other than money as motivating employees, such as the enjoyment of work and self-actualization. Some basic provisions of the theory are:

1. Management is responsible (as in Theory X) for organizing the elements of production in the interest of economic goals.

2. People are not by nature passive or resistant to organizational needs but have become so as a result of experience.

3. People have within themselves motivation, potential for development, capacity to assume responsibility, and readiness to direct their behavior toward organizational goals. Management does not create these characteristics but makes possible their recognition and development.

The essential task of management, therefore, is to arrange organizational conditions and methods of operation so that people can achieve their own goals best by directing their own efforts toward organizational objectives.

Likert developed his management ideas after extensive research at the University of Michigan's Institute for Social Research, which he directed. In 1961, Likert published his widely recognized work *New Patterns of Management*, which incorporated his conceptualization and operationalization of what he called "a newer theory of organization based on the management principles and practices of the managers who are achieving the best results in American business and government" (Likert 1961, p. vii).

Central to Likert's (1961, p. 223) model is the classification of systems of organization, based on operating characteristics, into four types ranging from authoritative to participative. His categories are exploitative authoritative, benevolent authoritative, consultative, and participative. Leadership and supervision are crucial to the most sophisticated stage of participative management (System 4). The leader using this system is supportive, approachable, and interested in the well-being of subordinates. The leader builds the subordinates into cohesive, effective, cooperative problem-solving teams and expects high quality performance from himself and from others. Therefore, System 4 organization has excellent communication, high motivation, and capacity for reciprocal influence — the cornerstones of participative management (p. 674).

Recognizing research findings that indicate that supervisory and leadership practices, effective in some situations, yield unsatisfactory results in others, Likert (1961, p. 95) sets some conditions: The subordinate's reaction to the supervisor's behavior always depends upon the relationship between the supervisory act as perceived by the subordinate and the expectations, values, and interpersonal skills of the subordinate. To communicate effectively, a leader must always adapt his or her behavior to take into account the expectations, values, and interpersonal skills of those with whom he or she is interacting.

Likert realized that, in order to create the conditions for effective supervision, organizations must establish an atmosphere and create circumstances that enable and even encourage every supervisor to deal with the people he or she encounters in ways that fit the values and expectations of the people. Likert qualified his "new theory" with various modifying variables and conditions. He underlined the importance of the need for more research on implementation and for requiring sufficient time to introduce the different management system. He recommended pilot testing of the newer theory in a particular company, as he pointed out the essential cooperation and acceptance of those at the top of the organization.

Nevertheless, Likert's theory faced skepticism, and his evidence was not universally viewed as convincing. The relationship between participation, satisfaction, and productivity proved to be problematic and controversial. Likert (1961, p. 96) claimed that "differences in the amount of participation between the subparts of an organization tend to be related to differences in productivity and job satisfaction." He asserted that, the greater the amount of participation within a unit, the greater the productivity of that unit — and the greater the satisfaction of its members. No doubt, the contributions of contemporary leading scholars in human relations represent important advancements to organizational management. The more germane question, however, appears to be: What is the overall significance of the human relations school to the development of public administration knowledge and skills?

Human relations actually had more impact in the business organization than in public administration. Business organizations experienced gradual modification in management attitudes, as well as changes in labor demands. Ideas such as worker participation in decision making, improving working conditions, safety, recognition, satisfaction, motivation, and fringe benefits found themselves integrated in the contemporary management lexicon and in labor-management bargaining arguments. The concept of employee involvement or worker participation promises workers autonomy over their jobs and gives managers a powerful tool to improve productivity and quality. Recent investigations reveal that real employee involvement "is sinking into the core of Corporate America," but at a slow rate (Hoerr 1989, p. 56). Suspicions come from some labor unions, who charge that participation is cooptation and a new form of the old age speed-up. Nevertheless, a 1987 survey by the General Accounting Office found that 70 percent of 476 large companies had installed the most common employee involvement form, problem-solving committees, usually known as "quality circles" (p. 58).

In public organizations, however, recent organizational processes that are grounded in human relations perspectives such as organizational development, team building, job enrichment, and participatory leadership have met restrained receptions. This is not to say that the public sector remains unaffected by employee-oriented managerial techniques that are grounded in human relations. On the contrary, government employees are involved at many agencies, ranging from the U.S. Postal Service to the New York Sanitation Department.

The point is that human relations impact on the practice of public administration has been, on the whole, incidental and indirect. Managers of public agencies work in a different environment, usually regimented by laws and regulations supported by a hierarchical order of authority on many aspects of employment and employee relationships with employers. Public agencies mostly deliver services, and, incidentally or not, service industry in the private sector also has been less receptive to these managerial techniques than the manufacturing sector. Indeed, published data indicate that the team idea is mushrooming throughout manufacturing, but it is rare in the service industries, which account for more than 70 percent of employment in the United States (Hoerr 1989, p. 59). Other external and internal factors also prevented any large-scale adoption of human relations concepts and techniques in government.

Judged from a humanist perspective, certain distinctive features of public administration frequently are misinterpreted or dismissed as anomalous management. We notice, for example, expressions of surprise at the failure of "organizational democracy" to penetrate the "barriers to innovation embedded in the structure and culture of public bureaucracy" (Smith 1984, p. 453). Ultimately, such a view regards the inherent characteristics of public bureaucracy simply as obstacles to organizational democracy. At the same time, some of the critical aspects of public bureaucracy are dictated by the democratic political theory itself, which provides that external and internal controls over bureaucracy be exercised through action by executives, legislators, courts, and the electorate. This sort of process is inherently inconsistent with managerial democracy, which envisions employees sharing the power in the form of self-management or full participation in decision making.

Human relationists' claims about organizational democratization leading to increased responsibility and accountability of administrative actions and creating an environment of "mutual reciprocity" to replace reliance on formal hierarchy in relationships among members of a working unit have been more inspirational than commonly practiced management. The weakness of such reasoning reveals itself when failures are rationalized or explained away as odds or forces that appear to be stacked against organizational democracy, or, as McGregor and Likert claim, the not-infrequent failure of the new ideas is the result of the workers' long socialization to classical management techniques.

For public administration, one may argue that problems in applying the human relations tonic probably are as related to the medicine itself as to the characteristics of the recipient.

Considering that an increase in workers' autonomy, power, and opportunity for creativity, causes employees' job satisfaction to increase, leading to increased productivity (Smith 1984, p. 459). Nevertheless, the link between satisfaction and productivity still is tenuous and lacking in definitive evidence. Thus, public administration has not been profoundly affected by the human relations theory at its early stage of development or its more recent humanistic emphasis, despite its appeal within the corporate sector and in university classrooms.

The opposite conclusion, however, could be equally misleading. To assume that public organizations are not concerned with employee-oriented managerial processes or that public management applies the opposite of the human relations perspectives is to ignore the imperatives of the political environment and the necessity of adapting management practices to it (Lynn 1981, p. 84). Indeed, since the turmoil of the 1960s, public administration has been experiencing fundamental changes of its own, both in its practice and in its teaching.

Public administration today indicates greater emphasis on policy questions, revival of concern with ethics of public service, higher receptivity to new methods of operation and technology, and continuation of the efforts of professionalization of public service that were in motion before the turn of the century (Frederickson 1980, p. 4). Management of public organizations seems to develop in harmony with society's wants, which inspired enactments for the protection of public employees against unfair managerial practices and for ensuring affirmative action in recruitment of public servants.

During the 1960s, the society experienced a tremendous amount of social change; not the least of its consequences is the enactment of the Civil Rights Act of 1964, giving official approval to the process of eliminating discriminatory practices. This act specifically prohibits discrimination because of race, color, religion, sex, or national origin in all employment practices, including hiring, firing, layoffs, promotion, wages, training, disciplinary action, and other terms, privileges, conditions, or benefits of employment (Title VII of the Civil Rights Act of 1964). Subsequent governmental actions prohibited age discrimination in employment. Also, improvements were made in the mechanisms of investigation, conciliation, and litigation of discriminatory employment practices as well as in the promotion of affirmative action policy.

Thus, public employment has developed policies and programs for human rights instead of human relations in the workplace. In this regard, public organizations, at all levels of government, have been in the forefront of progressive policies of merit system, due process, and protection of employees against capricious managerial decisions. The conscious effort to internalize values of social equity in public service, emphasized by the "New Public Administration" scholars, underlines the commitment to equality within the public organization and toward its larger community

(Frederickson 1990, p. 228). Admittedly, these changes were not applauded by all nor were they without cost. Claims of decline in productivity and motivation to work are among the most often repeated criticisms. Also, one may say that government has been more successful in checking abuses and negative decisions within public service than in promoting positive values of responsibility, accountability, and professional performance.

Finally, it is incorrect to conclude that public service has not responded to the ideals of participatory management. Since World War II, substantial progress has been achieved in bringing into managerial decisions of large organizations the ideals and techniques of democracy through greater participation by employees (Mosher 1968, p. 17). Generally, justification of employee participation in public organizations is made on grounds such as better decisions because more knowledge and opinions would be brought to bear, better morale and less resistance to change, greater degree of self-actualization, and greater degree of commitment to organization and a larger stake in its decisions (pp. 17–18).

Critical of classical theory and offering alternative views, the human relations approach was subjected to scrutiny and criticisms of its own. In fact, critical opinions of the volume by Roethlisberger and Dixon were expressed in the *American Journal of Sociology* in 1940 and even earlier (1937) in the *Political Science Quarterly* (see Perrow 1979, p. 94). Other critics have provided a steady barrage over the years directed against elements of humanist ideas about organizations.

First, human relations theory is criticized for assigning a negative role to conflict in organization and for assuming that cooperation and equilibrium in management's image and on its terms are the desirable state. Also, the theory fails to conceptualize the larger institutional picture of the economic order that would reveal inevitable conflicts between divergent interests of management and workers. The impacts of technology, increasing depersonalization of work relationships, and the progressive rationalization of tasks add to the fears and insecurities of employees, which are not adequately accounted for by human relations (Perrow 1979, p. 95).

Similarly, observes Crozier (1964, p. 244), most human relationists have tended to shy away from power problems within the organization (although they prepared the way for an understanding of power relationships), preferring to study interactions in their most physical aspect, without taking into account the hierarchical systems of domination. They can explain the emergence of spontaneous leadership but not the impact of authority imposed from the top and the concomitant struggle for power.

Second, a most controversial postulate of human relations deals with employee participation in decision making. There is no disagreement that participation reflects democratic values, encourages commitment to shared decisions, and enhances self-control by the employees. The controversy surrounds the claim by humanists of a link between participation and productivity. The suppositions that participation increases satisfaction and that satisfaction is reflected in improved productivity have been described as "tenuous," "simplistic," "naive," and "in error" (Eddy 1981, p. 31; Perrow 1979, p. 133).

The criticism here may be mistargeted. The problem, we believe, is when employee satisfaction is viewed as an end purpose of the organization against which the organization's success or failure is measured. Employee satisfaction, in this case, becomes a focal point of management actions. Often, this leads to losing sight of the instrumental aspects of organization as a tool of rational action to achieve certain goals and policies of value to society. It is almost the antithesis of the traditionalists, who view the individual as subservient to organizational needs and concerns. The humanists reversed the relationship by viewing the organization's purpose to be to satisfy its members and to maximize their interests. In reality, the relationship is best exemplified by the Barnard-Simon-March perspectives. The incentives produce motivation and commitment to organizational mission. Individual goals and organizational purpose are legitimate concerns that must be harmonized and balanced to maintain a productive relationship and reach the desirable stage of inducement-contribution equilibrium between the individual and the organization. The substitution of individual or organizational goals does not serve either in the long run.

Third, human relations advanced many "motherhood" notions in management, focusing on friendly, open, honest, self-actualization interaction within the organization. Many converts were impressed by such ideals and with the fact that employee satisfaction and "love and truth" are desirable conditions in the workplace. Management and disciples of this thinking sought to inculcate the employees with these values through sensitivity training, group dynamics, and organizational development techniques. Nonetheless, the zeal frequently generated excesses so that human relations became a "fad and a bag of tricks" (Eddy 1981, p. 30), with some of its provisions elevated to ideological dogma taken with deep faith and not measured against organizational reality. Others saw in this a school of management that is "manipulative, insincere, and, most importantly, as ignoring the reality of economic life" (Rush 1978, p. 36).

Fourth, Charles Perrow (1979, p. 144), in a scathing attack on the human relations, agreed with the criticisms and advanced a few of his own. He sees little empirical support for human relations theory and asserts that extensive efforts to find that support have resulted in increasing limitations and contingencies and that the grand schemes such as Likert's appear to be "methodologically unsound" and "theoretically biased." Underlying this criticism is Perrow's belief that one cannot explain organizations by explaining the attitudes and behavior of individuals or even small groups within them. He concedes that one can learn a great deal about psychology and social psychology this way — but little about organizations. Even the knowledge of psychology and social psychology gleaned from such studies may be outmoded. William Eddy's (1981, p. 30) criticism is more evenhanded than that of other critics. He recognizes the early contributions of human relations to the field of personnel administration such that human relations became a synonym for enlightenment and people-oriented management. However, the human relations approach tended to commit the opposite fallacy of the traditional theories, notes Eddy. Instead of organizations without people, we now had people without organizations.

Finally, irrespective of the excesses of the human relations perspective and the exaggerated denials of the critics, this approach has enriched management with knowledge and skills widely applied in the management of human resources in modern organizations that no effective manager can ignore or dismiss. Specifically, the emphasis on individual development and self-actualization, participation of the employees in the management of their units, solving organizational problems through the techniques of teamwork and organizational development, and a myriad of other managerial techniques of job enrichment, communication, leadership, and motivation, all have been incorporated to different degrees in modern management. The worth of these techniques has been demonstrated in the private sector, in selected public management applications, and in Japanese management, among others. To gain the full advantages of these processes, managers must recognize their instrumental values and ignore their ideological bent — with the first, there is a place for their adaptation to organizational and managerial needs; with the second, rigidities prevail.

REFERENCES

Barnard, Chester I. 1962. *The Functions of the Executive*. Cambridge, MA: Harvard University Press.

Bennis, Warren G. 1970. *American Bureaucracy*. New York: Aldine.

Crozier, Michel. 1964. *The Bureaucratic Phenomenon*. Chicago, IL: University of Chicago Press.

Eddy, William B. 1981. *Public Organization Behavior and Development*. Cambridge, MA: Winthrop.

Frederickson, George H. 1990. Public Administration and Social Equity. *Public Administration Review*, 50, 2 (March-April).

____. 1980. *New Public Administration*. University: University of Alabama Press.

Herzberg, Frederick. 1978. The Motivation-Hygiene Concept and Problems of Manpower. In *Classics of Public Administration*, edited by Jay M. Shafritz and Albert C. Hyde. Oak Park, IL: Moore.

Hoerr, John. July 10, 1989. The Payoff from Work Participation. *Business Week*, p. 56.

____. 1961. *New Patterns of Management*. New York: McGraw-Hill.

Lynn, Laurence E., Jr. 1981. *Managing the Public's Business*. New York: Basic Books.

March, James G. and Herbert A. Simon. 1958. *Organizations*. New York: John Wiley.

Maslow, A. H. 1943. A Theory of Human Motivation. *Psychological Review*, 50 (July).

Mayo, Elton. 1933. *The Human Problems of an Industrial Civilization*. New York: Macmillan.

McGregor, Douglas. 1960. *The Human Side of Enterprise*. New York: McGraw-Hill.

Mosher, Frederick C. 1968. *Democracy and Public Service*. New York: Oxford University Press.

Perrow, Charles. 1979. *Complex Organizations: A Critical Essay*, 2d ed. Glenview, IL: Scott, Foresman.

Presthus, Robert. 1965. *Behavioral Approaches to Public Administration*. University: University of Alabama Press.

Roethlisberger, F. J. 1978. Management and Morale. In *Classics of Public Administration*, edited by Jay M. Shafritz and Albert C. Hyde. Oak Park, IL: Moore.

Rush, Harold M. F. 1978. The World of Work and the Behavioral Sciences: A Perspective and an Overview. In *Classics of Organizational Behavior*, edited by Walter E. Natemeyer. Oak Park, IL: Moore.

Scott, William G. 1982. Barnard on the Nature of Elitist Responsibility. *Public Administration Review*, 42, 3 (May-June).

Smith, Michael P. 1984. Barriers to Organizational Democracy in Public Administration. In *Critical Studies in Organization and Bureaucracy*, edited by F. Rischer and C. Sirianni. Philadelphia, PA: Temple University Press.

7

The Synthesizers: Search for Completeness and Realism

Formal organizations are more than collections of people induced to perform in accordance with established norms or systems of authority structures, hierarchically designed for maximum efficiency of production. To limit our focus to either people or structure of the organization is to depict an incomplete, if not distorted, picture of organizational reality. Both dimensions of the organization are interwoven, and neither is representative of its totality. Indeed, a major problem of the traditional and the human relations theories of organization is that each sees only one dimension of the organization and ignores, or neglects, the development of the others.

What conceptual frameworks of the organization, then, can offer greater comprehensiveness, synthesis, and realism? To develop such a framework, one must recognize the organization as an organic entity with meaningful connections among its various elements. Organizations are interacting people within determinable structural patterns for the purposes of attainment of definable goals. Successful organizations also acquire knowledge of their environments and reach an accommodating stance with crucial forces outside organizational boundaries. Just as the holistic view of the human body recognizes various interacting subsystems and parts, a comprehensive view of the organization encompasses people, goals, structure, process, and environmental exchanges. Applying partial, preconceived frameworks of analysis inevitably leads to incomplete consideration of relevant variables. A segmental view, however, is not necessarily faulty and even may be unavoidable under certain circumstances, but the section must not be mistaken for the total organization.

Let us assume an organization is facing performance problems caused by employee absenteeism, low morale, or similar human-related concerns. It is most likely that the management analyst seeking to design solutions for these problems would benefit by skills and techniques grounded in the behavioral perspective. On the other hand, if the problems impeding performance are related to definition of responsibility, lack of control, poor procedures, or lack of coordination among subunits, the analyst is compelled to pay greater attention to the structural variables that cause or contribute to the problems.

Thus, a relevant segmental view of the organization is useful for those wanting to focus on the problem and its solution without ignoring the remaining organizational characteristics. When the segmental view is equated with the total organizational view, it leads to a conception of an "organization without people or people without organization." As Louis C. Gawthrop (1984, p. 5) appropriately concludes: "The compartmentalized intellectual schema of discrete entities that has characterized our approach to public sector administration in the past is sadly outdated."

Consequently, the structures of public organizations are strained, and the intellectual capacity to redesign these structures to be more effective in dealing with the complexities of change is circumscribed by the state of our managerial knowledge and skills. The irony is that some of the most frequent causes of failure in organizational change efforts come from an incomplete and often superficial understanding of the multiple causes of a problem. Incomplete understanding leads to sketchy diagnosis, which results in a deficient action plan and often targets for change only a few of the critical organizational elements (Beer 1980, p. 15). Perceiving the organization as a system, changing and adapting to meet the needs of its environment, is an alternative approach for attaining greater synthesis and relevance.

SYSTEMS ANALYSIS

A system is "an organized or complex whole; an assemblage or combination of things or parts forming a complex or unitary whole" (Johnson, Kast, & Rosenzweig 1963, p. 4). The system approach is not new and has been vigorously applied in the past in various fields of knowledge. An early and widely recognized use of the systems approach in social sciences is by Talcott Parsons (1951) in his study of social structures.

Parsons developed global sociological models of social systems and subsystems that influenced our thinking about organizations in several ways.

Applying systems analysis to organizations stresses an open-system perspective that avoids the oversimplifications of the traditional closed-system approach. The open-system perspective emphasizes the close relationship between a structure and its supporting environment. The relationship is reciprocal in the sense that the environment provides inputs and support to the structures in expectation of receiving desirable outcomes of services or goods. Processing inputs to yield those desirable outcomes, to be utilized by some outside group or system, is an important element of the systems perspective. In fact, complex systems may consist of chains of processors, connected both hierarchically and laterally, called subsystems. Often, the output of one such subsystem may become an input of another.

A basic advantage of open-system analysis is that it permits integration of the so-called macro approach of the sociologist and the micro approach of the psychologist (Katz & Kahn 1982, pp. 9–11). Sociology lacks precise formulations that encompass the motivational and behavioral dynamics in the organization. Psychology deals with very few significant variables in the total situation, leading in the direction of universal principles through inappropriate means (p. 11). Thus, the integrative power of the system framework facilitates the notion of unity and wholeness of the organization, underscoring the overall objective and function of the system, rather than focusing on its components.

Common Characteristics of Open Systems

Systems analysts agree on the most common characteristics of all open systems (Johnson, Kast, & Rosenzweig 1963; Katz & Kahn 1982; Thompson 1967; Beer 1980; Harmon & Mayer 1986). The following is a summary of these characteristics as applied to organizations.

Input is energy imported from the external environment.

Throughput transforms the energy available into action, product, service, or thought pattern.

Output is exported to the environment.

Energy exchange is cyclical; the product exported into the environment furnishes the sources of energy for the repetition of the cycle of activities.

Survival of the system is dependent on importing sufficient energy from its environment and converting it into valuable outputs that allow further reinvestment and development. This maintenance source is necessary to arrest the entropic process — a universal law of nature in which all forms of organization move toward disorganization or death. Human efforts and motivation are critical sources of maintenance support in all organizations.

Information input and feedback regulate the system and help the dynamic process of adjustment to demands and needs by monitoring the input of information and the actions that result.

The steady state and dynamic homeostasis mean constancy in energy exchange to assure survival but not a state of motionlessness or true equilibrium.

In differentiation, diffuse global patterns are replaced by more specialized functions.

"Equafinality" means that a system can reach the same final state from differing initial conditions and by a variety of paths.

Systems Theory and Public Management

The quest for integration of new management ideas into a general framework serving traditional managerial functions goes back to the early years of this century. Clearly, the classic theories, and scientific management in particular, sought to serve such an integrationist role. However, achieving unity and comprehensiveness continued to challenge (and elude) organizational research and development. The systems perspective offered realistic possibilities in this regard and, consequently, received general acceptance in management literature.

The maturation of the systems concepts followed their noticeable success in the military area during World War II, when the so-called operations research was applied to various nonmilitary problems in industry and government. Assisted by computer capabilities, systems analysts applied their techniques to various areas of policy problems. In many state and national units of government, attempts were made to apply complex systems analysis to critical decision-making problems. As West Churchman (1968, p. x) points out, in practically every office of government, there were operations researchers, management scientists, and system scientists, all attempting to look at the problems of the U.S. government through the systems approach.

The techniques became as venerable as the concepts themselves. Data gathering and data analysis became a high priority, providing information about overall performance of the system. Inherent in the systems approach is the notion that there is an objective way to study and evaluate the system and how it works. Science is the medium. Always, the overriding concern is the overall objective and how to achieve it using prescribed standards.

The public management processes that invested great energies to harnessing systems analysis are public budgeting, decision making, organizational diagnosis and design, and policy analysis. The overlapping among these processes is obvious. They became the arena of vanguard techniques such as linear programming, decision trees, simulation, time-series analysis, flow charting, and program evaluation and review (Gortner, Mahler, & Nicholson 1987, pp. 406–407). Program budgeting and its successor, planning-programming-budget systems (PPBS), became the most visible management processes committed to the new techniques of systems analysis. The first effort of program budgeting, wrote David Novick (1965, p. x), "is simply the rational ordering of inputs and outputs, in which the initial emphasis is on the identifiable outputs — major objectives of government processes." After structuring the problem, program budgeting utilizes a wide range of analytical tools such as cost-benefit analysis, statistical economic data, and needs assessment.

The application of systems analysis techniques in the Department of Defense (DOD) under Secretary Robert McNamara in the 1960s brought about two basic changes. First, programs for new weapons systems were set up in packages, instead of one at a time. This changed the overall perspective in weapons procurement, and long-range planning became more involved. Therefore, various managerial processes had to be invested to set goals, devise schedules, and establish basic accounting guidelines. The goal is always to maximize the input-output ratio. Second, a resource management system was established to assist supervisors and leaders in management control. Intended or not, the application of PPBS resulted in a more centralized DOD. Many military officers did not like the PPBS, and, several years from its inception, they seem to remember only the shortcomings, despite the fact that basic structures continued to exist long after the apparent demise of PPBS.

Criticisms of Systems Analysis

The term "system" has a very broad spectrum of concepts and, as an approach, has weathered continuing evolution, changing from its initial set of general notions to a defined framework of specific and interrelated concepts and characteristics (as summarized above). The early fluid state of systems analysis appeared to relegate the systems concepts to assumptions and givens. Herbert Simon (1960, p. 15) referred to systems analysis as something "you do without being conscious of." He considered it to be mainly a "set of attitudes and a frame of mind rather than a definite and explicit theory."

Many lessons are learned from the application of systems analysis in the DOD, the most publicized systems analysis implementation in the public sector. Most basic from these lessons is that input-output ratio is not useful when data are statistically incorrect. Moreover, a management system such as PPBS does not have the means to ensure that the approved plan would be carried out or resources actually used in the way decision makers had intended. The DOD experience indicates that communication between programming systems and managerial accounting systems and between financial planners and people who carry out the plan was always poor.

Finally, the systems approach is composed of concepts and methods that have met strong criticisms in the literature on two grounds. One is that systems analysis is essentially conservative and biased in favor of the status quo. It tends to accept existing conditions as givens in its analysis and cannot handle radical departures in a field such as public administration, in which change is a constant concern. Another major dissatisfaction with systems analysis is that it must be supplemented by specific middle-range theories and techniques of application to give it greater relevance and specificity. Middle-range propositions become necessary to extend macro views of organizations to the realm of actual and operational managerial processes. Being easier to verify and measure, middle-range propositions provide important realism to the systems approach.

THE NEOBUREAUCRATIC PERSPECTIVE

We have suggested earlier that perceiving the organization only in accordance with the classic bureaucratic model (an efficient machine with structure, hierarchy, rules, offices, tasks, positions, and so forth) is deficient. Also, limiting the focus to the individuals in the organization, as human relations theorists have done, sacrifices significant elements of the organizational reality. Organizations are more than their structures and rules, and although they consist of collections of individuals, they have a life of their own and pursue goals and values independent from those of the individuals within them.

The neobureaucratic perspective is another attempt to bridge the gap or to extend the classic bureaucratic model to deal with greater organizational complexities. Both the neobureaucratic perspective and the classic model seek to maximize organizational rationality by enhancing the objectives of efficiency and effectiveness. However, the assumptions concerning the individual and the organization in the neobureaucratic approach are different from those in the classic model. In addition, the neobureaucratic unit of analysis, in which variability at the individual and organizational levels is manifested, is the decision making.

Simon, in his influential work *Administrative Behavior* (1961, p. xii), considers a complex organizational decision "like a great river, drawing from its many tributaries the innumerable component premises of which it is constituted." His dissatisfaction with traditional administrative theory is widely publicized in the literature (see his famous critique of the principles of administration, cited earlier). What Simon offers instead is a framework of analysis that permits a realistic investigation of administrative decisions.

A significant element in Simon's perspective is the objective environment surrounding choice. Mainly he defines this environment in terms of its intraorganizational reality, such as hierarchy, control, a rewards system, and the work group itself. Each alternative behavior leads to definite anticipated consequences. Knowledge about the consequences of behavior is, thus, identified as a primary influence on choice. The second influence lies in the preferences of behaving individuals. Hence, the problem of choice is one of describing consequences, evaluating them, and connecting them with behavior alternatives. Individual choice takes place in an environment of "givens," that is, premises that are accepted by the subject as bases for choice. However, Simon recognizes various limits on human rationality, such as incomplete information, imperfect prediction of the future, and the inability of the human mind to consider all possible alternatives. Thus, for Simon, administrative rationality, even if grounded in means-ends cognitive reasoning processes, remains limited, "bounded rationality."

A major effort to harmonize and integrate existing diverse theoretical formulations of organization theory was undertaken by James March and Simon in *Organizations* (1958), which achieved unsurpassed eminence in the organizational literature of the 1950s and 1960s. Organizations, March and Simon point out, impinge on so many aspects of our society that bits and pieces of organization theory and empirical data can be assembled from a wide range of sources. They include practices, scientific theory, bureaucratic theory, behavioral and psychological studies, and many others.

March and Simon identify the limitations of classic organization theories and propose extensions and adaptations of their provisions to include elements not dealt with before. They declare that these three important modifications have had sustained impact on organizational analysis (March & Simon, 1958, pp. 33–35).

First, the motivational assumptions underlying classic theories are incomplete and, consequently, inaccurate, because they are based on viewing the organization as a simple machine. Accordingly, organizational leaders are limited in their achievement of goals only by constraints imposed by the capacities, speeds, durabilities, and costs of these simple machines. In this model, the environment of the individual and the system stimuli are determined by severe assumptions and expectations. March and Simon recognize that the classic theories are neither totally wrong nor should they be totally replaced. What is needed, in their view, is an expansion of organizational conceptualization to accommodate additional aspects. They offer an "influence theory" based on the stimuli that impinge on the individual, the psychological frame of reference that is evoked by the stimuli, and the response or action that results.

A stimulus may have unanticipated consequences because it evokes a larger or different set than expected. The stimulus may include elements not intended by the organization hierarchy when providing it. The individual responding to the stimulus may mistake it for another and, therefore, not respond at all or respond differently from what was expected. These "pathological" processes show, according to March and Simon (1958, pp. 35–36), how unanticipated consequences restrict the adaptiveness of the organization to the goals of the top administrative hierarchy.

Contemporary literature on bureaucracy devotes considerable attention, much more than that provided by the classic models, to the problems of managing organizations. The areas of motivation and the congruences of individual behavior and organizational demands, for example, have become central to organizational analysis because they are reflected in the motivation to produce. At the same time, as March and Simon (1958, p. 82) explain, motivation to produce is a function of the evoking of action alternatives for the individual, the consequences of evoked alternatives by the individual, and the values attached to consequences by the individual. Each of these aspects is partly under the control of the organization but partly also determined by extraorganizational factors, such as general economic conditions.

Second, there is little appreciation in the classic organization theory of the role of intraorganizational conflict of interests in defining limits of organizational behavior. March and Simon (1958, pp. 112–136) consider conflict to be the breakdown of the standard mechanisms of organizational decision making. Individual and group conflicts within an organization are differentiated from other types of conflict, such as the interorganizational conflict. Both the organizational environment and the characteristics of the organization contribute to the amount of individual conflict within the organization. March and Simon argue that intergroup conflict may result from a perceived need for joint decision making and the existence of differences in goals or perceptions or both. Conditions under which these conflicts occur are, in part, predictable from a knowledge of the organization. An organization reacts to conflict, March and Simon (1958, p. 129) point out, by four major processes.

1. Problem solving. Identify a solution by stressing the importance of assembling information, increasing search behavior, and placing considerable emphasis on evoking new alternatives.
2. Persuasion. This assumes that goals of individuals may differ but that, at some level, objectives are shared and disagreements over subgoals can be mediated by reference to common goals.
3. Bargaining. Disagreement over goals is taken as fixed, and agreement (without persuasion) is attempted. Solutions are sought on the basis of shared values of "fairness" and "obviousness" (similar to persuasion). Bargaining may become a test of strength and persistence or may degenerate into threats, falsification of position, and gamesmanship.
4. Politics. This is a process in which the basic situation is the same as in bargaining — there is intergroup conflict of interest — but the arena of bargaining is not taken as fixed by the participants.

In summary, the processes of problem solving and persuasion are based on analysis and greater use of information. However, bargaining and politics are more of a power play and a forceful perception of status, often resulting in strain on the organization and alienation of the losing side.

Third, classic organization theory gave little consideration to the constraints placed on the human being by his or her limitations as a complex information-processing system. The "Thinking Man," Simon (1979, p. x) says, "is capable of expressing his cognitive skills in a wide range of task domains: learning and remembering, problem solving, inducing rules and attaining concepts, perceiving and recognizing stimuli, understanding natural language, and others." The recognition of the human information-processing system in organization theory opens the door to a variety of research in cognitive psychology, particularly those processes that affect rational behavior.

The information-processing revolution, as it is often referred to in the literature, has been intensified by the use of computer programming languages and techniques to express, to test, and to predict behaviors. At the same time, we have come to appreciate the limit of human intellectual capacities in comparison with the complexities of problems that individuals and organizations face. Thus, we seek simplified organizational and managerial models that capture the main features of a problem without being mired in its complexities.

March and Simon (1958, p. 169) conclude that, by operating under such simplified organizational models, "satisficing" replaces optimizing. Thus, alternatives of action and consequences of actions are discovered sequentially through search processes, and a variety of programs are developed to serve alternatives and choices and to be executed semi-independently.

The neobureaucratic model of organization accepts the notion of hierarchy in which leaders and supervisors set goals and individuals execute them because the goals meet the individual's own personal values. Routinization of work, communication techniques, and sequential processes of problem solving as well as past decisions and financial commitments (sunk costs) contribute to simplify administrative problems and stabilize organizational behavior. Influence and control are attained by altering the premises, the "givens" of choice.

The updating and extensions of the classic approaches offered by the neobureaucratic perspective infused organization theory with greater sophistication and realism, particularly in the realm of individual motivation, cognitive factors, and decision processes. This work also influenced public administration because of its appeal to practicing managers. Simon's observation, for example, that limitations of time, information, and resources force managers to settle for "satisficing" solutions injects a note of realism that tempers otherwise idealistic expectations about managers as rational problem solvers (Harmon & Mayer 1986, p. 150).

It is important to note Charles Perrow's (1979, p. 145) conclusion that, despite severe criticisms of the classic administrative theory, March and Simon unwittingly have provided the bureaucratic model (Max Weber) with more substance, complexity, and believability without reducing organization theory to propositions about individual behavior. The preoccupation of the neobureaucratic analysis with intraorganizational variables, however, relegated external environmental influences to the periphery of its concern. For managing public organizations, the political and economic considerations have been of primary importance on what can or cannot be done in the domain of these public institutions.

Finally, there is no doubt that the infusion of Weber's bureaucratic model or Frederick Taylor's structural analysis with behavioral variables and considerations of individual choices is a considerable advancement of our understanding of modern organizations. This advancement, however, does not satisfy the concerns of organization theory activists who seek concepts that emanate from higher commitment to values of democratization, equity, and social responsibility of public organization management. For instance, Simon's view of efficiency only in terms of results, as a phenomenon that can be evaluated objectively, is rejected by those who consider results and their effects as inseparable from their larger frameworks of consciously held values. As in the tradition of political theory, practice follows theory and action follows values and priorities (Davis 1996, p. 43).

OTHER FRAMEWORKS

Three other significant contributions to managing public organizations with claims of synthesis and realism deserve special attention: new public administration, public choice theory, and action theory (critical and interpretive theory).

The New Public Administration

Influenced by the Vietnam War and the many social ills that inflicted the society in the 1960s and 1970s (poverty, prejudice, and alienation of young people), the new public administration represents an intellectual response to such immediate societal needs. The new public administration literature reflects criticisms and dissatisfaction with prevalent organizational and managerial thinking as well as a search to meet the challenging task of developing alternative options.

The collection of articles often referred to as the "Minnowbrook Perspective," edited by Frank Marini (1971), is the most widely known product of this development. George Frederickson, Dwight Waldo, Todd LaPorte, and Michael Harmon are some of the contributors to the project.

What is new about the new public administration? The proponents advance notions often repeated in the writings of participants in the Minnowbrook conference. In brief, the ideas that express commitment of the new public administration are a significant probing of critical issues facing public administration in modern society, a movement in the direction of normative theory and philosophy and away from positivism and scientism, an attempt to achieve relevance of public administration theory, a call for social equity and justice as superior values of public managers, and a call for adaptation to new societal needs and focus on client relations with public agencies (Waldo, in Marini 1971, p. xvi).

Because public organizations are becoming the major vehicles for social change, the direction of change is increasingly important. More attention to the impact of public organizations on surrounding social conditions is required in evaluating either analytical questions or emerging theories of organization. LaPorte argues that "the purpose of public organization is the reduction of economic, social, and psychic suffering and the enhancement of life opportunities for those inside and outside the organization" (in Marini 1971, p. 32).

The new public administration attempts to forge a new synthesis of the field, drawing on traditionalist and humanist organizational theories. Themes of relevance and disenchantment with the underlying theoretical premises of mainstream social science research and its positivistic tendencies are frequent. Adapting public organizations to a changing environment and developing new organizational forms are recognized as crucial challenges. These new forms are to be more tuned to issues of relevance, participation, confrontation, value involvement, and relations with clients. Specifically, the public organization favored by the new public administration is responsive to its clients, is decentralized, allows for workers' and citizens' participation in decision making, provides for the development and training of its employees, abides by professional codes of ethics, and is committed to equitable production and distribution of its outputs of services and goods.

Although the emphases differ, there is very little in the new public administration that is inherently inconsistent with, say, human relations and even neobureaucratic concepts. Sensitivity to environmental changes and concerns for equity and social justice are not contradictory to the values of previous organizational models, nor do these models subscribe to opposite views. The crucial test of the new public administration, therefore, is not dependent on pronouncements of "new" values to be served or dissatisfaction with existing managerial theory and practice. It is more important to ask whether a new alternative theoretical framework is being proposed to advance administrative knowledge and practice. We think not, and others agree (see Denhardt 1984, p. 108).

Public Choice Theory

Public choice theory is critical of bureaucratic organization and central coordination of decision making in government. Public choice means that individual choices and preferences constitute the basis of organizational action, unlike the classic administrative perspectives that sacrifice these choices. Organizational arrangements are viewed merely as decision-making arrangements that establish the terms and conditions for making individual choices (Ostrom 1973, p. 3).

Public choice theories are grounded in economics and politics with spillovers to administration. Most relevant to our interest is the focus on the administrative organization as a vehicle for constructing a theory of democratic administration. Vincent Ostrom in *The Intellectual Crisis in American Public Administration* (1973) is representative and, thus, a basic source of this analysis.

Ostrom offers a paradigm for public administration that would reshape its theoretical assumptions and patterns of practices. To achieve such an enormous task, Ostrom levels a lengthy attack on the classic and neobureaucratic administrative models. He argues, for example, that "Woodrow Wilson and his contemporaries made an explicit paradigmatic choice in rejecting the political theory articulated by Hamilton and Madison in *The Federalist*" (Ostrom 1973, p. 99). Ostrom criticizes bureaucracy's monopoly on technical expertise and knowledge that leads to the dependency of political authorities and consequently results in administration replacing politics as the paradigm of government.

Ostrom's (1973) proposed alternative is a theory of democratic administration that limits the exercise of political power, advocates overlapping of jurisdictions and fragmentation of authority, and also rejects the separation of politics and administration. The assumption is that multiorganizational arrangements stimulate and encourage competition among government agencies, in contrast to the notion of a single center of power controlling administrative units. Efficiency, therefore, is related to the diverse preferences of consumers and not to be defined strictly in terms of producer efficiency.

Two types of governmental activities, consistent with the precepts of public choice theorists, may help to explain some administrative issues: privatization and special purpose districts at the local level.

Privatization

Public choice economists liken the provision of services by government to monopoly of production. The government, as the sole supplier of a service to an area, has no incentive to search for lower cost, eliminate inefficiencies, or modernize procedures for such service. Consequently, only the competitive market place produces goods and services efficiently, in contrast to monopolies (DeHoog 1984, p. 4).

By privatizing and contracting out public services, for example, market forces of competition are reintroduced to public service delivery as the less expensive alternative. The proponents of privatization and contracting out of governmental services list among the advantages revealing the true costs of production and eliminating waste through competition for contracts, limiting budget growth in government, reducing public personnel costs, and giving greater flexibility in the use of personnel and equipments (DeHoog 1984, p. 6). Although cost saving is cited by city managers and county administrators as the primary reason why their governments contract out, other advantages are also realized, such as avoiding large initial costs, producing better management information, and providing specialized skills (Fisk, Kiesling, & Muller 1978, pp. 6–8).

At the same time, studies indicate that contracting out may produce serious disadvantages, such as the deterioration of quality of service because of cutting corners for maximizing profitability. Also, the critics cite increasing chances of corruption, the possibility of a contractor not completing the operation, opposition by labor unions, and problems of enforcing public policies (Fisk, Kiesling, & Muller 1978, pp. 7–8). An important negative consideration about contracting out is that, when costs of developing the contract and monitoring its implementation by government are included, either cost savings are lower than claimed or savings diminish altogether.

To what extent does the inclusion of private producers represent democratization of public administration or rejection of the bureaucratic model? Are privatization and contracting out more than a mere search for traditional efficiency (cutting costs) in times of shortfall of revenues? Does privatization offer wider choice to customers? Public choice theory seeks to "restore" political authority to primacy, after presumably being taken over by bureaucracy; instead, privatization often has resulted in the dilution of this authority.

Inherent in the public choice theory is the notion of individual self-interest that motivates the utility maximization drive in individual and organizational decision making. However, self-interest is too general to explain behavior and all individual choices. Moreover, public choice relies on marketlike structures of decision making for improving the performance of government and serving the self-interest of the citizen. The difficulty of defining self-interest is compounded by the fact that existing institutional, political, and economic contexts influence citizens' notions of self-interest. Also, the market as a principle of organization may underline certain values that contrast with those of bureaucracy. We raise in particular at least two major objections. One objection is that the market, as an organizational force, is inadequate to deal with issues of equity, human development, maintenance of public authority, or enhancement of community (Harmon & Mayer 1986, p. 281). The second objection is based on the experience of the 1980s, when political and economic forces pushed for a nineteenth-century style of "free banking," in which government would get out of the business of regulating and supervising banking. In theory, Robert Kuttner (1990, p. 16) points out, "informed consumers would differentiate between institutions that made risky loans and ones that made prudent investments; high rollers would have to compensate for risk by paying higher interest rates, it would all equilibrate, just as in the textbook." All that was required was "perfect information" on the part of depositors. After a decade of experience in the deregulation of the credit market, we are finding out that, on balance of pluses and minuses, all benefits to entrepreneurial innovation were canceled out many times over by the cost of the savings and loan bailout (p. 16). Consequently, the assumption by advocates of privatization that the private sector is almost always more efficient and more productive than the public sector is questionable in light of the record of the U.S. business sector during the past 20 years.

Special Purpose Districts

Perhaps one of the best arenas for approximating the public choice perspective in government is the operations of special purpose districts. They are created to solve functional problems of service delivery, generate revenues, and develop infrastructure facilities for public use, such as airports, seaports, and housing. Reliance on these districts has increased dramatically in recent years to slightly fewer than 29,000 units across the country (Porter 1987, p. 9). Thus, special purpose districts offer alternative choices to citizens in dealing with local governments by dramatically increasing the fragmentation of local authority and weakening central coordination and control. A major justification of these districts is the need for more responsive public organizations and for the development of independent sources of revenue.

In practice, special purpose districts have not always been the embodiment of democratic administration sought by public choice theorists. Fragmentation and duplication resulted in fiscal competition, lack of economies of scale, loss of public accountability, and lack of public access. As a rule, Manning Dauer (1980, p. 9) points out, special purpose districts are not carefully monitored by citizenry and are, therefore, easily dominated by self-interest cliques.

A democratic theory of administration, Ostrom (1973, p. 132) claims, will not be preoccupied with simplicity, neatness, and symmetry but with diversity, variety, and responsiveness to the preferences of constituents. However, serving these desirable values has been the exception rather than the rule in the practices of the special purpose districts. Finally, it is not entirely clear what the appropriate organization would be with the implementation of the public choice perspective, nor do we know how such an organization would operate when a system of multiple or different organizational arrangements is adopted to replace single centers of production in the public sector.

The public choice theory is not a viable organization theory and does not offer an adequate model of management for the public sector. It may be difficult to disagree with the principles of public choice, but it is less convincing that fragmentation and duplication of public service, for example, are the proper means for serving those values. The main thoughts of the public choice perspective that received the greatest attention in the literature so far have been supremacy of politics over administration (a political perspective) and market competition (an economic concept). Both are insufficient propositions for administering or organizing people to accomplish specific legitimate goals of public policy.

Action and Critical Theories

These theories are also premised on the idea that the principles of the classic organization theories have failed, faltered, or weakened. Hence, the search continues for an alternative theory, recognizing that no consensus has emerged on a model of public administration theory and practice that is appropriate for the contemporary political, economic, and social contexts.

The common features of the action theory and the critical theory are much more than the shades of different emphases that may be established between them. For the purpose of this synopsis, therefore, we shall treat them as one and the same. Our discussion relies on works by Harmon (1981), Harmon and Richard Mayer (1986), and Robert Denhardt (1981, 1984).

Action theory aspires to be the alternative to the classical perspectives, offering a theory of knowledge and science "quite different from that which underlies the current mainstream of social science and administrative thought" (Harmon 1981, p. 4). The main elements of the action theory are as follows:

1. Antipositivists' views. In imitating natural science methodologies, social science is tied to a positivistic reliance on the notion of behavior, which is an inadequate basis for comprehending the social world. Instead, social science should be grounded in the idea of action, which directs attention toward the subjective meaning of people's everyday social experience (Harmon & Mayer 1986, p. 284).

2. A normative theory of public administration. Empirical concerns, such as accurate description and explanation, are inextricably tied to normative evaluation and social ethics. The conventional distinction between "empirical" theory and "normative" theory is misleading and unproductive (Harmon & Mayer 1986, p. 284).

3. The primary value in the development of a normative theory for public administration is mutuality, which is the normative premise derived from the face-to-face relation (encounter) between active persons (Harmon 1981, p. 5).

4. Modern organization theory, in its narrow focus on purposive-rational action, reinforces bureaucratic domination and produces individual alienation and citizens' distrust. As long as one party holds power in any dialogue, Denhardt (1981, p. 63) claims, the resulting communication will prevent the parties from arriving at consensus. Under a hierarchical system of domination, the individual is locked into personal alienation and the organization emerges as a battleground for the struggles of numerous contenders. Therefore, a critical approach to the theory and practice of public organizations would be concerned with exposing patterns of power and domination, both within bureaucracy and in its relations with the citizens who are served by it (Harmon & Mayer 1986, p. 327).

5. Public administration in theory and in practice is concerned with the rules and processes used in making and in legitimating decisions. Decision rules and institutional processes associated with them are the primary ingredients of organization "structure." Five kinds of rules are, or can be, employed in public organizations: hierarchy (unilateral decision), bargaining or market rules, voting, contract, and consensus (Harmon 1981, p. 5).

The effect of particular decision rules on the quality of the processes by which social meanings are negotiated and the compatibility of various rules with the normative theory of the action paradigm are the primary criteria for the normative assessment of decision rules. The consensus rule logically satisfies these criteria better than the rules of hierarchy, bargaining, voting, and contract (Harmon 1981, p. 5).

The action and critical theories are grounded in complex philosophical schools of European origin. They offer profound and innovative departures from all existing theories of organization. Their solid, normative conceptualization is particularly appealing to those who seek balance to the excesses of the empiricists, statisticians, and quantifiers of behavior.

Why these theories have had little impact on the practice of managing public organizations is not totally evident. One may speculate about certain factors that may be relevant, such as the newness of the concepts to U.S. students of the field, the abstract style of analysis, and the lack of operational thrust. Action and critical organizational thinking may prove to be the perspective with the greatest potential for dealing with certain limitations of contemporary organizational analysis. To reach this potential, action theory requires greater concern for the organization and its task-related problems than the preoccupation with global (societal) prescriptions.

CONCLUSION

The new public administration, public choice theory, and action theory are distinct in many aspects but similar in more elements than appear on the surface. They are critical of the classic theories, dissatisfied with the "scientific," rationalistic slant, cognizant of the political and social needs in the environment, and unhappy with the alienation of the individual in modern organizations. They differ from each other in the prescriptive power of each conceptualization. None of these theories has been successful in offering operational organizational alternatives that address the anomalies of classic or modern organizational theories and practices, which they have so adeptly delineated and criticized. Their values as a group are in their focus on certain organizational and societal problems, more than their contributions to organizational theory and practice.

The neobureaucratic conceptualization, on the other hand, stands out for sustained and fundamental expansion of the boundaries of our knowledge of organizations and their practices. By infusing the bureaucratic, classic model with sociological and psychological variables and by specifying decision making as the unit of analysis to explain variability of individual and organizational behavior, March and Simon provided valuable contributions to organizational analysis. The expansion of the bureaucratic analysis into the motivational, cognitive, and conflict resolution processes is the major development of organization theory and practice in the second half of this century.

REFERENCES

Beer, Michael. 1980. *Organization Change and Development*. Santa Monica, CA: Goodyear Publishing.

Churchman, C. West. 1968. *The Systems Approach*. New York: Dell Publishing.

Dauer, Manning J. 1980. *Florida's Politics and Government*. Gainesville: University Presses of Florida.

Davis, Charles R. 1996. The Administrative Rational Model and Public Organization Theory. *Administration and Society*, 28, 1 (May).

DeHoog, Ruth Hoogland. 1984. *Contracting Out for Human Services*. Albany: State University of New York.

Denhardt, Robert B. 1984. *Theories of Public Organization*. Belmont, CA: Wadsworth

____. 1981. *In the Shadow of Organization*. Lawrence: Regents Press of Kansas.

Fisk, Donald, Herbert Kiesling, and Thomas Muller. 1978. *Private Provision of Public Services: An Overview*. Washington, DC: Urban Institute.

Gawthrop, Louis C. 1984. *Public Sector Management, Systems, and Ethics*. Bloomington: Indiana University Press.

Gortner, Harold F., J. Mahler, and J. B. Nicholson. 1987. *Organization Theory: A Public Perspective*. Chicago, IL: Dorsey Press.

Harmon, Michael M. 1981. *Action Theory for Public Administration*. New York: Longman.

Harmon, Michael M. and Richard T. Mayer. 1986. *Organization Theory for Public Administration*. Boston, MA: Little, Brown.

Johnson, Richard, Fremont Kast, and James Rosenzweig. 1963. *The Theory and Management of Systems*. New York: McGraw-Hill.

Katz, Daniel and Robert Kahn. 1982. *The Social Psychology of Organizations*, 3rd ed. New York: John Wiley.

Kuttner, Robert. July 23, 1990. The Real Culprit in the Thrift Debacle: Deregulation. *Business Week*.

March, James G. and Herbert Simon. 1958. *Organizations*. New York: John Wiley.

Marini, Frank, ed. 1971. *Toward a New Public Administration*: The Minnowbrook Perspective. Scranton, PA: Chandler Publishing.

Novick, David, ed. 1965. *Program Budgeting*. Cambridge, MA: Harvard University Press.

Ostrom, Vincent. 1973. *The Intellectual Crisis in American Public Administration*. University: University of Alabama Press.

Parsons, Talcott. 1951. *Structure and Process in Modern Society*. New York: Free Press.

Perrow, Charles. 1979. *Complex Organizations: A Critical Essay*, 2d ed. Glenview, IL: Scott, Foresman.

Porter, Douglas. 1987. Financing Infrastructure with Special Districts. *Urban Land*, (May).

Simon, Herbert A. 1979. *Models of Thought*. New Haven, CT: Yale University Press.

____. 1961. *Administrative Behavior*, 2d ed. New York: Macmillan.

____. 1960. *The New Science of Management Decision*. New York: Harper &
    Row.
Thompson, James D. 1967. *Organization in Action*. New York: McGraw-Hill.

8

Decision Making and Communication

Students of public administration seek to understand how public organizations function, just as the economists try to figure out how the economy works or the political scientists attempt to explain the political process. The task is not simple in any of these cases. Issues facing public administrators are especially complicated: data often are incomplete, and principles and rules of operation almost always are relative to many uncontrollable and unpredictable factors. There also is the problem of observers' personal preferences and biases that add conceptual diversity and complexity to organizational analysis.

As a starting point for understanding public organizations, we underline common elements that largely are supported in the literature. All public organizations consist of interacting people, have specific and nonspecific structural patterns, and seek to accomplish authoritative missions. Thus, the public organization and the people employed by it enjoy official, defined status when rendering their duties. People employed by public organizations are public servants who perform numerous roles at various levels of authority. They function at the front line of operations as police persons, fire fighters, public schoolteachers, tax collectors, and administrators of various regulatory processes. Public servants also are top managers who occupy the higher echelon of organizational hierarchy as city managers, county administrators, and other types of public executives. At this level, administrators are more involved in public policy decisions and in issues of planning, implementation, evaluation, and organizational change in order to effectively respond to needs and interests of their publics.

The basic challenge facing public organizations is how to use resources efficiently and how to serve their publics effectively. To accomplish their missions, organizations must be served by competent leadership that facilitates the performance of numerous fundamental managerial functions, such as decision making and communication, discussed in this chapter, and other functions, analyzed in the coming chapters.

DECISION MAKING

Public management requires making choices among options and alternatives; managers spend significant amounts of their time deliberating decisional options. The process of choice often calls for determination of the rationality and ethics of the choice as well as acquiring relevant knowledge about it. Sometimes, assumptions made by administrators are proven wrong, and the anticipated results of their decisions never materialize. Under these conditions, theory loses its guiding force to those working on the forefront of the service, and administrators are left with trial-and-error techniques in dealing with problems facing them.

In reality, the process of decision making remains one arena where the theory and practice are intertwined and mutually enriched by the practical experience of management. Indeed, the theory-practice connection is crucial in public administration not only for maintaining realism and relevance in the field but also as a source of change and renewal of managerial concepts and processes.

Public administrators are called upon to render decisions that, singularly or cumulatively, shape their organizations and the services they deliver. The pervasiveness of decision making in the entire modern organization has made the process of deciding a very attractive item on the research agenda of numerous disciplines and fields of knowledge as well as of public administration. Among the early and influential contributions to the literature of decision making are those by Herbert Simon. In 1948, Simon (1961, p. 1) argued that choice prefaces all action and that administrative theory should be concerned with the processes of decision and of action. He pointed out that decision making has been neglected by administrative theory because of the wrong belief that decision making is confined to the formulation of overall policy. In fact, for Simon (1960, p. 3) decision making is synonymous with managing. Such conclusions significantly focus the analysis on decision processes as the means of fulfilling the aspiration for developing a science of administration.

PROGRAMMED AND NONPROGRAMMED DECISIONS

Differentiation between decisions is essential for describing them and for determining their vital features and processes. The distinction of programmed from nonprogrammed decisions is not new (Selznick 1957), but it was Simon (1960, 1961) who popularized the notion. Programmed decisions are routine and repetitive and can be automated. Their purposes are clear and specific; quantification of these types of recurring decisions is not a problem. They take place in uniformity, as in classifying and delivering the mail, making payroll, keeping records, and numerous other actions of public agencies, in which decisions are applications of standard operating procedures.

Decisions are nonprogrammed to the extent that they are novel, unstructured, and consequential. Usually, such decisions involve policy-making, goal setting, or independent personal judgment. "There is no cut-and-dried method of handling the problem," Simon says, "because it hasn't arisen before, or because its precise nature and structure are elusive and complex, or because it is so important that it deserves a custom-tailored treatment" (1960, p. 6). Therefore, in the absence of specific procedures for dealing with unstructured decision situations, a great deal of traditional administrative judgment, intuition, and creativity is required in responding to demands for new programs or new policies. Here, examination of goals and the development of new policies are decisions of consequence and are not routine. Setting new directions or new goals in health, education, defense, welfare, or foreign policy are examples of nonprogrammed decisions.

Today, beyond expectations only few decades ago, programmed decisions have been automated and computerized. From preparing payrolls to providing general information, from sorting the mail to auditing income tax returns, programmed decisions are handled automatically. However, nonprogrammed decisions remain mostly the domain of disciplined human judgment. Disciplined judgment means clear vision of what is needed, heavy reliance on information, and application of dependable processes of evaluation of information before a final choice is made. These are decisions that seriously affect the welfare of the organization and involve higher risks as well as greater uncertainty.

The term most commonly used by managers and organization analysts is "strategic decision" rather than "nonprogrammed decision." Strategic separates those decisions with profound effects on the organization, its future, and its prospects within current environmental constraints from routinized, everyday operational decisions. Strategic decisions typically are made by teams, including line and staff managers, with abilities to think creatively as well as to comprehend the issues that matter for the organization, its mission, and its community. Also, strategic decisions often involve high risks to the organization and its management; consequently, coalitions form, conflicts emerge, and the sense of uncertainty intensifies. Sound strategic decisions weave together various important elements of organizational management to produce far-reaching improvements in quality and quantity of output, to restructure the organization, to adapt its mission, to secure its resources, or to bring it closer to its community. As to the rationality of the strategic decision processes, it remains limited by numerous constraints. Rationality of decisions is bound by incomplete information, pressures of time, limited available resources, and difficulties of overcoming resistance to change from within and from without the organization.

Fact and Value Separation

Closely related to programmed and nonprogrammed differentiation is the attempt to establish distinctions between fact and value elements in the decision process. Again, Simon (1961, pp. 4–5) sets the arguments for this separation. He considers small decisions that govern specific actions as inevitable instances of the application of broader decisions relative to purpose and method. Each decision involves the selection of a goal and a behavior relevant to it. Such a goal may, in turn, be mediate to a somewhat more distant goal, until the final goal is reached. Decisions leading toward the selection of final goals are value judgments, according to Simon (pp. 73, 74), and decisions involved in the implementation of such goals are factual premises. This separation of means and ends, fact and value, and, finally, politics and administration in the decision process has proven to be very controversial and has generated some of the most intellectually stimulating debates in the literature of public administration over the past 50 years. The whole philosophy of logical positivism and its role in the development of public administration theory and process became the central subject of this debate.

Logical positivism is described as a tough-minded school of thought that abhors metaphysics, dismisses ethics, emphasizes empiricism, and places a high premium upon rigorous, logical analysis (Waldo 1955, p. 44). The most popular discussions on fact and value elements in public decision processes often turned out to be a recitation of the pluses and minuses of logical positivism itself as a philosophy or as a methodology. The debate between Simon and Dwight Waldo on the issue is informative; thus, we underline the critical points on both sides of this debate.

Factual propositions, Simon (1961, pp. 45–46) maintains, are statements about the observable world and the way in which it operates. Factual propositions, consequently, may be tested to determine whether they are true or false. To determine whether a proposition is correct, it must be compared directly with experience — with the facts — or it must lead by logical reasoning to other propositions that can be compared with experience. Consequently, focusing on factual and observable premises of decision making is the unavoidable path to administrative science.

Waldo (1955, pp. 63–64) and others reject the logical positivist view on several grounds. In the decision-making process, fact and value are organically merged, and the separation is not possible. The assumption by logical positivists that the ends of action are defined, specific, and nonproblematic is questionable. Less accepted also is the derivative proposition that leadership may become dispensable and the organization can be absorbed into a technological context.

The critics also see logical positivism as an extension of the rationalist tradition and continuation of the movement toward a science of administration. However, as Waldo (1955, p. 64) concludes, logical positivism opens the door to a meaningless and instrumentalist view of means that is value blind. Paradoxically, despite the commitment to the ideals of a science, Waldo points out that the effect of logical positivism may be to limit or retard actual scientific advance, that is, search for regularities in the social realm.

Descriptive and Prescriptive Decision Models

An administrative decision is a choice between and among alternatives or a judgment based on the evaluation of a single option. Students of public organizations must establish a clear distinction between decision models that are concerned with the methods of actual decisions and those concerned with prescribing optimal decisions. The study of decisions as they are made, including those aspects of the decision process that inhibit effective decision making, results in descriptive models. In contrast, prescriptive models focus on the selection of the optimal choice and how a decision "should" be made, often suggested in a mathematical formula (Bazerman 1990, p. 8).

The literature of decision making in government and in business includes the work of psychologists, political scientists, statisticians, economists, anthropologists, sociologists, and mathematicians, as well as students of public and business administration. This broad spectrum of research interests necessitates that we establish some boundaries of inquiry. Therefore, our primary concern is with the actual decisions and how they are made in the context of public organizations. Based on such experiences, four influential decision models are selected for further discussion: rational, incremental, bounded rationality, and variation of consensus building models.

The rational model assumes that the decision maker is a rational person who follows logical steps and makes perfect decisions. Rationality requires clear definition of values and goals to be maximized by the decision as well as complete knowledge of the alternatives and their anticipated consequences. In this type of decision, analysis is comprehensive and takes into account every important relevant factor. This model has been attributed commonly to economists, who have a clear and consistent system of preferences, knowledge of choices, and tools of computation that permit selection of optimal choices (Novick 1965; Simon 1961; Bazerman 1986). The major, specific steps followed in a rational decision-making process are:

1. Define the problem clearly and accurately.
2. Develop all relevant alternatives.
3. Gather complete information about each alternative.
4. Establish complete criteria of cost, time, and other specifications.
5. Evaluate the criteria according to the goals.
6. Assess each alternative on each criterion.
7. Calculate and select the alternative with the optimum value.

The incremental model does not assume a clear, final definition of goals (objectives) of decisions in government. This approach begins with the existing situation, in which means and ends often are intermixed. Analysis is limited and focused on alternatives that can be agreed upon or accepted. This decision-making process is pragmatic and primarily is concerned with reaching an agreement among parties involved. The decisional tools of the incremental approach are less of the objective calculations and systematic evaluations utilized by the rational man and are more of the bargaining and compromising techniques that provide for proportional representation of interests, minimize conflict, and lead to an agreement.

Just as the rational model often is associated with economists, the incremental model generally is associated with politics and the political approach to public administration. Discussions of the incremental model, as David Rosenbloom (1986, p. 290) points out, develop a dual argument: first, that the incremental approach is, in fact, the approach most characteristic of U.S. public administration and, second, that it is the model that should be relied upon.

The incremental model has been popularized in studies of public decisions of allocation of resources. Aaron Wildavsky's *The Politics of the Budgetary Process* (1984) is one of the most widely known references that promote the incremental approach in budgetary decisions. "The largest determining factor of the size and content of this year's budget," says Wildavsky (p. 13), "is last year's budget." From this perspective, decisions on the size and shape of the budget are matters of serious contention among presidents, Congress, political parties, administrators, and interest groups who vie with one another to have budget decisions reflecting their preferences. Charles Lindblom (1959, 1980) is another leading proponent of the incremental approach in public policy decision making. Lindbloom and many others in his camp view the making of public policy as a response to short-term political conditions, by small increments, according to events and developments, not according to rational, information-based analysis.

The incrementalist decision maker primarily is concerned with reaching an agreement on a final outcome. The method used is bargaining that utilizes various tools, including policy concessions, side payments, persuasion, and skillful use of limited information. The process is inherently political and often degenerates into power plays among contending forces who seek to influence the final decision by building alliances and attempting to manipulate the rules of the game more than by searching for fair or equitable solutions. The process is realistic and widely used but often is uncertain and even suspect. The outcomes of incremental decisions, with selective reliance on facts and evidence, largely depend on the participants' ability to reach an agreement over who gets what.

The bounded rationality model is based on the recognition of the inherent limitations of the rational model when applied to government. In a real situation of decision making, the values are not always as clearly defined as the rational model assumes. Knowledge of the consequences is always fragmentary, incomplete, or totally unavailable. Lack of information on the problem, the alternatives, the criteria, and the impact of choosing a certain alternative seriously limits the judgments of decision makers. Time and cost constraints, in particular, limit the search for full information.

An important limitation also is imposed by the imperfections of human perceptions in the selection of information as well as in its utilization. The human cognitive ability is limited naturally and can evoke or retain only limited information on the problem and the alternatives for its solution. The enormous progress in the development of computational tools and the so-called information revolution have aided and advanced man's cognitive capability. However, they have not freed humans of biases, self-interest, and biological limitations to reach totally rational decisions in modern organizations.

Thus, our experiences in administrative organizations, as well as administrative theory, indicate that, although human behavior in organizations may not be totally rational, at least in substantive ways, it is intended to be so. This is the model of decision making in public organizations that Simon advanced nearly four decades ago. "Administrative theory is peculiarly the theory of intended and bounded rationality — of the behavior of human beings who *satisfice* because they have not the wits to *maximize*" (1961, p. xxiv).

The consensus building models involve more than one decision strategy and may use various decision rules. One such decision strategy, which is widely used in government, is voting. The voting method is not limited to selection of policymakers at the various levels of government; it is also the main method for decision making used within government on a daily basis. County commissions, city councils, employee groups, advisory citizens councils, and employees of public organizations vote on policies or solutions to problems. The process assumes the existence of a measure of information, discussion of the problem requiring a decision, and knowledge and acceptance of the decision rules in advance.

Voting also means equal participation in public decisions by affected parties and aggregation of their preferences. Municipalities resort to referenda for settling various debates over public decisions on taxes, zoning, form of government, and other significant policies. Administrative organizations rely on voting by their employees to measure support for certain public policy decisions, such as health insurance coverage, salary contracts, or certain rules affecting modes of operation. The outcome of a decision made as a result of the voting method may be binding, as in referenda on local taxes, or may be advisory, when the purpose is to find out preference or level of support for a policy choice. Voting is almost always a decisive method to establish aggregate preferences and, hence, a consensus for some choice of action.

A second popular strategy of decision making is through agreement of the experts who act in a jurylike process. They hear the evidence, argue their positions, and render judgments that merge into a final decision. This method is used by review boards of various types, evaluation committees, university tenure and promotion committees, planning commissions, engineering teams, or professional groups when making or recommending a decision.

The method and the premises of group decisions are similar to those of voting but differ in two basic assumptions. The group consists of a small number of participants, and, generally, they are experts on the subject. Thus, their judgment is a distillation of knowledge about the problem and its solution, whether acting in advisory or executive capacity. When the mandate is binding, the decision outcome has legal, moral, and expert power of influence. Even when the judgment of the group is only advisory, it usually exerts such significant expert and moral influence that deviation from such judgment requires convincing justification by those who have the executive authority.

When the group of experts deliberates a decision, assisted by a consultant, and follows certain steps in a process that leads to an aggregate outcome, they may be using a simplified form of the Delphi technique. Members of the group usually are experts (not representatives of interest groups), the group is usually small in number, interacts, and seeks to develop consensus decisions. The technique is used in organizations for planning, forecasting, and establishing priorities among activities and programs.

Applications of this method vary with the subject and with the context. However, the Delphi process is basically an approach of refining group judgment by attempting to arrive at some form of consensus, through the utilization of informed opinions. Harold Gortner, J. Mahler, and J. B. Nicholson (1987, p. 261) underline these steps of the process.

First, establish clear, operational question or problem for the group to work on. This is the consultant job.

Second, generate ideas in writing from all participants, about the question or the problem before discussions begin, in order to maximize the variety of views.

Third, conduct discussions in an environment that does not inhibit diversity of opinions, but does discourage lobbying for any part of the decision and prevents domination by powerful members. A "mindset" attitude and a "groupthink" situation also are real drawbacks to guard against. In any event, the process involves a carefully controlled feedback between rounds of discussion and communication to the participants a summary of the results of previous discussions. Thus, a consensus is reached which establishes the outcome in clear, specific, and manageable numbers of prioritized items.

Finally, an approach that merges judgments of people with basic computational techniques for decision making is introduced by Thomas Saaty (1988) for a wide range of applications in government and in corporations. Saaty (p. 4) recognizes the need to view the problems in an organized but complex framework that allows for interaction and interdependence among factors and still enables us to think about them in a simple way. He calls it the Analytic Hierarchy Process (AHP) and describes it in a book-length volume in addition to a computerized decision support system that integrates the theory with a fairly easy to use software for professional decision makers. Saaty (p. 5) describes the process of the AHP as basically a method of breaking down a complex, unstructured situation into its component parts; arranging these parts, or variables, into a hierarchic order; and assigning numerical values to subjective judgments to determine which variables have the highest priority and should be acted upon to influence the outcome of the situation.

This way, Saaty believes, the AHP provides an effective structure for group decision making by imposing discipline on the group's thought process, maintaining cohesiveness, and helping reach a conclusion. Making decisions through voting or group action does not include another widely used strategy based on the individual initiative of the leading manager, supported by the senior staff. More decisions are made this way by top public managers than we all acknowledge. Even in institutions of collegial administration, such as the university, individual decisions are routinely communicated downward by senior administrators accompanied with rationalization and claims of support and input from employees to these unilateral decisions.

Opposition to decisions communicated downward may exist at any time but may not be sufficiently unified to block even unpopular decisions. One reason is that senior managers almost always have some loyal support from the inner circle of their staff. Other employees may assume that higher knowledge and wisdom are dictating the decision and, hence, acquiesce. Such specific application of organizational hierarchical power by superiors (bosses) over employees has a legitimate role in the bureaucratic model, because power is transformed into authority. However, this interpersonal power, with its hierarchical dimension, that is common in most organizations does not explain all forms of power one encounters at the workplace. There is a "recognition that power is, first of all, a structural phenomenon, created by the division of labor and departmentation that characterize the specific organization or set of organizations being investigated" (Pfeffer 1996, p. 359). When this type of power is transformed into authority, it becomes fairly institutionalized. For illustrations, consider the common practices of departments of budgeting, audit, and personnel in a public organization. They often transform their respective mandates into legitimate authority that, in practice, is a structured power.

Finally, a type of power often develops as alliances and groups use various political tactics ranging from disinformation to granting support or withholding it from managerial decisions to force concessions from management that they will not get otherwise. This political power or influence over decision making is not necessarily legitimate or authoritative. Although such power may produce positive results when invested to promote common interests, it often is used by groups for self-serving reasons and to feather the nests of those in that circle. Many university programs and departments have been ravaged by feuds instigated by such paralyzing political groupings that managed to halt all actions not serving their individual interests. It must be added that such events are endemic to collegial management and less likely in settings with pronounced hierarchical authority of decision making.

Managers who have experience and entrepreneurial vision also frequently utilize hierarchical decision-making methods to introduce fundamental changes to public organizations. Many strategic changes that vitalize and reshape an organization are traceable to individual initiatives at all levels of government. Although efforts are made to communicate to the rest of employees and to enlist their support, such a method of decision making, in conception and in implementation, often is associated with the individual initiator.

The rational and the limited rationality models are search models that probe data, explore alternatives, and evaluate them before the choice is made. In this regard, both perspectives are seeking the appropriate solutions or policies, although through different tools of analysis and levels of commitment to optimum outcomes. The rational model relies on complete data and complex analysis, including operations research, mathematical modeling, computer simulation, experimental design, the analysis of variance, linear and nonlinear programming, and many other statistical techniques to determine optimality. In practice, however, for many reasons (including lack of familiarity, limited data, limited time, and cost constraints), such procedures are rarely used by public managers in making decisions.

The limitations of the rational-comprehensive model are not necessarily advantages of the incremental approach. In fact, the incremental process undermines important traditional values of public administration such as economy, efficiency, and effectiveness (Rosenbloom 1986, p. 292) and often results in political alliances and power centers that dominate decision processes in the organization. Moreover, the approach is criticized for its inherent conservative outlook that seeks adjustments to the status quo and avoids radical departures.

Public managers are always facing competing demands for their time and attention. Often, the problems and the needs cannot wait for the discovery of optimal solutions, and they may not have their own past to adjust incrementally. Indeed, frequently, managers act intuitively or after a brief and expedited data analysis and evaluation. As Robert Behn and J. W. Vaupel (1982, p. 5) point out, "when a decision must be made without very much time or data, the specialized techniques of decision analysis are not very helpful." Quick analysis, they wrote, requires a sharp pencil or perhaps a pocket calculator rather than the latest generation of computers. Training managers to think analytically and to proceed systematically in making decisions is more important than increasing the level of complexity of their research or expanding the collection and processing of information — a common pitfall of academic training of managers in decision making.

The dynamics of the decision-making process in public organizations usually benefit from the effective use of certain techniques by managers, such as simplifying the decision process by defining its basic components. The process also should recognize elements of subjectivity in the merit evaluation of each option and in stating preferences of final outcome. Associating characteristics of scientific, independent, or rational approaches to these judgments will not obscure their inherent subjectivity.

Equally important for public managers is the realization that uncertainty is a constant challenge that could jeopardize all assumptions and predictions of the decision maker. Because many public decisions are based on forecasts of future developments, public managers need to be aware of probabilities, familiar with data, and experienced in making judgments. Examples of uncertainty in public decisions are many, such as: estimates of financial cost in the budget depend on future economic changes, such as in prices and wages; deregulation may not achieve its anticipated impact on business practices; the cost of operating a municipal fleet of vehicles may change dramatically because of the fluctuation of prices of oil; and maintaining a healthy reserve fund for a local government depends on its fortunes of not having to endure unpredictable natural disasters such as floods or earthquakes or to live through the impact of severe economic recessions.

Predictions or forecasts will always have an element of uncertainty and surprise. However, public managers' reliance on past observations (relative-frequency), their own good sense of the situation, their trained judgment, and the collective judgment and experience of their employees are some of the tools that can be used to check this uncertainty. The use of collective understanding of employees in a public organization when logic, intuition, and data fail to resolve the problem is an underutilized management process. Thinking together, agreeing on a decision collectively, and benefiting by the different senses and thought processes of all involved individuals is to reduce biases and self-serving managerial actions.

Also, decisions made are not necessarily decisions implemented. Therefore, the practicality and realism of a decision — indeed, its rationality — are inseparable from its chances of implementation and monitoring. U.S. public organizations are under pressures of dwindling resources, unbalanced budgets, and the need to do more with less. Participative techniques of decision making have not realized their potential improvement of productivity through encouraging employee input in the making and the implementation of public decisions.

In conclusion, the development of decision-making skills among public managers has not been well-served by the bipolar approach to decision analysis in training and in academic administrative education. Generally, decisions are classified into rational (scientific) and incremental (political). The variations of decision techniques found in the real life of public organizations are not adequately represented when reduced to these two perspectives. Bridging the gaps among various perspectives and synthesizing the applicable techniques from several approaches may be essential to deal with the situation faced by the manager to reach a professional solution. The manager is not a scientist or a politician. As professionals, managers need to select their tools according to tasks as well as to situations surrounding them.

POLICYMAKING AND DECISION MAKING

Policymaking, broadly speaking, is decision making calculated to deal with overall objectives by enunciating a body of principles to guide action. Just like decision making, an effective policymaking process requires clear goals, evaluation of possible alternatives, and selection of the appropriate course of action after balancing the probable consequences of available alternatives. The development of a public policy may involve more than one decision by one center of power. Governments develop policies on issues of general interest to citizens ranging from health care, housing, and education to crime fighting.

Is policymaking, then, different from decision making? The answer in a general sense is, no, it is not, although policy emphasizes certain aspects of the decision process more than others. Sometimes, policymaking may involve several decisions that sequentially evolve into the formal policy. Often, policy is determined at the top of the organization, although decisions are made at all levels. Also, policy, being a choice of some alternatives, is more attuned to issues of values and preferences of policymakers as well as of clients and citizens at large than are administrative decisions. Public administration has been struggling to come to terms with this issue. Indeed, this is the most fundamental question behind the call for a new public administration that is more mindful of normative and ethical values in the field, as we discussed earlier.

Public administration's interest in policy has many dimensions, not the least of which is that policy is an element in the performance of the political system. More importantly, public administration shares the concern for the effect of public policy along with many disciplinary areas, particularly economics. Finally, policy analysis may be more attuned to the comprehensive values of its constituents and to the symbolic meaning of its context than is public administration, which seems to deal pragmatically with more circumscribed issues and to search in earnest for solutions to concrete organizational problems.

An important distinction must be made between policy output and policy impact. Policy output is tangible and concrete (building an additional 100 miles of roads) or symbolic (support of the democratization trend in Eastern Europe). When a choice is made and a policy is defined by the national government, for example, one expects this choice to be expressed in the form of a statute, a congressional resolution, a presidential executive order, a set of departmental regulations, or a budgetary allocation. The process of choice that delineates expected outputs is very significant to public organizations because it also provides the framework for their goals and objectives. However, these goals and objectives, preceded by choice of public policy, may not tell us very much about performance unless it accurately measures impact. Issues related to organizational performance are the subjects of coming chapters.

COMMUNICATION

Emphasis on participatory management and the efforts to create appropriate conditions for cooperation and team building largely depend on effective communication in modern organizations. Leaders, managers, supervisors, and teams of various types would not be able to function effectively without communication within and without the organization. Decisions will have little chance of implementation without adequate attention to when, how, and to whom these decisions must be communicated.

In a narrow sense, communication is the transmittal of information from one source to another. It involves a source, a message, a destination, an instrument, and — sometimes — feedback. The process of information exchange appears neutral and frequently is reduced to its technical elements and the skills necessary for manipulating them. However, communication also is a process of influence and control as well as of sharing ideas and feelings.

Traditional organization theories heavily emphasized hierarchical — downward — communications to convey duties, responsibilities, and other directives to employees. Organization charts, for example, unmistakably dictate and illustrate the channels and directions of communication. The human relations school focused on groups and individuals in the organization and argued for balancing the structural outlook with concerns for the human relations and behavioral consequences. Thus, the human relationists legitimized the informal channels of communication.

Viewing the organization as a system expanded the scope of issues of communications to include complex interactions and interdependence among parts of the organization as well as with the environment. Finally, the current technological revolution has solved many technical problems, expanded capacities, and facilitated what was impossible a few years ago in all aspects of communication. The practical significance of effective communication to organizational management is difficult to exaggerate. Communication is essential for defining and operationalizing goals, influencing the social process within the organization, resolving conflicts, and shaping important aspects of decision making throughout the administrative unit. Moreover, communication serves two fundamental purposes of maintaining the cooperation necessary among employees through an effective communication framework and providing support for organizational goals, programs, and mission.

For public organizations, communication takes another form of significance because of accountability, which necessitates well-defined, reliable, and accessible methods of recording and reporting information. Concerns for accountability and openness of public transactions are of growing significance because of the complexity of governmental relations as well as the increasing emphasis on the customer in the delivery of public service.

The common view of communication as the process of encoding of messages by the sender and decoding of these messages by the receiver through some medium or channel (Berlo 1960) is correct but incomplete. In a broader sense, communication is more involved in managing the organization, particularly in decision making and leadership, than has been recognized by practitioners or in the literature. Indeed, very early, Chester Barnard (1962, p. 82) recognized that an organization comes into being when there are persons able to communicate with each other and who are willing to act to serve a common purpose. Thus, communication is a fundamental element of organization. Barnard (pp. 89–90) also distinguishes between communication techniques in the informal and formal organization. The first is more generalized and diffuse; the second is the responsibility of the executive, who controls, manipulates, and directs it toward serving the purpose of the organization. Formal communication conveys information through formal channels that follow lines of authority. Informal communication is not limited to the lines of authority.

Various schemes of classification recognize the many dimensions and characteristics of effective communication — verbal and nonverbal, oral and written, formal and informal, internal and external, and intentional and nonintentional. Each one of these dimensions identifies with certain skills and underlines certain problems that could facilitate or inhibit effective communication. The literature is extensive on these skills, particularly for business organizations (Stone 1989; Timm 1986; Sussman & Krivonos 1979; Allen 1977).

As an interactive process of influencing others, communication assumes many forms, simple and complex. Because a major objective is to influence behavior and attitude, communication cannot be limited to its instrumental elements. Effective communication requires more than the tools of transmittal of messages. To achieve its purposes, communication requires credibility and consistency on the part of the communicator as well as willingness to communicate thoughts and feelings openly and honestly.

Interpersonal communication suffers when organizational communication begins to break down. For example, poorly defined organizational structure, which obscures lines of authority and responsibility, creates communication barriers that reduce cooperation between members of departments and blur employees' understanding of departmental functions.

Improving downward, upward, and horizontal communication encourages free flow of information, increases employee involvement, and reduces alienation. The individual's communication efforts are influenced by the larger organizational setting. Public organizations tend to emphasize formal communication for maintaining management control and for collection of information and feedback necessary for making decisions and communicating them to the rest of the organization. Public managers and their staffs often circumvent the slow and inflexible formal communication by developing interpersonal communication in all directions. Such informal systems or networks are vital for organizational functioning. Whatever the method of communicating policies, decisions, or any type of information, ascertaining its nature and its vitality is an important challenge for the receiver. Is the communication a command, advice, data for common knowledge, or feedback about some operation? The manager needs to establish the nature of the information and his or her confidence in its reliability before acting on it.

Similarly, the informal process presents suggestions and transmits messages in various directions and with amazing speed. Public managers are more successful in conveying information downward through official channels than in receiving employees' opinions and suggestions. Recognizing and removing barriers to upward communication are essential for releasing the enormous potential for innovation and change from ideas originating from employees in the organization. Employees who have firsthand knowledge of the job must feel that management is interested, supportive, and protective of the free flow of information in upward directions.

Training programs for developing communication skills are numerous and are being peddled across the country by consultants, training institutes, and academic programs. Most of these programs identify problems or obstacles to effective communication and present a variety of techniques and skills for dealing with them. Improvements are possible in three major communication-related areas: interpersonal, organizational, and technological.

At the interpersonal level, skills are developed in writing, speaking, listening, body language, dealing with gossip, vocal qualities, facial qualities, attitudes, and so forth. Thus, interpersonal communication is not limited to the use of words. Messages often are effectively transmitted through actions, gestures, or tone of voice. The common wisdom that "actions speak louder than words" is appropriate in a managerial sense as well. Also important for the manager is to realize the potency of informal communications, which often develop through social interactions among people in the organization and outside. Informal groups can generate a culture of cooperation and loyalty to the organization and its policies or instigate the deterioration of such values. Because of their effects on behavioral norms and work habits, the manager must give adequate attention to perceptual, semantic, emotional, and many other real barriers to interpersonal and informal communications.

At the organizational level, the focus of developing effective communication tends to be on clarity of goals and policies, methods of formal reporting, and use of hierarchical (downward) communication versus free flow of information in all directions. Formal communication in the organization ensures orderly exchange of information and enhances the predictability and reliability of organizational behavior. Also emphasized at this level are the existence of evaluation and monitoring processes, the level of specialization, norms for dealing with informal communication, and standard operating procedures of communication. However, organizational barriers to communication are common and may originate in the hierarchical structure, in the supervisory style, or in the organizational culture. Management that practices selective interactions, limited to the in-groups, or exhibits tendencies to secrecy, for example, is using the organizational structure to stifle open and effective communications to all without exclusions and discrimination.

At the technological level, the greatest advancements in communication have taken place in the past few years. The information revolution changed the traditional tools and produced many technologies to serve the needs of modern organizations in telecommunication, word processing, computerization, and numerous programs of storing and retrieving information for the use of managers. Decisions increasingly are made using data and analysis when it was not possible before. The surge of wireless communication brought many important tools such as cellular phones, pagers, facsimile machines, and other devices that increasingly are being used to improve and expedite the communication process.

In summary, effective communication affects all the managerial processes of the organization, strengthens relationships, reinforces goal-directed behavior, creates bonds of confidence and trust, reduces distortions of views and actions, improves morale, reduces grievances, minimizes employees' fear of change, and facilitates making better decisions. The interesting thing about public organizations is that, often, the communication process is taken for granted until barriers develop and damage is done. Public managers, as decision makers and as organizational leaders, can use the tools of effective communication for overall improvement of managerial functions on a continuous basis.

REFERENCES

Allen, Richard K. 1977. *Organizational Management Through Communication.* New York: Harper & Row.

Barnard, Chester I. 1962. *The Functions of the Executive.* Cambridge, MA: Harvard University Press.

Bazerman, Max A. 1990. *Judgment in Managerial Decision-Making,* 2d ed. New York: John Wiley.

Behn, Robert D. and J. W. Vaupel. 1982. *Quick Analysis for Busy Decision Makers.* New York: Basic Books.

Berlo, Davis K. 1960. *The Process of Communication: An Introduction to Theory and Practice.* New York: Holt, Rinehart & Winston.

Gortner, Harold, J. Mahler, and J. B. Nicholson. 1987. *Organization Theory: A Public Perspective.* Chicago, IL: Dorsey Press.

Lindblom, Charles E. 1980. *The Policymaking Process,* 2d ed. Englewood Cliffs, NJ: Prentice-Hall.

____. 1959. The Science of "Muddling Through." *Public Administration Review,* 19 (Spring).

Novick, David, ed. 1965. *Program Budgeting.* Cambridge, MA: Harvard University Press.

Pfeffer, Jeffrey. 1996. Understanding the Role of Power in Decision Making. In *Classics of Organization Theory,* 4th ed., edited by Jay M. Shafritz and J. Steven Ott. Belmont, CA: Wadsworth.

Rosenbloom, David H. 1986. *Public Administration: Understanding Management, Politics, and Law in the Public Sector.* New York: Random House.

Saaty, Thomas L. 1988. *Decision Making for Leaders.* Pittsburgh, PA: RWS Publications.

Selznick, Philip. 1957. *Leadership in Administration.* New York: Harper & Row.

Simon, Herbert A. 1961. *Administrative Behavior,* 2d ed. New York: Macmillan.

____. 1960. *The New Science of Management Decision.* New York: Harper & Row.

Stone, Florence M., ed. 1989. *The AMA Handbook of Supervisory Management.* New York: AMACOM.

Sussman, Lyle and Paul Krivonos. 1979. *Communication for Supervisors and Managers.* Sherman Oaks, CA: Alfred Publishing.

Timm, Paul R. 1986. *Managerial Communication: A Finger on the Pulse.* Englewood Cliffs, NJ: Prentice-Hall.

Waldo, Dwight. 1955. *The Study of Public Administration.* New York: Random House.

Wildavsky, Aaron. 1984. *The Politics of the Budgetary Process*, 4th ed. Boston, MA: Little, Brown.

9

Organizational Leadership

Leaders in organizations today are learning that the survival of their institutions often depends on understanding change and complexity in their internal and external environments and, accordingly, adopting new methods for managing such change. More than any other position in the organization, a leader is critical for promoting adaptation and modification. Leaders are primarily responsible for making necessary change to meet new needs and demands, even if "leadership rarely rises to the full need for it," as James Burns (1978, p. 1) remarks.

For our purpose, leadership is the process of influencing the behavior of others — subordinates, followers, peers, or a community — to accomplish defined objectives. There is much less argument over the idea that a leader needs to have influence, a group to influence, and goals worthy of exerting influence. Difficulties in studying leadership surface in defining goals (what and why) and designating methods for achieving them (how). Over the years, researchers have focused on leaders' roles, personal traits and qualities, style of operation and skills, and behavior and development. Such investigations also covered the leaders' impact on followers and a variety of situational and contextual factors affecting the leader's performance. The tendency in the literature to concentrate on one aspect of leadership or another seems unavoidable, particularly when sources of information frequently are memoirs, biographies, case studies, and surveys of small groups.

It is not surprising, for example, after a brief examination of the holdings of a university library, to develop an exaggerated sense of chaos and inconsistency in the literature. This partly is because of various narrow disciplinary interests focusing on their own questions and pursuing their particular disciplinary concerns: political science, social psychology, organization studies, and sociology. Another part of the reason is that, as Barbara Kellerman (1984, p. ix) points out, "the work that exists in this area tends to be prescriptive rather than descriptive." Consequently, few areas in social science have generated more research and less consensus than leadership, leading Burns (1978, p. 2) to conclude that "leadership is one of the most observed and least understood phenomena on earth."

At the outset, therefore, we need to set some preliminary boundaries. The focus here is primarily on organizational leadership, where results of a leader's efforts usually are tangible and observable. One is able to examine (and to measure) outcomes and impacts of leadership activities in areas such as setting goals, affirming values, motivating employees, resolving menacing conflicts, developing teamwork, and enhancing overall performance. Specifying leaders of public organizations also serves to differentiate them from other types of leaders, such as national, religious, or corporate. Realistically, however, leaders share certain attributes but drastically differ in others, particularly those related to role, expectations, and context.

Leaders in the corporate United States, for example, hold a different value structure and a wider set of managerial techniques and latitudes than their counterparts in government. In public organizations, leaders influence and are influenced by followers in order to accomplish legitimate goals and tasks, and usually they are not alone at the helms. Heads of government agencies follow orders of presidents, legislators, and governors as well as conform to existing laws and constitutional provisions. Such sharing of responsibilities is not entirely consistent with perceptions of leadership as located solely at the top of large organizations and institutions, directing policy for the entire nation (Nanus 1989, p. 6).

Research on leadership since World War II has inspired many theories and models that reveal divergent views and shifting attention. Each approach or phase of research "signals a change of emphasis rather than the demise of the previous approach(es)" (Bryman 1996, p. 277). The four perspectives reviewed here accent substantive theoretical components as well as explain practical implications to studying leadership. The perspectives are traits, action-behavior-style, contingency, and transformational.

THE TRAIT THEORY

The trait theory is based on the assumption that certain identifiable individual characteristics distinguish leaders from others. This perspective achieved prominence in the 1940s and 1950s, when recruiters for positions of organizational leaders defined the job in terms of discovering those individuals possessing leadership traits from birth. Researchers, therefore, sought to establish personal qualities or traits of leaders and to develop means for recognizing them. The objective was to clarify what physical and personality characteristics and what abilities distinguish successful from not-so-successful leaders.

Consequently, many lists of desirable qualities have been circulating from hand to hand and from one training workshop to another. The list of leadership traits (Table 9.1) became widely known after R. M. Stogdill's survey (1948) and has been quoted in several subsequent works (Bass 1981; Bryman 1986, p. 21). After failing to provide conclusive evidence that general qualities and abilities could be discerned (Bryman 1986, p. 18), several studies questioned whether natural leaders do exist. Stogdill's (1948) review is the most influential (subsequently extended to cover literature until 1970) and is considered the turning point of disillusionment with research into traits (Bryman 1986, p. 18). At the same time, a surge of research interests in leadership advanced alternative perspectives on the subject, which contributed to further decline of the traits approach and to development of alternative theories.

Dissatisfaction with the trait theory is the result of its inherent limitations. The assumption of certain inborn qualities of leaders, because they "are born and not made," neglects the crucial issues of leadership development and training (Adair 1983). Subsequent research rendered old notions of traits inadequate, particularly that no agreement on the qualities has been forthcoming. As Frederick Thayer (1981, p. A4) indicates, if leadership traits exist, social research never discovered them; hence, the idea was abandoned some time ago. He concludes that, if we discover such traits, we will need a caste system to segregate "natural leaders" from followers, perhaps a new theory of "divine right kings" (p. A5).

LEADERSHIP ACTION-BEHAVIOR APPROACH

Changing the focus of leadership research from the traits to the actions of the leader is a consequence of two significant factors. First is the inherent weakness of the trait theory and its limited utility in guiding the identification, selection, and development of managerial leaders. Second is the

TABLE 9.1
Stogdill's Personal Traits of Leadership

Physical Characteristics
    Activity, energy, appearance, grooming
Social Background
    Education, social status, mobility
Intelligence and Ability
    Intelligence, judgment, decisiveness, knowledge, fluency of speech
Personality
    Adaptability, adjustment, normality, aggressiveness, assertiveness, alertness, ascendance, dominance, emotional balance, control, independence, nonconformity objectivity, tough-mindedness, originality, creativity, personal integrity, ethical conduct, resourcefulness, self-confidence, strength of conviction, tolerance of stress
Task-Related Characteristics
    Achievement drive, desire to excel, drive for responsibility, enterprise, initiative, persistence against obstacles, responsible in pursuit of objectives, task orientation
Social Characteristics
    Ability to enlist cooperation, administrative ability, cooperativeness, popularity, prestige, sociability, interpersonal skills, social participation, tact, diplomacy

---

Source: Bryman 1986, p. 21.

evolution of behavioral thinking in management, particularly after the Hawthorne studies and the emergence of the human relations theory of management.

The action perspective is concerned with leadership effectiveness; hence, it focuses on what leaders do — their style and their behavior — more than on their personal traits. Leadership effectiveness is defined in terms of "how well the leader's group performs its assigned functions" (Fiedler & Chemers 1974, p. 7). Just as a conductor is judged by how well the orchestra plays, a football coach is judged by how well the team plays, or a general is evaluated by how well the troops perform, the effectiveness of the organizational leader is largely measured in terms of achieving the goals of the organization.

The literature often traces early research interest in this direction to the work of K. Lewin, R. Lippitt, and R. K. White (Bryman 1986, p. 36). They organized two clubs of ten-year-old children engaged in a work task over a three-month period. Three styles of leadership were applied. In the authoritarian style, the leader determined policy, work methods, and organization. The leader also was aloof and personal in criticisms or praise of the group members. In the democratic situation, policy matters and procedures were decided collectively; the leader made suggestions and remained objective in praise or criticism. The laissez-faire leader was nonparticipatory and allowed the group complete freedom.

The experiment applied three styles of leadership on four groups in different order and gathered information about reactions and results. The findings are summarized as follows:

Authoritarian leadership generated aggression, hostility, in-group scapegoating, more dependence on the leader, and the existence of high latent discontent. However, the groups evidenced a tendency to be more productive.

Democratic leadership generated greater work motivation and a friendlier environment. It was preferred to authoritarian leadership by the group members.

Laissez-faire leadership resulted overall in less quantity and quality of work performed.

These findings were expanded by the human relations approach and its preoccupation with supervisory and leadership styles of management and their impact on workers' attitudes and productivity (Bryman 1986, p. 36). The Ohio State Leadership Studies were conducted to examine and measure leaders' performance and behavior rather than human traits. Utilizing interdisciplinary teams, the studies focused on leadership activities. The massive accumulation of possible descriptors of leaders' behavior was eventually reduced to more than 100 items, which then were incorporated into a research instrument named Leader Behavior Description Questionnaire. The analysis of the Ohio State studies reveals four predominant factors in leadership behavior:

the consideration factor: camaraderie, mutual trust, liking, and respect,

the initiating factor: ability to organize work tightly, structure work context, provide clear-cut definition of role responsibility, and be active in getting the work at hand fully scheduled,

production emphasis: motivating employees to greater activity by emphasizing the mission or job to be done, and

sensitivity: awareness of social interrelationships and pressures.

The findings of the Ohio studies that received the greatest emphasis in the initial data are consideration and initiating structure. These two factors have been touted as independent dimensions of leader behavior and have had an important influence on contemporary research of leadership (Bryman 1986, p. 43). However, despite the magnitude and the impact of efforts, the general methodology of the Ohio studies and the assumptions made have been criticized on the following grounds.

First, leadership is conceptualized through perceptions and observations of groups as well as accounts of leaders themselves of what they do. This created a measurement problem as to whether such data constitute measurement of actual leaders' performance or outcomes of perceptual and attitudinal assessments, namely, assumed theories of leadership by each individual have an impact on how they rated the behavior of leaders, undermining the findings of the Ohio researchers (Bryman 1996, p. 279).

Second, the fact that leaders covered in these surveys have supervisory positions, within hierarchical settings, indicates an exclusion of leadership that may exist outside formal allocation of responsibility and control. Naturally, if leadership is defined in terms of influence, then we need people to be influenced. As Fred Fiedler and Martin Chemers (1974, p. 9) point out, "it is difficult to speak of the leader who does not have a group." However, the literature occasionally recognizes leaders other than incumbents, such as informal leaders without a formalized structure.

Third, perhaps one of the most surprising factors about the Ohio State studies is their failure to include situational variables that moderate the relationship between leadership behavior and outcome (Korman 1966; Bryman 1986). The general context of the organization (technology applied, size, relations with the environment) may not be part of leadership style, but it, nevertheless, affects the groups' responses and the final outcome of leadership style. Also, subordinates' performance and leadership behavior do influence each other and cause adjustments and changes on either side of the relationship.

The Michigan studies started in the 1940s when a group of researchers at the Survey Research Center, University of Michigan, embarked on studying group performance, motivation, organizational structure, and leadership practices. The researchers were mostly psychologists and were directed by Rensis Likert, whose name became synonymous with the efforts.

Like the Ohio studies, the Michigan research also conceptualized leadership behavior in terms of two dimensions: employee centered and production centered. Differences between the two research efforts, however, are significant. The Michigan studies utilized company records, focused on productivity, and relied on extensive descriptions of behavior from supervisors' reports. The Michigan researchers were dominated by psychologists; the Ohio teams were interdisciplinary with a sociological orientation.

The more recent works to come out of the Michigan research proposed more flexible conceptualization and established distinctions among three types of leadership skills (Mann 1965, pp. 79–80; Bryman 1986, p. 68).

Human relations skills roughly correspond to employee centeredness and denote sensitivity to underlying principles of human behavior, relationships, and motivation.

Technical skills are the ability to use knowledge, methods, and equipments to achieve specific tasks.

Administrative skills refer to an awareness of the broader organizational context and its goals as well as the administrative skills, which include the capabilities of organizing, planning, coordinating, and personnel development.

Enormous research conducted by those associated with the Institute of Social Research, University of Michigan (headed by Likert until his retirement in the late 1970s) has been cited in connection with Likert's model (Perrow 1979, p. 115). Likert's model appeared in his book *New Pattern of Management* (published in 1961 and winner of several awards and wide acclaim). Likert's model recognizes four "systems" of organizations: exploitative authoritative (approximates Max Weber's bureaucratic model or Douglas McGregor's Theory X), benevolent authoritative, consultative, and participative (System 4). Managers who use System 4, Likert (1981, p. 675) says, "create System 4 organizations which have excellent communication, high motivation, and capacity for reciprocal influence." System 4 is based on participative management and expresses the dimensions of leadership emphasized in the more recent Michigan studies. In Likert's System 4 (1981, p. 674), a leader is recognized as supportive, approachable, friendly, easy to talk to, interested in the well-being of subordinates; builds the subordinates into cohesive, highly effective, cooperative problem-solving teams linked together by persons who hold overlapping membership (subordinates are not pitted against each other in hostile, competitive relationships); helps subordinates with their work by seeing that they are supplied with all necessary resources, and subordinates are kept informed of overall plans so they can plan their work more effectively; has high performance, no-nonsense goals and expects high quality performance from herself or himself and others.

Criticisms of the Michigan studies are not totally different from those directed against the Ohio studies. In both, reliance on group averaging techniques in dealing with subordinate accounts of leader behavior, with little actual observance of such behavior, underlines the perceptual and attitudinal elements in the findings. Both studies neglect informal leadership as well as situational elements that modify the leader's behavior, even if the Michigan studies are less deficient on these factors than the Ohio studies.

In conclusion, studies of leadership style reduce behaviors and actions to fixed categories. More recent research findings negate rigid, universalistic categories of leaders' behavior and, instead, suggest variations of behavior according to situations. In other words, leaders change their style of operation and adjust their behavior, but the question that remains unanswered is, what instigates such change and in relation to what.

Undoubtedly, studies of leadership action (style, behavior) are substantive advancements (relative to what preceded them); these studies focus our attention on the actions of leaders and their influences on people, the organization, and productivity. Consequently, evidence related to participative systems, employees' satisfaction, and organizational productivity became repeated themes in literature on leadership and organization.

THE CONTINGENCY APPROACH TO LEADERSHIP

The change from traits to style and, more recently, to contingency theories is neither accidental nor an independent development. The shift of perspective is fully connected to the development of organization theory and process. The basic contingency model is a confirmation of the absence of a universally appropriate style of leadership and, further, that the outcome of the style is contingent on situational factors. Thus, high on the research agenda of proponents of contingency theory is the need to operationally specify the particular "conditions under which one kind of leader behavior will be superior to another and conditions which influence the leader behavior itself" (Hunt & Larson 1974, p. xv).

Results of contingency research vary in scope and emphasis. For example, a leader's behavior may be influenced by interactions among management ideology, technological sophistication, and time (Taylor 1974). George Farris (1974) places emphasis on leadership as a superior-subordinate mutual influence process described in the notion of feedback loops. Performance is implicitly and explicitly considered by Farris to influence leadership via feedback loops, as in systems models.

Fiedler, widely credited with articulating the early versions of the contingency theory, maintains that the type of leader required in order to enhance performance of the group is situationally contingent. Fiedler focuses on the extent to which the situation is favorable to the leader (degree of situational control). After reviewing several of Fiedler's publications, Alan Bryman (1986, p. 128) concludes that Fiedler underlines three components of the situation that facilitate the leader's influence over the group: leader-member relations, the quality of personal and affective relations between the leader and the group; task structure, clear and unambiguous tasks that facilitate the leader's position; and position power, the extent to which a leader has the ability to administer rewards and punishments to group members and to enforce compliance.

TRANSFORMATIONAL LEADERSHIP

Transformational leadership has been popularized in Burns' seminal work, *Leadership* (1978). Leadership for Burns (1978, p. 3) is linked to collective purpose, and the effectiveness of leaders is judged by actual social change, measured by intent and by the satisfaction of human needs and expectations. Transformational leaders are distinguished from transactional leaders. In the latter case, relations of leaders to followers are mere exchanges of one thing for another. A transforming leader "looks for potential motives in followers, seeks to satisfy higher needs, and engages the full person of the follower" (p. 4). Depictions of visionary, charismatic, or transformational together reveal a new conception of the leader "as someone who defines organizational reality through the articulation of a vision which is a reflection of how he or she defines an organization's mission and the values which support it" (Bryman 1996, p. 280).

In a broader sense, distinctions of transforming and transactional leadership comprise a model of individual and organizational performance that identifies variables involved in what is sometimes identified as "first-order" and "second-order" change (Burke 1994; French & Bell 1995, pp. 3–4). The first-order, also called "transactional," is evolutionary, adaptive change in which features of the organization are changed but not its fundamental nature. Second-order change, transformational, is revolutionary, fundamental change in which the nature of the organization is altered in significant ways (French & Bell 1995, p. 85). The transactional and transformational concepts come from leadership research in which it was observed that some leaders are capable of obtaining extraordinary performance from followers, but other leaders are not (Burns 1978; Tichy & Devanna 1986; French & Bell 1995, p. 87). Transformational leaders are those who "inspire followers to transcend their own self-interest for the good of the organization and who are capable of having a profound and extraordinary effect on the followers" (French & Bell 1995, p. 87). Transactional leadership, on the other hand, implies an ordinary exchange between leader and follower that maintains normal, satisfactory functioning of the organization.

Transformational leadership essentially is concerned with strategic issues that affect the mission of the organization. Philip Selznick's (1957, p. 24) classic work on leadership separates "routine" from "critical" decision making and views leadership in terms of significant effects on the overall condition of the organization. Actually, Selznick argues that a theory of leadership will necessarily reflect the level of sophistication we have reached in the study of organization. He recognizes that much failure of leadership results from an inadequate understanding of its true nature (Selznick 1957, p. 24). The default of leadership occurs when leaders fail to set goals (define the mission of the enterprise) or when goals, however neatly formulated, enjoy only a superficial acceptance and do not genuinely influence the total structure of the organization (Selznick 1957, p. 26).

Certainly, the success of transformational leadership entails particular requirements that include, first, the presence of a congruous culture, broadly shared by individuals and having discernable influence on organizational performance. In this situation, culture is characterized by consistency, organization-wide consensus, and clarity (Frost, Moore, Louis, Lundberg, and Martin 1991, p. 11). A deeper understanding of cultural issues in organizations, Edgar Schein (1985, p. 2) points out, "is necessary not only to identify what goes on in them but, even more important, to identify what may be the priority issues for leaders and leadership." Schein views organizational sides of the culture and leadership as "two sides of the same coin." Indeed, he contends, "the only thing of real importance that leaders do is to create and manage culture and that the unique talent of leaders is their ability to work with culture" (p. 2).

A second requirement for the success of transformational leadership is empowerment of people through participation in managing the organization. Employee participation is not a new notion in organizational analysis. Human relations perspectives, particularly Likert's System 4 and McGregor's Theory Y, made participation a central theme of their ideas. Today's teambuilding, quality circles, Total Quality Management, and the reinvention movement all extol empowerment of people in the organization as a key to good performance. Participation is crucial in order to "energize greater performance," produce better solutions to problems, and greatly enhance acceptance of decisions (French & Bell 1995, p. 94).

Accordingly, links between participation and leadership are explicit and fundamental. "I define leadership," Burns (1978, p. 19) concludes, "as leaders inducing followers to act for certain goals that represent the values and motivations — the wants and needs, the aspirations and expectations — *of both leaders and followers.*" These goals consume considerable leaders' efforts; they are the vision, the purpose, or the mission, as others have labeled them. Regardless of terms, leadership is about an imaginative idea of change and the ability to bring it about. Clearly, an image of the future, a vision, by itself is insufficient to create what some authors call abilities of leaders "to get extraordinary things done in organizations" (Kouzes & Posner 1990, p. xvii). It is difficult to think of a leader without followers who accept the leader's vision as their own. "You cannot command commitment, you can only inspire it" (p. 9). To get others to buy into the future image of the organization, a leader also utilizes the process of communication to explain the purpose, to develop trust, and to effectuate appropriate means for change.

The allegory in Belasco and Stayer's *Flight of the Buffalo* (1993), is based on a comparison of buffalo and geese. Buffalo, it seems, follow one leader blindly, and if that leader errs in judgment or meets with some disaster, the rest of the herd is at peril. It is explained that this is the reason these magnificent animals were so easily slaughtered in the early West. Experienced hunters merely dispatched the "lead buffalo," and the others stood around waiting to be shot. In contrast, geese fly in the readily recognizable V formation, with each individual in the formation taking the lead and being responsible for the direction and welfare of the entire flight. If your employees usually are waiting around for some direction or leadership, this reveals your style of leadership — the buffalo style.

CONCEPT PRECEDES PRACTICE

Conceptual analysis and evaluation of leadership is significant for its operational thrust, not merely for its theoretical symmetry and elegance. If leadership is a set of natural personal traits, then identification and recruitment of organizational leaders are exercises in the discovery of the persons with these traits for selection, placement, and development. If leaders are born, then elaborate and extended training may be superfluous, unessential, or wasteful.

Alternatively, if leadership emerges mainly from actions and behaviors, then our task is to identify these effective actions and behaviors and learn from them. Expansion of our conceptual schemes to include the contextual modifiers of behavior would result in a more realistic picture of effective leadership and the situational factors that influence it. Implications to learning, training, and development are obvious, namely, that situational analysis expands our theoretical and practical concerns from the person and the office to all surrounding relevant forces that impinge on the leader's performance. These relevant factors encompass the type of subordinates, the structure of the organization, and the task itself.

The traditional theories of organization (scientific management, administrative management, and the bureaucratic model) offer a clear and simple view of leadership. In these approaches, leadership usually is located at the top of the hierarchy and performs managerial functions such as planning, organizing, budgeting, coordinating, and monitoring the overall performance of the administrative unit. This strong-executive model naturally enjoys the powers of legitimacy, punishment, and reward used in getting the task accomplished efficiently and effectively. Although emphasizing reliable, stable, and consistent performance, traditional views of leadership respect hierarchy and reward those who follow the rules while getting the job done. This task orientation also assumes a rationally structured organizational setting.

Leadership is conceived differently in organizations managed according to human relations viewpoints or applying recent managerial practices, such as team building and quality circles, for example. In 1938, Chester Barnard's *The Functions of the Executive* (1962) offered a precursor to current views stressing the centrality of leadership to task accomplishment. The executive, according to Barnard (p. 217), coordinates all aspects of the organization through communication, promotes and secures efforts, and formulates and defines purpose of the organization. To secure enduring cooperation in the organization, the executive authority lies in the subordinates, not in any coercive instrument. As a result, a cardinal principle for executive conduct in good organizations is "orders will not be issued that cannot or will not be obeyed" (p. 167).

This managerial principle, Thayer (1981, p. A20) points out, is considered identical to the political doctrine of "consent of the governed." Barnard (1962, p. 169) recommends that orders not be issued outside the "zone of acceptance" in each individual. To be accepted by employees, communicated executive orders must be authoritative, understood, consistent with the goals of the organization, and compatible with the personal interests of those affected. Also, orders must be implementable within available resources. The zone of acceptance will be wider or narrower depending upon the degree to which the inducements exceed the burdens and sacrifices that determine the individual's adhesion to the organization.

The contingency and the transformational perspectives of leadership also relate activities of the leader to conditions in the organization and attitudes and skills of subordinates. For example, empowering employees and developing organizational culture are conducive to change; they also are primary responsibilities of a leader. In brief, leading through conceptual analysis of problems and goals promotes application of logical systems thinking and yields better use of intellectual capacities of leaders. Realistic concepts help the leader to cut directly to the core of issues, to sort out what is significant, and to demonstrate competence in dealing with complex problems.

LEADERS AND MANAGERS

The literature offers two-strand analysis of leadership, frequently underlining differences between leaders and managers. Differentiating leaders from executives is established explicitly in Selznick's *Leadership in Administration.* In this, Selznick (1957, p. 3) searches beyond the logic of efficiency, which applies mostly to subordinate units with defined operating responsibilities, limited discretion, set communication channels, and a sure position in the command structure. He notes that the logic of efficiency, thus, loses force as we approach the top of the pyramid. Similarly, despite the considerable interest generated by the human relations approach, we are left with what Selznick (1957, p. 4) refers to as "a sense of inadequacy" when we try to see the whole enterprise and how institutional change is produced.

Selznick (1957, p. 4) considers the leader a "statesman" who presides over the organization and infuses it with the values of its community, thus, transforming it from an expendable tool to an institution valued by its environment. Not surprising, this analysis finds that most organizations are led by default and that people at the top do not lead but, instead, retreat to executiveship, practicing managerial technologies such as planning, budgeting, and staffing.

Political scientists distinguish leaders in terms of power, authority, and position. In the process, goals and motives of power holders as well as their skills and resources are crucial in the analysis (Burns 1978; Kellerman 1984). Often, in public administration literature, manager is used interchangeably with leader. Conventions of business administration, however, are inconsistent, although the distinction between leaders and managers is noted increasingly (Bennis & Nanus 1985; Nanus 1989; Zaleznick 1989).

The distinction between manager and leader frequently is pronounced to lament the rarity of effective leadership at the top of corporate organizations — too many managers and too few leaders. As Burt Nanus (1989, p. 6) points out, there are plenty of excellent managers in organizations who schedule, budget, plan, or coordinate the efforts of subordinates, but leadership is another thing entirely. What is it that leaders do that is different? Nanus (p. 7) proposes that leaders take charge, make things happen, dream dreams, and then translate them into reality; attract the voluntary commitment of followers, energize them, and transform organizations into new entities with greater potential for survival, growth, and excellence; and empower organizations to maximize contributions to the well-being of their members and to society.

Nanus' perspective is in agreement with Selznick's views on leaders and executives, in which the leader is expert in defining the mission of the organization, defending its integrity, resolving its conflicts, and infusing it with values. In a catchy phrase, Warren Bennis and Nanus (1985, p. 21) sum up the difference as "managers are people who do things right and leaders are people who do the right things." Actually, a convergence of views on leadership functions has been in the making since the 1980s. In practical terms, these functions include, but are not limited to, the following:

Provide future-oriented actions
    Diagnose organizational needs
    Develop long-range vision and mission
    Design strategies for achieving broad goals
    Initiate change
Maintain cooperative team approach
    Lead through actions by setting an example
    Treat people equally
    Foster independence and project-oriented actions
    Negotiate and persuade for acceptance of own views
    Reward goal accomplishment
    Use personal loyalty for motivating people
    Promote employee compatibility
    Encourage cooperation and effective interactions
    Communicate organizational values
Promote result-oriented actions
    Develop sensible and reasoned plans
    Deal directly with problems

Monitor implementation of strategies
Take corrective actions
Recognize opportunities and take initiatives
Guard integrity of the institution and its processes
Resolve threatening conflicts
Represent the organization to its environment
Act as catalysts between systems and people
Respond to community needs
Bolster organizational values of innovation.

Distinctions between managers and leaders may not be so simple in real situations. Yet, without significant operational thrusts, popular notions (or clichés) abound, such as: "Leaders master the context, managers master the content." "Managers administer and leaders innovate." "Managers maintain, leaders develop." The manager's eye is always on the bottom line and often accepts the status quo; the leader challenges it.

In defining the manager's job, Henry Mintzberg (1990, p. 168) considers leadership as part of what managers do. He delineates three important roles for the manager with formal authority and status. These roles extend beyond the traditional tasks of planning, organizing, coordinating, and controlling. They are interpersonal roles — figurehead, leader, liaison; informational roles — monitor, disseminator, spokesperson; and decisional roles — entrepreneur, disturbance handler, resource allocator, negotiator.

Instead of a clear line of demarcation between the functions of leaders and managers, a flexible approach is more functional. Roles of leaders and managers may overlap and intermix, and, certainly, they are complimentary. More often than not, effective leaders are also effective managers, and vice versa. The conclusion that "leadership begins where management ends" (Kouzes & Posner 1990, p. xvii) is valid only when the two functions are complementary. Such a conclusion is not accurate when it implies that leadership and management are distinctive, autonomous, or entirely separate functions.

Indeed, few city managers, county administrators, or public executives at any level of government would agree to the separation of functions in the first place. Effective public managers assume leadership roles when they influence policy and people, overcome constraints, set directions, and take aggressive actions. Limiting their functions to efficiency considerations is neither realistic nor desirable. The effective manager is the backbone of operations — makes decisions, monitors processes of spending funds, ensures legitimacy of daily transactions, and maintains efficient and equitable reward systems. Perhaps, the manager may be considered a transactional leader who emphasizes organizational decision making and spends much of his or her time making sure lower level managers (supervisors) are making effective operating decisions. To a large measure, the manager's job becomes to review lower level decisions and to lead subordinates by example, persuasion, demonstrated superior knowledge and skills, and ethical conduct. Managers use new techniques and information, mobilize support, and exercise control over performance. Managers are known for skill in solving problems; leaders are known for being masters in designing and building institutions and are the architects of new approaches to the future of the organization.

Finally, the supervisory level in the organization is the front line operation of management. Supervisors are practicing managers in their relatively small domains, although usually they exercise less than executive authority. However, as supervisors influence their followers and are influenced by the top leaders and managers of their organizations, they do exert a modifying influence on the exercise of leadership. Supervisors are connected upward and downward with leadership channels that determine outcomes. Consequently, a leader's success in public organizations includes the supervisory level, usually affected by similar, if more constricted, considerations of power and influence. These functions of the manager and the supervisor may be summed up in the following:

Manager
    Maintains effective functioning of management
    Mobilizes financial and human resources to achieve defined goals
    Plans, organizes, staffs, and coordinates
    Sets ethical and professional standards of performance
    Maintains effective communication among unit members
Supervisor
    Provides technical and operational know-how to staff
    Motivates staff
    Attends to bureaucratic routine
    Complements the manager's functions and activities
    Evaluates staff
    Reports on the performance of the unit and its workers.

BASES OF INFLUENCE

Abilities of leaders and managers of public organizations to influence subordinates are much greater with the presence of important foundations of power. However, having a basis of power, as Mintzberg (1996, p. 414) points out, is not enough. "The individual must act in order to become an influencer, he or she must expend energy, use the basis of power." Most widely recognized vehicles for influencing others in the organization are constellations of positional and personal strengths. They have been grouped and defined by John French and Bertram Raven (1959) as follows:

Reward power is based on the belief that a person has the ability to offer positive rewards to another person for his or her obedience and loyalty. In the organizational context, such rewards may include pay raise, promotion, and public recognition.

Coercive power is based on the perception that a person has the ability to punish another person, psychologically or physically, in order to attain compliance with orders. In the organizational context this may include termination of employment, reprimand, demotion, transfer, and withholding privileges.

Legitimate power is based on the recognition that one person has the legal right to prescribe behavior for others in particular situations according to prescribed rules. Examples in the managerial field are operational rules and regulations issued by a manager to the employees of his or her unit.

Referent power covers the psychological identification with a particular individual or group as a result of respect and admiration for their leadership style, professional values, or other favorable human characteristics. An illustration is when employees are able to say: "We do what our manager tells us to do because he or she cares; this manager is trusted, hard-working, and interested in the welfare of the employees."

Expert power is demonstrated or perceived knowledge and skills of an individual in a specific field that induce others to follow or comply with his or her orders and wishes. In organizations, subordinates tend to obey or comply with the desires of the leader when those desires are accepted as based on expert knowledge and superior ability in specific areas. Employees are satisfied with the leader's expertise because "he or she knows what they are doing."

Although reward, punishment, and legitimate powers usually are derived from the position of the individual in command, referent and expert powers are tied to personal or behavioral attributes. In public organizations, powers of formal positions (manager, director, supervisor) typically are defined by law or by regulations that allow all individuals in certain positions to have the same legitimate, punishment, and reward powers. Also, the manager is presumably a knowledgeable person who provides the organization with expertise and skills necessary for satisfying organizational goals. It is in these two areas, referent and expert powers, where large variations of leadership performance occur.

What about leaders who have no positional powers and, consequently, have no money or material rewards to offer, no promotions to make, and no performance evaluations to administer? Can a leader function in the absence of these formal methods of influence? Can a leader generate internal motivation and willingness on the part of others to want, voluntarily, to do what they are asked to do? The answer is affirmative, and history is full of illustrations indicating such possibility. Martin Luther King, Jr., Mother Teresa, Nelson Mandela, and Andrei Sakharov did not achieve their leadership status on the basis of positional powers as discussed above. Each is recognized as an outstanding leader in a defined area. Such leaders also may become organizational leaders as a result of their roles in nonorganizational settings.

Because leadership is defined in terms of influence, interaction becomes an essential medium for such influence to produce its desirable effect of compliance by the subordinates. Variations of subordinates, organizational structure, and the complexity of technology used necessitate changes in the methods of influence used by the leader. In fact, "the success of any leader depends on his or her ability to use the variety of available means of influence in a way that gains compliance and ensures a coordinated effort to achieve the goals of the group" (Gortner, Mahler, & Nicholson 1987, p. 297). Consequently, leaders must ask themselves what people want from their leaders. Typically, followers expect leaders to lead, to have a sense of purpose and the ability to evoke the trust of the followers — trust not only in the integrity and honesty of the leader but also in his or her competence to produce results, achieve success, and inspire followers to jump on the bandwagon.

The five bases of power described by French and Raven are broad categories and do not specifically delineate the many complex and subtle means of influence available to leaders of contemporary formal organizations. Gary Yukl (1989, pp. 20–21) adds other sources of power and influence, such as:

Control over information. A person's access to vital information and its distribution to others may lead to selected interpretation of information to peers and subordinates and, consequently, influence their perceptions and attitudes.

Control over the physical environment, technology, and organization of work. Yukl considers this important source of leader's influence as situational engineering or ecological control. The most widely known form of situational engineering is job design, which has potential influence on a subordinate's motivation, competition, autonomy, and sense of meaningful participation in accomplishing the task.

Other tools of influence. These include rational persuasion to convince a subordinate that suggested behavior is the best way to satisfy his or her needs. Inspirational appeal, for example, is effective in persuading a person to see the link between the requested behavior and some value that is important enough to justify the behavior. Indoctrination is an effective tool of influence when a person is induced to act through internalization of strong values that are relevant to the desired behavior.

Finally, recent institutional and cultural changes in the society add to the responsibilities of the leader. Employees expect individuals in high offices, consuming large resources, to be not only competent and knowledgeable about the task but also vigilant in upholding the laws and the values of the community. In the past 50 years, society experienced enormous change in values and expectations. Today, society is less tolerant of racism, sexism, and any such types of discrimination. Although court rulings repeatedly upheld constitutional rights of individuals, growing fear of abuse of these rights by public officials has resulted from recent legislative initiatives that give federal investigative organizations extraordinary powers of questionable constitutional legitimacy.

Despite altering the absolute immunity doctrine and replacing it with limited immunity ruling in order to allow citizens to sue public officials for illegal acts, recent legislative powers allowed to investigative agencies, such as the Federal Bureau of Investigation, have eroded individual rights. Under specific conditions, these agencies are not subject to judicial review and other due process protections traditionally granted to citizens. Society (citizens, mass media, professional organizations) expects higher standards of ethics and performance from public officials entrusted with public responsibilities. Within contemporary organizations, the participatory culture is taking root. At the workplace, employees expect that they be involved in organizational decision making. Overall, employees demand proper treatment, due process, and equitable distribution of material as well as symbolic rewards. The leader is not a free agent anymore, particularly in public organizations. It is increasingly more difficult for authoritarian leaders to apply their powers unchecked or without accountability.

LEADERSHIP TRAINING AND DEVELOPMENT

Discussions of leadership often ignore one of the most difficult questions, namely, how to prepare individuals for senior positions in public organizations and, after they reach such positions, how to provide them with relevant skills and knowledge for renewal and development. Even the existence of such information is debatable, and when available, it often is contradictory. Training and development for leadership have several components. The convergence of these components helps the establishment of suitable conditions for the emergence of leadership.

Academic preparation lays a general foundation, and graduate studies provide important focus and depth. Practical experience on the job generates functional knowledge about organizations and their operations. It is difficult to conceive of a starting position at a leadership level without prior work experience unless the person is born crown prince in a monarchical system. Most leaders start somewhere in the organization in nonleadership capacities. Through job enlargement and job enrichment, an employee also is enabled to assume more tasks and responsibility and to exercise greater autonomy and independence in making decisions.

Applied knowledge complements the formal education of managers and leaders. They are more likely to learn relevant skills if exposed to a variety of developmental experiences with appropriate coaching and mentoring by superiors and peers (Yukl 1989, p. 286). Career growth and development through training are commonly acceptable practices in both public and private organizations. Most corporations have executive management programs for the development of their staffs, with contents ranging from the specific and technical to the comprehensive and conceptual. A report by the Carnegie Foundation estimates that corporations spend nearly $40 billion each year for employee education, with about 30 percent of the total specifically spent on leadership training (Kouzes & Posner 1990, p. 288).

Executive education in the business sector is dominated increasingly by business colleges in well-established universities. Various rankings of these universities are published annually by popular business journals. The Master of Business Administration degree is being recognized more and more as the standard qualification for business executives, much more than the Master of Public Administration degree is for government managers. For various reasons, public managers do not seek out public administration programs for leading-edge thinking the way business executives do in relation to business schools. One reason, perhaps, is that most public administration faculty members have no practical experience in government and may not even be trained in public administration.

Leadership training (nondegree study) relies on various techniques and instructional methods such as case studies, problem-solving exercises, lectures, readings, simulations, films, and videotapes (Yukl 1989, p. 284). "Behavioral modeling is often used as an important part of leadership training" (Sims & Lorenzi 1992, p. 15). Special training programs for developing interpersonal skills usually include a heavy dose of human relations experiences to enhance the personal abilities of leaders in areas of conflict resolution, negotiations, social sensitivity, and developing trust and confidence of followers.

Other widely used techniques of leadership training include case studies, role-playing, and coaching. However, feedback and evaluation of training, although essential, remain most underdeveloped and problematic. How real is the contribution of training to knowledge and skills of the manager or the leader? How can one measure the effectiveness and impact of training efforts? What is the real feeling of the trainee about a training program? Questionnaires filled out by participants are not always effective for evaluation and feedback. Many of these surveys, because of poor conception and flawed design, do not get at the right information. Trainees also do not easily admit failure or uselessness of a program of which they have been part. Finally, organizers often exert exceptional efforts to please the participants through social and hospitality programs so that trainees feel well treated and do not want to appear ungrateful by giving poor grades to a training program.

CONCLUSION

Leadership has been conceived as a combination of personal traits, as a style of behavior and action, and as performance that is contingent on the organizational context. In all cases, leadership is a form of influence that results in desirable behavior by the influenced. In the process, leadership may utilize or manipulate several means of power to attain the desirable behavior or compliance. However, effective organizational leadership must be viewed as a collective responsibility that engages followers and leaders to respond to common goals and shared values.

However much we admire, discuss, and seek to understand leadership, agreement on major aspects of it remains illusive. Descriptions of leadership are abundant, such as infusion of the organization with vision, strategy, trust, collaboration, goals, motivation, direction, change, and so forth. Despite rich literature on leadership, the subject often is described as confusing and contradictory, partly because of "narrow research" and "lack of integrating conceptual frameworks" (Yukl 1989, p. 287).

At the same time, leaders are parts of larger social systems that incorporate social values and mores. Leaders inspire higher goals and values and implore others to attain them. They are the few that cause things to happen, usher in their happening, and remove the obstacles that stand in the way of their happening. In terms of performance, the consensus is that leaders perform a variety of functions that expand or contract in each position. Although people at the top do have greater leadership roles, others at the managerial or supervisory levels also are expected to demonstrate leadership skills when exercising their managerial duties. Thus, compartmentalizing roles by limiting leaders to the why or purpose and the manager to the how or the process of the operation is an inadequate distinction. In fact, each function complements the other and contributes to the proper performance of the organization. Positions are not exclusive, although leaders lead more than they manage and managers manage more than they lead. Finally, leadership is not a mysterious activity, as John W. Gardner (1989) points out. The capacity to perform leadership tasks is widely distributed in the population.

REFERENCES

Adair, John E. 1983. *Effective Leadership.* London: Pan.

Barnard, Chester I. 1962. *The Functions of the Executive.* Cambridge, MA: Harvard University Press.

Bass, B. M. 1981. *Stogdill's Handbook of Leadership.* New York: Free Press.

Belasco, James A. and Ralph C. Stayer. 1993. *Flight of the Buffalo: Soaring to Excellence, Learning to Let Employees Lead.* New York: Warner Books.

Bennis, Warren and Burt Nanus. 1985. *Leaders.* New York: Harper & Row.

Bryman, Alan. 1996. Leadership in Organizations. In *Handbook of Organization Studies*, edited by Stewart Clegg, Cynthia Hardy, and Walter Nord. Thousand Oaks, CA: Sage.

____. 1986. *Leadership and Organization.* London: Routledge & Kegan Paul.

Burke, W. Warner. 1994. *Organization Development: A Process of Learning and Changing*, 2d ed. Reading, MA: Addison-Wesley Publishing.

Burns, James MacGregor. 1978. *Leadership.* New York: Harper & Row.

Farris, George F. 1974. Leadership and Supervision in the Informal Organization. In *Contingency Approaches to Leadership*, edited by J. G. Hunt and L. L. Larson. Carbondale: Southern Illinois University Press.

Fiedler, Fred E. and Martin M. Chemers. 1974. *Leadership and Effective Management.* Glenview, IL: Scott, Foresman.

French, John and Bertram Raven. 1959. The Bases of Social Power. In *Studies in Social Power*, edited by Dorwin Cartwright. Ann Arbor, MI: Institute for Social Research.

French, Wendell L. and Cecil H. Bell, Jr. 1995. *Organization Development*, 4th ed. Englewood Cliffs, NJ: Prentice-Hall.

Frost, Peter J., Larry Moore, Meryl R. Louis, C. C. Lundberg, and Joane Martin. 1991. *Reframing Organizational Culture*. Newbury Park, CA: Sage.

Gardner, John W. 1989. *On Leadership*. New York: Free Press.

Gortner, Harold, J. Mahler, and J. B. Nicholson. 1987. *Organization Theory: A Public Perspective*. Chicago, IL: Dorsey Press.

Hunt, James G. and Lars L. Larson, eds. 1974. *Contingency Approaches to Leadership*. Carbondale: Southern Illinois University Press.

Kellerman, Barbara. 1984. *Leadership: Multidisciplinary Perspectives*. Englewood Cliffs, NJ: Prentice-Hall.

Korman, Abraham K. 1966. "Consideration," "Initiating Structure," and Organizational Criteria — A Review. *Personal Psychology*, 19, 349–361.

Kouzes, James M. and Barry Z. Posner. 1990. *The Leadership Challenge: How to Get Extraordinary Things Done in Organizations*. San Francisco, CA: Jossey-Bass.

Likert, Rensis. 1981. System 4: A Resource for Improving Public Administration. *Public Administration Review*, 41, 6 (November-December).

___. 1961. *New Pattern of Management*. New York: McGraw-Hill.

Mann, F. C. 1965. Toward Understanding of the Leadership Role in Formal Organization. In *Leadership and Productivity*, edited by R. Dubin. San Francisco, CA: Chandler.

Mintzberg, Henry. 1996. The Power Game and the Players. In *Classics of Organization Theory*, 4th ed, edited by J. M. Shafritz and J. S. Ott. New York: Wadsworth Publishing.

___. 1990. The Manager's Job: Folklore and Fact. *Harvard Business Review*, (March-April).

Nanus, Burt. 1989. *The Leader's Edge*. Chicago, IL: Contemporary Books.

Perrow, Charles. 1979. *Complex Organizations: A Critical Essay*, 2d ed. Glenview, IL: Scott, Foresman.

Schein, Edgar H. 1985. *Organizational Culture and Leadership*. San Francisco, CA: Jossey-Bass.

Selznick, Philip. 1957. *Leadership in Administration*. New York: Harper & Row.

Sims, Henry P., Jr. and Peter Lorenzi. 1992. *The New Leadership Paradigm*. Newbury Park, CA: Sage.

Stogdill, R. M. 1948. Personal Factors Associated with Leadership: A Survey of the Literature. *Journal of Psychology*, 25.

Taylor, James C. 1974. Technology and Supervision in the Postindustrial Era. In *Contingency Approaches to Leadership*, edited by James G. Hunt and Lars L. Larson. Carbondale: Southern Illinois University Press.

Thayer, Frederick C. 1981. *An End to Hierarchy and Competition*, 2d ed. New York: New Viewpoints.

Tichy, N. M. and M. A. Devanna. 1986. *The Transformational Leader*. New York: Wiley and Sons.

Yukl, Gary A. 1989. *Leadership in Organizations*. Englewood Cliffs, NJ: Prentice-Hall.

Zaleznick, Abraham. 1989. *The Managerial Mystique: Restoring Leadership in Business*. New York: Harper & Row.

10

Organizational Culture

Traditional theories of organization offer managerial practices that are readily recognizable in many contemporary public and private organizations. The hierarchy in many organizations, conspicuously pronounced, illustrates reliance on authority structure to provide the capacity to organize specialized employees into a coordinated work force. Other crucial elements of traditional management include explicit control mechanisms, specified individual responsibilities, and clearly detailed rules of operation.

Traditional theories of management have proven to be utilitarian, if controversial. The ideas of Luther Gulick, Frederick Taylor, and Max Weber are associated with more managerial deficiencies and problems in current literature than these authors could have anticipated. Unfair as it may be, in the minds of students of management, Theory X by Douglas McGregor (1960) is an approximation of the traditional schools. Theory X assumes that people are fundamentally lazy and irresponsible and need to be monitored constantly. The association of negative techniques with traditional management often is accentuated with criticisms that aim at emptying traditional schools of their significance.

The development of the human relations perspective contributed significantly to the steady adaptation of the basic tenets of traditional management, even with the human relations bifurcation into several distinct frameworks that both compete and overlap. Several modern frameworks are grounded in the basic thinking of the human relations school, but each has attained autonomous standing on its own. McGregor's Theory Y and Rensis Likert's System 4 are presented above. Theory Y assumes that people are fundamentally hardworking and responsible; thus, management needs only to support, develop, and encourage employees. Likert's System 4 organization is based on participative management with a cohesive work force, open communication, high motivation, and a capacity for reciprocal influence between leaders and subordinates. A recent and expanding perspective is based on viewing the organization either as a culture-producing entity or as a cultural system (Peters & Waterman 1982; Smircich 1983; Ouchi & Wilkins 1985; Schein 1985; Frost, Moore, Louis, Lundberg, & Martin 1985).

DEFINING ORGANIZATIONAL CULTURE

Culture is not always easy to define in specific terms. In a sense, culture is the "social or normative glue that holds an organization together" (Smircich 1983, p. 344). In another view, it signifies shared values and beliefs that give people a sense of identity. Culture facilitates commitment to larger goals than one's own (Peters & Waterman 1982), influences behavior, and enhances stability and orderly development of the organization (Meyer 1981; Ouchi 1981; Smircich 1983). To John Van Maanen and Stephen Barley (1985, p. 31), "Culture implies that human behavior is partially prescribed by a collectively created and sustained way of life that cannot be personality based because it is shared by diverse individuals." New employees in the organization often hear coworkers telling them about existing acceptable norms of behavior, as conveyed by these statements: "this is the way it is done around here"; "in this organization, people are very high on regular attendance, quality of service, and physical fitness"; "they really don't care if you socialize during work hours"; and "don't make waves." Such sayings mean some behavioral norms are mediating between formal structures and informal voluntary patterns. These norms are reflections of organizational culture and constitute significant contributions to the delineation of acceptable standards of work and conduct by employees.

Some of the difficulty in defining organizational culture stems from the fact that important elements of the concept deal with fluid and symbolic characteristics, more than concrete ones. Often, culture is not seen, but its consequences and manifestations are continually encountered within the organization. As Jay Shafritz and J. Steven Ott (1996, p. 373) point out, organizational culture "is comprised of many intangible things such as values, beliefs, assumptions, perceptions, behavioral norms, artifacts, and patterns of behavior." The realization of the significance of culture in shaping human behavior within the organization has been one of the fastest growing research interests in management in the past few years.

In the literature, Meryl Louis (1985, p. 74) finds three basic components of culture: first, the content, which is the totality of socially transmitted behavior patterns, style of social and artistic expression, and a set of common understandings; second, the group, which is a community of population, a society, an organization, a unit; and third, the relationship between the content and the group, which decides the characteristics of the group — peculiar, common, or different from other groups.

In this analysis, organizational culture is distinguished from societal or national culture, which we discuss earlier as an element of the external environment. This distinction does not mean the two concepts (or clusters of concepts) are mutually exclusive. On the contrary, both levels of cultural analysis (organizational and national) result in behavioral regularities of people subjected to these cultures, because they invariably influence each other. Nevertheless, making such distinctions is important to avoid the confusion that often results from equating the organization with its larger setting and because national culture is recognized as a crucial element of the external environment. Organizational culture is influenced by societal culture but not totally determined or defined by it. Organizational culture may have within it many other subcultures. Also, a sophisticated, rational organizational culture, for example, a modern hospital or a factory, may operate — successfully — within a traditional societal culture. Importing technology, skills, and knowledge by an organization, for example, often widens the discrepancy between its own culture and that of the larger society.

Edgar Schein (1985, p. 2) believes that organizational cultures are created by leaders and that one of the most decisive functions of leadership well may be the creation and management of culture. Thus, we must learn to analyze organizational cultures accurately in order to understand why organizations act as they do and why leaders have some of the difficulties they have. Schein (1985, p. 24) also is concerned with the impact and analytical significance of the concept of organizational culture, particularly for these three reasons:

Organizational cultures are "feelable" and have real impact on a society, an occupation, an organization, or a group.

Individual and organizational performance, and the feelings that people have about their organizations, cannot be understood unless one takes into account the organization's culture, which can determine the degree of effectiveness of the organization.

Organizational culture as a concept has been misunderstood and confused with other concepts, such as "climate," "philosophy," "ideology," and "style." Indeed, psychologists prefer using the concept of organizational "climate" to focus on "shared perceptions" of organizational policies, practices, and procedures, both formal and informal (Reichers & Schneider 1990, p. 22). Some prefer climate over culture because the first reflects or describes individual cognition or belief regarding important organizational properties such as managerial trust, supportiveness, or participativeness in decision making (Rousseau 1990, p. 159). However, advocates of climate admit the overlap with culture, which has a deeper and more comprehensive set of meanings, and agree that climate simply is a manifestation of culture (Reichers & Schneider 1990, p. 24).

To cultivate the potential benefits of cultural analysis, we first must build a common frame of reference and apply it in a theoretically appropriate manner. A considerable part of organizational culture is transmitted through processes of social learning and communication of a set of cognitions shared by members of the organization. At the same time, shared cognition is reinforced by a socialization process within the organization that transmits to employees common normative beliefs, shared assumptions, and general expectations. It is helpful to understand larger interests in causes and processes of cultural development, but the more important issue is the effect of culture on organizational performance and organizational change. From the public administration perspective, the crucial purpose of organizational cultural analysis is managerial, not anthropological. The primary concern is the effective functioning of the organization rather than studying culture per se, without any expression of preference or value judgment, as an anthropologist would do.

Researchers emphasize different elements in defining culture, and, consequently, they collect different types of data. Consider the following major cultural elements underlined by various researchers and described by Denise Rousseau (1990, p. 157):

physical manifestations and material artifacts of cultural activity, such as logos, badges, pins, blue suits, office furniture;

structures giving patterns to organizational activity such as decision making, coordination, and communication mechanisms;

behavioral norms that define member beliefs regarding acceptable and unacceptable behaviors and promote mutual predictability;

values and beliefs that determine priorities assigned to certain outcomes, innova-
tiveness, risk taking versus risk avoidance; and

unconscious assumptions, not directly knowable even to members.

Researchers show a tendency to choose their particular layer of culture
and apply one of a multiplicity of methods in researching it. In this
context, it must be indicated that organizational culture tends to guide and
influence action, not necessarily determine it. Norms developed and
incorporated in individual and group behaviors often are mixed with
myths, symbols, and assumptions. However, education and training, as
well as the "information revolution" touching every community, are
dispelling many of those myths and undermining the grip of traditional
cultural norms. Nowhere is this observation more true than in developing
countries, where new or modified norms frequently are replacing old
ones. In pluralistic systems, competition among cultures within the organization prevents dominance by any; hence, it affords the organization and
its management a measure of choice. In brief, organizational culture is not
static or totally dependent on national culture; organizational culture
changes all the time and may influence the world around it as much or
more than it is influenced by it.

CULTURE AND PUBLIC ORGANIZATIONS

In terms of application, studies of organizational culture pursue several
tracks, with varying rationales and differing results. Studies of corporate
culture seek to delineate the ways various organizational dimensions are
interrelated and how they influence process and outcome (Smircich 1983,
p. 354). Thomas Peters and R. H. Waterman (1982, p. 26) point out that
"the excellent companies seem to have developed cultures that have incorporated the values and practices of the great leaders and thus those shared
values can be seen to survive for decades after the passing of the original
guru." In public organizations, bureaucratic culture interests researchers
who seek understanding of the rules of organizational intervention and
coordinated action to serve legitimate (and symbolic) objectives. Cultural
analysis of organizations attempts to discover how organizations differ in
their views of time, space, and relationships to the community, as well as
how they differ in honoring truth, public trust, and loyalty of employees.

"Unless we have searched for the pattern among the different underlying assumptions of a group and have attempted to identify the paradigm
by which the members of a group perceive, think about, feel about, and

judge situations and relationships, we cannot claim that we have described or understood the group's culture" (Schein 1985, p. 111). Thus, as students of organizations, we are expressing a desire that the workplace be designed to function as a community, in contrast to the traditional emphasis on authority structure, division of labor, impersonal interaction, and reliance on rules. Studying the organization as a community inevitably underlines the cultural variables that make organizations more productive and the people in them more satisfied and more committed to their jobs. Viewing the organization as a community highlights its organic nature and its exchange with its environment as an open system.

The complexity of cultural analysis often is manifested in methodological difficulties for researchers. Cultural assumptions are not always obvious or observable, and cultural elements are varied and changing. Revealing patterns of organizational culture requires painstaking methodologies, which are not fixed to quick surveys and quantitative research. In their reference on *Varieties of Qualitative Research*, Van Maanen, Dabbs, and Faulkner (quoted in Shafritz & Ott, 1996, p. 421) describe a growing wave of disenchantment with the use of quantitative quasi-experimental research methods for studying organizations, mainly because they have produced very little useful knowledge about organizations over the past 20 years. In fact, one researcher argues that "quantitative assessments conducted through surveys is unethical in that it reflects conceptual categories not the respondent's own, presuming unwarranted generalizablity (Schein, quoted by Rousseau 1990, p. 161). More and more, Shafritz and Ott (1996, p. 421) note, the organizational culture approach is turning to qualitative research methods such as ethnography and participant observation.

Cultural analysis cannot avoid utilizing qualitative methods of observation as well as employing quantitative techniques. Also, cultural analysis requires disciplined exploration and observation, effective interviewing, discovery of critical incidents, and informed comparisons. The researcher cannot escape in-depth analysis of assumptions and competent description of meaningful patterns by taking refuge in statistical manipulations. As Peter Frost and his colleagues (1985, p. 16) point out, "adopting a cultural perspective may lead to an important epistemological synthesis wherein a much richer set of organizational variables is studied using a deeper theoretical frame of reference and a broader range of acceptable methods of analysis."

Thus, the subject demands a broad range of methods of study applied in creative ways. The topic of organizational culture is young and still mostly at the conceptual stage. There is a dearth of empirical data and a compelling need to elaborate and augment theoretical formulations to be useful in data collection and analysis.

APPLICATION AND UTILITY

The advantage of cultural analysis in studies of public organizations has been demonstrated by several authors at the conceptual and the practical levels. One such example is a study by Wallace Walker (1986) about changing organizational culture in the U.S. General Accounting Office (GAO). Walker (1986, p. 8) suggests that true organizational change is manifested in altered behavior patterns by public professionals and that to alter behavior, an organization's culture must be transformed. To do that, organizational design must be changed. An organizational design is composed of current and past arrangements that agency elites have fashioned to contend with conditions imposed by their environment.

Walker illustrates his perspective through a study of the major cultural change experienced by the GAO. He points out that one sees a major shift within the GAO from a culture of control at the time of its creation in 1921 to its present-day culture of oversight. According to Walker (1986, p. 7), an organization's culture consists of its ideology, rituals, myths, and knowledge. To successfully implement a strategy to change these cultural elements, one must consider the organization's historical experiences, including the traditional demands of the task environment, the character and latitude of the leaders appointed in the past, the organization's career elite, and the statutory mandates under which it functions (pp. 8–9).

Walker emphasizes the importance of leadership and personnel management in changing organizational culture. The need is crucial for leadership in public organizations to be attuned to the environment around it in order to initiate changes that may be necessary for the organization to survive. Also central to the process is the necessity of planning, developing, and executing personnel management programs to support the desired change within the organization. Training programs, for example, assist employees in accepting the new values and designs.

In Walker's strategy for organizational change, structure develops from consultation, experimentation, and adaptation to provide for patterning and differentiating relationships within the institution. Three structural factors are underscored by Walker (1986, p. 11), "each of which must be altered for public organizations to change: hierarchical arrangements, planning mechanisms, and the personnel system." In addition to their behavioral implications, these structural factors exert a determining influence on the manner in which professionals carry out organizational functions.

Another example of the application of organizational culture in public organizations is the study of the U.S. Department of State by Donald Warwick (1975). In this study, culture is a significant element in the analysis of the external as well as the internal environments of the organization. Warwick's analysis of the internal environment examines the pressures for hierarchy and rules in the Department of State, which he determined to "arise from the goals, culture, and internal structure" (p. 97).

Michael Lipsky's *Street-Level Bureaucracy* is another example of the application of organizational culture to achieving deeper knowledge of bureaucratic behavior. Street-level bureaucrats, regarded as low level employees, actually occupy critical positions in U.S. society because of their large numbers, their discretionary actions, and growing citizens' demands for their services. Lipsky (1980) contends that their large numbers as teachers, welfare workers, police officers, and similar occupations mean that most of public budgets are expended just to pay them. They make decisions that tend to be redistributive as well as allocative. They determine who is eligible to receive the service at the expense of the taxpayers. They are agents of social control and exercise wide discretion in decisions about citizens with whom they interact. In conflict with these values are the constraints on their behavior imposed by limited resources, increasing demands for service, and increasing popular pressures for more efficient and effective service.

Pressures and counterpressures seem to have trapped the street-level bureaucrats "in a cycle of mediocrity," according to Lipsky (1980, pp. 38–39). Contributing to these conflicting positions are the difficulties of measuring job performance, goal ambiguity, inadequate information, and absence of a market mechanism of evaluation. Working under strain, these employees attempt to do a good job, but the job is, in a sense, impossible to do in ideal terms. Thus, the job becomes "client processing," which develops a mentality of its own. Finally, the culture in which the agency is embedded affects the behavior of the street-level bureaucrats. Citizens' attitudes toward the poor, the politics of the society, the restrictive patterns of practice in public organizations, the legitimacy of the political system, and the agreement on responsibility for social needs all determine the patterns of behavior and the value system of the public organization. Thus, characteristics of the task as well as societal culture appear to develop a particular organizational culture that perpetuates certain performance standards and behavioral patterns.

Despite these few studies, analysis of organizational culture in the public sector is much more limited than in the corporate world. The reasons are related to the concept of culture itself as well as the nature of public organizations. The concept of organizational culture is limited by its highly subjective determinations and, surprisingly, the lack of agreement in the literature on what culture *is*. Culture has to be studied against a broad backdrop of basic assumptions and purposes. Thus, without answering Smircich's (1983, p. 354) precise question — "useful for whom and for what purpose" — the utility of the cultural framework will remain confined.

For a considerable time, U.S. managers and organization theorists have been seeking to discover the "secret" of Japan's organizational and managerial success. The answer has almost always led to the phenomenon of organizational culture. Economist Alan Blinder (1991, p. 22) explains the Japanese "secret" this way: The Japanese seem to have broken down the "us vs. them" barriers that so often impair labor relations in U.S. and European companies. They do so by creating a feeling that employees and managers share a common fate. In the Japanese company, people, not machines, are the most important asset and, therefore, are to be valued, nurtured, and retained. Blinder observes that Japanese chief executives are not dictators; they run their companies by consensus and teamwork, and important ideas and decisions bubble up from below at least as frequently as they come down from on high. Clearly, we are told that the Japanese organization has been transformed into a functioning community and that the organizational culture is a key factor in managing people in this manner.

In the United States, the tension and contradictions between values of professional management and the negative influences of internal politics in all types of organizations often are difficult to ignore. Subjective considerations are abundant in decisions made by most organizations, including universities. However, what is objectionable, from the professional management perspective, is the subversion of the process of decision making through selective use of information, the primacy of power and personal consideration, and the abusive use of the participatory process to advance selfish motives and personal control.

Subjective factors determine how people view policy, evaluate decisions, and relate to others. Despite the difficulty of generalizing about such subjective elements, Simile Cubbert and John McDonough (1985, p. 5) note that claims of having "open-door policies" and wanting candid reports by higher-ups in organizations have convinced only a few people that they can "tell it straight" or voice criticism without cost to them. Advancement in human relations techniques and communication methods have not ended the dominance of power and hierarchy in the organization.

Despite efforts to pay people fairly, reward them for accomplishments and technical know-how, and offer them legal protection from arbitrary use of power, employees increasingly believe that their rewards are dependent on organization politics and whom you know more than the actual contribution.

In contrast to the cultural norms of the Japanese organization, the U.S. organizational culture is much more politicized, allowing leaders and managers to benefit themselves, reward allies, and build political powers. Undoubtedly, many exceptions exist, but the U.S. organizational culture, which is undergoing fundamental change at the present, primarily is not built on team cooperation, participatory decision making, or collective good. Claims of these values are abundant in all public organizations. However, application is the exception rather than the rule. Often, the U.S. organization operates with a split personality and dual sets of norms. The written rules and policies apply to the majority, and unwritten and rarely talked about benefits and privileges attach to the powerful and politically dominant. Studying the latter condition is like watching a submarine race. To appreciate this discrepancy, one needs only examine the rewards of the top executive class in U.S. corporations and those of the rest of the employees. The average annual income of U.S. executives in relation to the average pay of their employees, for example, is three times higher than in Japan. Looking at this indicator in a different way, one finds similar results, namely, studies of major U.S. corporations show that, in the 1980s, the average salary of chief executive officers (CEOs) was 110 times that of an average worker. In contrast, the average Japanese CEO makes just 17 times the salary of a typical employee; German CEOs made about 21 times the average salary. The annual salary of the president of General Motors, when announcing (December 1991) a plan to close 21 factories and lay off 74,000 workers, was four times the combined salaries of the heads of Toyota and Nissan of Japan, two major competitors (Nader 1991, p. 5C).

William Ouchi's Theory Z is in the genre of organizational theories that emphasize culture and rely on the cultural element in explaining organizational and managerial behaviors. Ouchi (1981) seeks to reconcile Japanese management and certain U.S. practices into a framework that crosses cultural boundaries. Because of its cultural foundations, further delineation of the theory is relevant.

In 1981, Ouchi proposed a management framework that represents aspects of modern Japanese practices. Subsequently, Theory Z gained wide popularity in the United States. Its elements have been frequently cited, applauded, and criticized (Joiner 1985; Kaplan & Ziegler 1985). The central elements of Theory Z are:

Employment within the organization is long-term; employees are provided in-house education and training and benefits that permit sharing in the prosperity and the adversity of the organization.

The management process ensures cooperation and teamwork among employees.

Decision making typically is consensual, participative, and arrived at through open communication, after complete discussion, and within an atmosphere of trust.

Promotion and remuneration are seniority based with periodic job reassignments made so employees will develop and maintain a holistic view of the organization.

Emphasis is on group activity and projects in which managers share in the effort, respond to subordinates' initiatives, and maintain broad participation within a system of implicit controls.

Firms organized as "industrial clans" tend to result in happier, more involved, and, hence, more productive workers than firms organized in a hierarchical, bureaucratic mold. Hierarchy imposes external controls; the clan utilizes internal controls that are rooted in integrated beliefs, values, and shared objectives. Such shared beliefs, values, and objectives are learned through socialization within an environment of trust, subtlety, and intimacy. Trust means that the workers are willing to sacrifice short-term personal gains for long-term benefits of the firm. Subtlety modifies behavior in response to complex and changing human relations. Intimacy produces a sense of communal responsibility and emotional well-being.

Thus, we notice that the fundamental premises of Theory Z are essentially culture bound. In this perspective, culture provides the linkages that maintain the collectivity. Consequently, changing the organization, or people's behavior within it, is possible only by changing the culture itself — which is a slow and difficult process (Ouchi 1981, p. 88). In fact, interventions by the practitioners of Organization Development (OD) invariably are concerned with enhancing the adaptive mechanisms within organizations (Smircich 1983, p. 345). OD interventions often are directed at the cultural subsystem to allow for the questioning of values and norms under which people operate (Smircich 1983, p. 345; French & Bell 1995, p. 5). These activities inform us that culture is important and must be made receptive to far-reaching organizational change.

A Type Z organization is known to develop certain deficiencies and shortcomings, however. Such organizations experience loss of professionalism because, as Ouchi (1981, pp. 90–91) acknowledges, the emphasis is on working teams that submerge the highly specialized into broader functions. Also, Ouchi notes that Type Z organizations have a tendency to be racist and sexist, a paradox when Z organization promises equality of opportunity to minorities who, undoubtedly, have much greater hurdles to overcome.

In relating the above studies (in which culture is a critical factor) to public organizations, we are faced once more with special constraints imposed by the environment. The nature of these constraints is determined by the nature of public sector goals and the methods that establish them. Serious limitations are placed on the public manager's authority by laws, media scrutiny, political considerations, and patterns of funding. In comparison with the corporate world, government goals are harder to define or specify, and government reform strategies are more difficult to formulate and implement. Undoubtedly, in these factors lies a major part of the explanation for the small inroads made by the cultural frameworks in public administration studies. In fact, similar arguments are advanced in explaining why the techniques of OD have had less than dramatic achievements in public organizations (Stupak & Moore 1987).

Organization development is defined in different ways, depending on the assumptions and emphases of the author. Edgar Huse (1975, p. 18) regards organization's culture, or climate, as the key to change. Similarly, organizational culture is prominent in Wendell French and Cecil Bell's perspective on OD. They define OD (1995, p. 28) as: "Organization development is a long-term effort, led and supported by top management, to improve an organization's visioning, empowerment, learning, and problem-solving processes, through an ongoing, collaborative management of organization culture — with special emphasis on the culture of intact work teams and other team configurations — utilizing the consultant-facilitator and the theory and technology of applied behavioral science, including action research."

Central to the above perspectives on OD are the tasks of creating a culture that supports the institutionalization and use of social technologies to facilitate diagnosis and change of interpersonal, group, and intergroup behavior, especially those behaviors related to organizational decision making, planning, and communication (Huse 1975, p. 13). Essentially, the definitions by French and Bell as well as by Huse assume a dynamic culture, a value system, that interacts with and adapts to changes in social knowledge and technology about human behavior. When culture fails to respond, its change becomes essential. In this situation, the dilemma becomes how to change the organizational culture. Huse (1975, p. 13) suggests a process that must precede the institutionalization of these social techniques. Entry, the first step, is aimed at establishing a felt need for change. Normative change exposes as many organizational members as possible to the new social norms. Structural change involves placing advocates of OD in positions where they have the power, prestige, and flexibility to conduct further OD projects. It is important, as Huse (1975, p. 13) points out, that the stress is on changing the climate of the organization through changing social norms, with little attention paid to changing the design of the organization itself.

Once more, the issue of utility is compelling. The literature conveys near agreement that certain public sector characteristics constitute significant constraints in the face of OD interventions (Golembiewski & Sink 1979; Burke 1980; Lynn 1981; Stupak & Moore 1987). A survey of the literature by Robert Golembiewski and David Sink (1979, pp. 5–7) lists 13 such constraints that limit the freedom of action by public managers. These legal restrictions include lack of economic incentives and market indicators, diverse constituencies of public managers, volatile political-administrative interface, procedural regularity and rigidity, short-term frame, and weak claims of command and delegation. Because of these constraints, conclude the authors, the common wisdom conveys that "attempts to improve a public organization's problem-solving and renewal processes through OD intervention have either failed, been modified considerably, or just not tried" (p. 1). Based on the authors' examination of the above constraints in 44 urban OD applications, they concluded that such constraints are found to be "confounding."

Despite certain obvious constraints on public managers, advocates of OD (Golembiewski 1990, p. 5) maintain that OD intervenors are valuable not only for what they do to the organization "but also — perhaps, especially — for the values they represent." This argument is grounded in the belief that OD's efficacy stems from its basics of participation, involvement, and commitment, which in turn rest on their "human rightness."

Consequently, the claims in the literature that OD has not been as successful in public organizations as in the private sector are explained as perhaps the result of theoretical progress lagging behind practical achievements (Golembiewski 1990, p. 4). Even optimistic assessments acknowledge the obstacles facing OD applications in public organizations but continue to aspire for recognition of OD as a significant "mini-paradigm" in the conceptual development of public administration. In conclusion, this chapter indicates that organizational culture is a formidable force that shapes behavior and value systems of the working people. Culture is an overall influence that (through symbols, norms, shared cognitions, and various intangibles) sets patterns of human behavior and develops collective understandings in the workplace. We know, for example, that some organizational cultures are more tolerant of corruption, nepotism, waste, and other forms of unsavory managerial conduct. Other organizational cultures are less receptive to such negative behavior and provide a variety of formal and informal monitoring systems to combat it. The growing importance of organizational culture is essentially the consequence of focusing on people as the crucial element in the organization and the need to inspire their cooperation as a collectivity in order to improve the quality of life at the workplace as well as to improve the overall organizational output.

However, culture is not a single variable that can be defined, isolated, measured, and controlled, nor is it a concrete act to observe and monitor. Cultural elements in the workplace are ubiquitous; culture touches every aspect of operations and people. Perhaps, one of the most significant consequences of organizational culture is its considerable impact on people in terms of the establishment of a consensus on standards of conduct and rules of operations that allow newcomers to interact successfully when joining the organization. It separates acceptable from unacceptable values; it sanctions and punishes; and, if not always visible, organizational culture cannot be ignored with impunity.

Can we change organizational culture? The answer is yes, but the process is slow and time-consuming, because it varies from place to place. Effective managers need to work with and even shape such a powerful force in the directions needed to accomplish the tasks of the organization and serve its mission. This is the difficult part of dealing with organizational culture. However, social learning, communication, socialization, and various techniques of human resources management may be the most effective tools to direct the influence of culture on shared values, common bonds, and collective consciousness to desirable organizational outcomes.

REFERENCES

Blinder, Alan S. November 11, 1991. How Japan Puts the "Human" in Human Capital. *Business Week.*

Burke, Warned. 1980. Organization Development and Bureaucracy in the 1980s. *Journal of Applied Behavioral Science,* 16, 3.

Cubbert, Simile A. and John J. McDonough. 1985. *Radical Management, Power Politics, and the Pursuit of Trust.* New York: Free Press.

French, Wendell L. and Cecil H. Bell. 1995. *Organization Development,* 5th ed. Englewood Cliffs, NJ: Prentice-Hall.

Frost, Peter J., L. F. Moore, M. R. Louis, C. C. Lundberg, and J. Martin. 1985. *Organizational Culture*. Beverly Hills, CA: Sage.

Golembiewski, Robert T. 1990. *Ironies in Organizational Development*. New Brunswick, NJ: Transaction Publishers.

Golembiewski, Robert and David Sink. 1979. OD Interventions in Urban Settings, I. *International Journal of Public Administration*, 1, 1.

Huse, Edgar F. 1975. *Organization Development and Change*. New York: West Publishing.

Joiner, Charles W., Jr. 1985. Making the "Z" Concept Work. *Sloan Management Review*, 26, 3.

Kaplan, David and Charles A. Ziegler. 1985. Clans, Hierarchies and Social Control: An Anthropologist's Commentary on Theory Z. *Human Organization*, 44, 1.

Lipsky, Michael. 1980. *Street-Level Bureaucracy*. New York: Russell Sage Foundation.

Louis, Meryl Reis. 1985. An Investigator's Guide to Workplace Culture. In *Organizational Culture*, edited by Peter J. Frost, L. F. Moore, M. R. Louis, C. C. Lundberg, and J. Martin. Beverly Hills, CA: Sage.

Lynn, Laurence E. 1981. *Managing the Public's Business*. New York: Basic Books.

McGregor, Douglas M. 1960. *The Human Side of Enterprise*. New York: McGraw-Hill.

Meyer, Alan. 1981. How Ideologies Supplant Formal Structures and Shape Responses of Environments. *Journal of Management Studies*, 19.

Nader, Ralph. December 29, 1991. Protecting Bloat at the Top. *Tampa Tribune*, p. C5.

Ouchi, William G. 1981. *Theory Z: How American Business Can Meet the Japanese Challenge*. Reading, MA: Addison-Wesley.

Ouchi, William G. and Alan L. Wilkins. 1985. Organizational Culture. *Annual Review of Sociology*, 11.

Peters, Thomas J. and R. H. Waterman. 1982. *In Search of Excellence*. New York: Harper & Row.

Reichers, Aron E. and Benjamin Schneider. 1990. Climate and Culture: An Evolution of Constructs. In *Organizational Climate and Culture*, edited by Benjamin Schneider. San Francisco, CA: Jossey-Bass.

Rousseau, Denise M. 1990. Assessing Organizational Culture: The Case for Multiple Methods. In *Organizational Climate and Culture*, edited by Benjamin Schneider. San Francisco, CA: Jossey-Bass.

Schein, Edgar H. 1985. *Organizational Culture and Leadership*. San Francisco, CA: Jossey-Bass.

Shafritz, Jay M. and J. Steven Ott. 1996. *Classics of Organization Theory*, 4th ed. Belmont, CA: Wadsworth.

Smircich, Linda. 1983. Concepts of Culture and Organizational Analysis. *Administrative Science Quarterly*, 28 (September).

Stupak, Ronald J. and Jerry E. Moore. 1987. The Practice of Managing Organization Development in Public Sector Organizations. *International Journal of Public Administration*, 10, 2.

Van Maanen, John and Stephen R. Barley. 1985. Cultural Organization: Fragments of a Theory. In *Organizational Culture*, edited by Peter J. Frost, L. F. Moore, M. R. Louis, C. C. Lundberg, and J. Martin. Beverly Hills, CA: Sage.

Walker, Wallace E. 1986. *Changing Organizational Culture*. Knoxville: University of Tennessee Press.

Warwick, Donald P. 1975. *A Theory of Public Bureaucracy*. Cambridge, MA: Harvard University Press.

11

Reforming Management of Public Organizations

The capacity of a society to manage its public policies and programs, not only effectively and efficiently but also fairly and creatively, defines most fundamental characteristics of such a society. In all countries, developed and developing alike, bureaucratic organizations are the main instruments for effecting public policies. Thus, building essential managerial capacities of public organizations requires a perpetual search for ways and means to enhance their overall competence in performing their designated functions. In the meantime, public administration literature regularly communicates dissatisfaction with traditional modes of managing human resources and the inability of management systems to change and to adjust according to desired public policy outcomes.

Management reform, therefore, is a search for more suitable approaches to accomplish policy objectives. Primarily, reform consists of upgrading employees' skills, improving operational effectiveness of organizations, inducing greater cooperation within the unit and better coordination with other organizations, and creating a receptive climate to innovation and change. In brief, management reform inevitably aims at reaching a higher level of overall performance (quantity and quality) within the limits of appropriated resources. Recent managerial perspectives seek to release the innovative and creative capabilities of employees by implementing processes that promise greater concern with results and more focus on quality. This is done, according to most of the new schools of management reform, through a host of techniques, including greater employee involvement in operational decisions. The assumption is that employees are the people who can do the most about change and innovation in the organization. Accordingly, we discuss here influential reform initiatives that have been widely debated, analyzed, applied, lauded, and condemned. In particular, we examine the following reform campaigns:

The drive for quality has come to the forefront of organizational management during the past two decades. It has acquired many designations, most familiar being Total Quality Management (TQM).

The reinvention of government is a movement that gained momentum after publication of David Osborn and Ted Gaebler's book (1992).

Bids to build performance management systems in order to relate cost to output, monitor performance, and satisfy the needs of the community are discussed in the next chapter.

Ventures to apply concepts and techniques rooted in the quality drive, reinvention, or performance-based systems permeate various levels of government in the United States as well as in many other countries. Evidently, these concepts and techniques are not mutually exclusive, and they even conflict. They are presented here as current, immediate tests of the efficacy of management systems everywhere. The following is a brief definition of basic features and some feedback on efforts to apply these reform perspectives.

THE DRIVE FOR QUALITY

The "quality drive" generated considerable debate and excitement in the management profession worldwide. In the United States, it has been referred to as a "quiet revolution" (Cohen & Brand 1993, p. xi). The immediate impetus came from the successes of Japanese industries in improving the quality of their products and the constant enhancement of productivity of their workers of which U.S. and Western industries took notice and moved expeditiously to emulate and to protect their shares of the world market. The unfolding of events in this regard is amply recorded in literature of business management and economics.

How is this relevant to managing government? We now have many concrete examples of attempted TQM applications in the public sector. Even with many false starts, often less systematic efforts, and with apparent exertion, managers of numerous public organizations boldly embraced the quality drive and attempted to cultivate its benefits.

Certainly, the new reality of public organizations has been confined by massive budget cutbacks, shortfalls of revenues, budget deficits, and public resistance to higher taxes during the past two decades. In the midst of this, particular managerial processes achieved prominence by appealing to practitioners, attracting attention in the academic community, and promising reduction in cost and improvement of quality of organizational performance. These concepts and processes are, in fact, related and even overlapping. TQM is the umbrella under which team building and quality circles, for example, find a hospitable environment.

Team building basically is a process of developing collective responsibility for professional and organizational renewal and effectiveness. Groups of employees join in such teams to look at their functions and determine what needs changing, how change might be accomplished, at what cost, and for what benefits. Team building is most effective when personal goals and team goals are harmonious and when the organizational culture is conducive to team actions.

During the diagnostic phase, the team identifies the problem to be addressed and the information needed, utilizing feedback to define and characterize the action to be taken. In the following phase, action options are transformed to specific operational steps with explicit estimates of resources needed. At the implementation phase, the team identifies impediments to implementation and deals with them. Finally, a successful team-building process must assess results and evaluate accomplishments as well as seek to solve unanticipated problems that may emerge. The consequences of the team effort will largely determine the importance of its role and its continuation. "Such introspection or reflection is useful, however, only to the extent that the group agrees to start doing, stop doing, or continue doing specific things" (Locke & Latham 1984, p. 4).

Quality circles are small groups of peers who meet regularly with or without supervisors to identify problems hindering production quality and to search for solutions to these problems. The final purpose is to help the organization achieve its goals by suggesting steps to enhance quantity and quality of production. Quality circles became popular management techniques in the 1980s with reports of successes attained by the Japanese industrial management. Incentives for employees participating in quality circles ranged from symbolic recognition of improvements introduced to sharing in the financial savings caused by suggestions made to management by these groups. By all indications, quality circles have been the exception rather than the rule in the public sector. Few governmental entities have tried them, and very few systematic assessments exist to indicate the consequences of their rare application.

Probably the most notable reason for the not-so-spectacular success of applying quality circles techniques in government is the weak support of top management. Quality-boosting efforts have often failed to win unwavering commitment of management leadership. Other factors contributing to the ineffectiveness of quality circles in government include not ensuring that participation is voluntary and not alleviating potential attendance problems because of conflicts with regular duties (Denhardt & Hammond 1992, p. 285). Indeed, in the public sector, competent use of quality circles is not attainable without allowing members of the circle direct access to top management to present their recommendations and without giving adequate recognition to participants (Hatry & Greiner 1984, p. 7).

TQM is the application of quality principles and the commitment to values of excellence in all activities of the organization. Total quality control emphasizes a comprehensive, integrated, customer-oriented approach to managing organizations. Consequently, TQM requires a defined managerial strategy that promises to achieve the desired standards of quality. The information available from practical experiences in the public and private sectors demonstrates some agreed-upon parameters. The fundamentals that seem to evoke the greatest acceptance may be summarized as follows (see Office of Management and Budgeting Draft Circular A-132, 1990, in Denhardt & Hammond 1992, p. 349; Jreisat 1992; Swiss 1992; Cohen & Brand 1993; Rago 1996):

1.   The employees continuously analyze work processes to improve their functioning and to reduce process variation. The employees themselves lead the search of all aspects of work to identify opportunities for improvement. Measurement and analysis of processes and output deal with information required to support total quality of processes, products, and services. Such information is to be complete, timely, accurate, useful, and clearly communicated to those who need it. Also, employee empowerment and teamwork require that management provides an environment that supports employee involvement, contribution, and teamwork.

2.   Training and incentives are provided in order to maintain consistently high quality and to prevent variability in production. Commitment to training and recognition of employees are essential to enable the employees to keep abreast of changing job requirements and to prepare them for greater responsibilities. Training must emphasize quality awareness and the use of tools and methods for continuous improvement.

3.   Quality is built into the product early in the production process (as an input), rather than being added on at the end (output). Because management by objectives (MBO) is used so often for individual measures, it is

considered a source of damaging variation into the system, leading the manager astray and causing disassociational influences on the individual in relation to the system and to the team. Quality results from people working within systems, not individual efforts.

4. The ultimate judge of quality is the customer; the final purpose is to satisfy customers. Focus on the customer means that management seeks ways to make employees aware of customers' needs, uses feedback data to improve processes and services, and continually adapts the strategic plan to make it more responsive to citizens' preferences. Quality assurance means that products and services are designed and verified to meet customer needs and expectations. Quality assurance systems are updated to keep pace with changes in technology, practice, and quality performance.

5. Quality attainment is not a static process; it requires continuous improvement of inputs and process. Such improvement necessitates strong worker participation and total organizational commitment. People working within systems, not individual efforts, is what counts, because quality is achieved only when managers create an organizational culture that focuses on and consistently produces quality products.

6. Top management leadership is directly and actively involved in the process of TQM. Managers take the lead in establishing the environment and culture that encourage change, innovation, risk taking, pride in work, and continuous improvement of service to customers. Through visible personal leadership, they communicate the organization's quality vision and goals as they provide the necessary resources.

7. Strategic planning requires that long- and short-range goals be established for quality improvement and that these goals be integrated into the strategic plan. Thus, strategic planning forces management to recognize what is fundamental for the organization by demanding definition of missions and goals.

In the business sector, elements of TQM are not much different from the above. A survey of 250 companies on the elements of their strategies for quality performance indicates that customer satisfaction is used by 87 percent; employee involvement is used by 85 percent; TQM is used by 68 percent; and self-management work teams are used by 35 percent (*Business Week* 1991, p. 38).

In terms of the background of TQM, all arrows point toward W. Edward Deming and John M. Juran as the preeminent champions of quality. Deming found his most loyal following in Japan, where he first described his method of total quality control in 1954. Juran furthered

Deming's objectives in Japan and applied quality to all aspects and all levels of the organization. In the early 1990s, both Deming and Juran are still active in pursuing their ideas of total quality control within the United States (Port 1991, p. 17).

Team building, quality circles, and TQM are three modern perspectives on how to create opportunities for employees to experience more satisfying and more productive work patterns within caring and successful organizations. To unleash creativity, build skills, and increase commitment of employees, managers have to change their own styles of leadership. Traditional structures need to adapt, and leadership behavior must pass the stage of "command-and-control" to a new era of participation and involvement by employees. The new managers enable, communicate, share, lead, and induce more than order or command.

TOTAL QUALITY MANAGEMENT IN GOVERNMENT: AN APPRAISAL

During the 1980s and before, the U.S. government encouraged the application of TQM throughout public agencies. In 1988, the Federal Quality Institute was created to lead in the quality drive in the public sector. So far, the departments of Defense, Agriculture, and Energy, and the National Aeronautics and Space Administration, the General Services Administration, the Environmental Protection Agency, and the Social Security Administration — all have brought TQM to the workplace (Cohen & Brand 1993, p. 14). True, in the process, many federal managers had help from central sources of information, lots of training, and many consultants; the Federal Quality Institute provided awards, published booklets, conducted seminars, and disseminated useful information to agencies seeking help in initiating the process (p. 14).

As James Bowman (1994, p. 129) reports, two-thirds of federal agencies are using some form of TQM. Thus, he concludes, "there is a growing realization that quality is as important in service industries as in manufacturing firms, and that quality awareness should permeate organizations from top to bottom." Nevertheless, studies of applications of TQM, in this name or in any other name, have had mixed reports. William Rago (1996, p. 227) argues that there have been many successes over the past four years in applying TQM but that they have been marked by a series of struggles that have roots in a mixture of uncertainty regarding the next step to take and in the need for the agency's senior managers to personally transform the way they go about their work. Rago concludes that, if the transformation of the agency culture is to occur, it must be preceded by this personal transformation.

The conclusions of the public sector endeavors in the realm of TQM are inconclusive at best. Even when improvements resulted from government applications, as in a study of the Internal Revenue Service (IRS), they were followed by many qualifiers, even by suggestions that the principles of public administration may be redefined as principles of TQM. In a case study of the IRS, Bonnie G. Mani (1995, pp. 147–157) presents empirical data describing the impact of TQM in the IRS and showing statistically significant differences of input and output before and after implementation. The study also affirms that training and commitment of top-level management are critical to the successful implementation of TQM. Actually, training began for all IRS senior executives and managers at an early phase (Mani 1995, p. 148).

Results of experiences at the local and state levels of government indicate a wide variation as well. TQM has been the guide and the pattern for implementing programs of improvement in many state and local governments. Frequently, adoption of TQM was preceded by more modest, but related, techniques, such as quality circles and team building. There are too few cases of irrefutable success; certainly, there are many false starts, signifying that all is not perfect on the TQM front.[1]

Once more, quality improvement requires strong employee participation, total organizational commitment, and conducive organizational culture. The environment of public organizations, the critics argue (Swiss 1992, pp. 356–362), is strikingly ill-suited to the TQM approach in its pure forms. There is insufficient modification of service, insensitivity to the problem of defining government customers, and inappropriate emphasis on input and process. Moreover, demands for top-level intensity and leadership commitment rarely can be met by the government culture and in service delivery, in contrast to manufacturing products.

The tenets of TQM, at least on the surface, seem to contradict the rationale of most government management reforms. Program budgeting, zero-base budgeting, MBO, and pay for performance all assume focus on output or performance, but, according to TQM rationale, such efforts are moving the manager's focus away from measuring inputs and processes toward results (Swiss 1992, pp. 357–358).

Another interesting objection to TQM's prescription is in dealing with citizens as customers of government. Citizens in a democracy are owners of government, argues Hindy Schachter (1995, p. 530). They elect leaders to represent their interests. A customer-centered model puts citizens in a reactive role limited to liking or disliking services and hoping that administrators will change delivery if enough customers object. Owners, on the other hand, play a proactive role; they decide what the government's agenda will be.

The lesson here is not that TQM is irrelevant or inapplicable in the public sector but, rather, that calibrating and adjusting TQM are essential steps for successful implementation in government. Actually, public management is not so removed from processes of quality in concept or in application. Traditionally, public organizations have relied on client feedback, often tracked and monitored performance, regularly searched for improvement, and even utilized measured employee participation, however modest. These concepts, one may argue, have been management axioms for decades. Resuscitating and systematizing these ideas in the form of a TQM approach is possible, if special aspects of public organizations are recognized and dealt with. Certainly, some notions of TQM are merely relabeling old ideas — "old wine in new bottles" or "new wine in old bottles." However, management analysts and consultants must change the way they present enduring principles periodically. Perhaps, if introduced without overselling, with sensitivity to government unique circumstances, reformed TQM can make a useful contribution to contemporary public management (Swiss 1992, p. 360).

REINVENTING GOVERNMENT

Reinventing government is a pretentious, attention-grabber title of a book that seeks to convey a sense of dramatic change of the system. The authors have been fairly successful in advancing the idea that what is needed is to transform the habits, culture, and performance of all public organizations. Osborne and Gaebler's *Reinventing Government: How the Entrepreneurial Spirit Is Transforming the Public Sector from Schoolhouse to State House, City Hall to Pentagon* (1992) offers their program of action for improving the system of managing government. The main elements of their recipe for reform, Richard Nathan (1995, p. 213) and others conclude, are to empower citizens, promote mission-driven entrepreneurial leadership in order to "steer rather than row," enhance competition and deregulate government by cutting red tape, foster "total quality management," decentralize government, and apply performance budget, civil service reform, and privatization. These ideas are not mutually exclusive; in fact, they are often contradictory. For generations, reformers have been attempting to separate certain activities from the political heat. Public management reforms regularly pursued the objective of enhancing expertise and professionalism and maintaining a balance of political accountability and intellectual input to processes of government. A wide range of methods has been utilized, such as civil service reform, budget reform, independent regulatory agencies, and numerous federal and state reorganization measures. Also, newer approaches, such as planning-programming-budget systems, MBO, policy analysis, and performance budget, have similar aims (Nathan 1995, pp. 213–214).

During the past few years, public administration has been saturated with reinvention ideas and words. Often, distinctions between reinventing government and applying TQM seem to fade in the discussions. Scholars have explained, compared, lauded, criticized, interpreted, and reinterpreted what Osborne and Gaebler or Deming said or failed to say, more than any other management author in the past decade (one needs only compute frequency of appearance of the terms "reninventing" or "TQM" in the tables of contents of *Public Administration Review* since 1993). Actually, when all else has been said and done, we began to "reinvent ourselves" and to compare the reinventing movement with every other administrative perspective in existence, including "the new public administration."

Indeed, H. George Frederickson (1996, pp. 263–270) finds six dimensions along which reinventing government and the "new public administration" may be compared: both attempt to respond to strongly felt administrative need to change, both seek relevance and responsiveness, both conceptualize organization similarly, reinventing has a stronger commitment to market approaches and closer appeal to popular electoral politics for executives — presidents, governors, mayors — and people with consulting money. However, Frederickson (1996, p. 263) sees the new public administration more concerned with issues of rationality, methodology, and epistemology and also prompted by incremental shifts toward democratic management practices and social equity.

It is in the application of reform that the reinventing movement made its greatest headway. The National Performance Review (NPR) was announced by President Clinton and Vice-President Gore on the White House lawn amidst ten-foot piles of government reports. The NPR received a very positive public reaction initially and helped the president's standing in the polls (Nathan 1995, p. 213). Amid high expectations and considerable fanfare, Gore presented the report of his NPR to Clinton and the public on September 7, 1993; also distributed at this event were cards that provided the philosophical goals of this exercise in "reinventing the federal government" (Moe 1994, p. 111). The cards contained such principles as: "We will invent a government that puts people first" by serving its customers, empowering its employees, and fostering excellence. Here's how: "We will create a clear sense of mission, delegate authority and responsibility, replace regulations with incentives, develop budget based outcomes, measure our success by customer satisfaction" (Moe 1994, p. 111). A few months and 200 consultants later, the results were in a 168-page report containing more than 800 recommendations. The ideas in the report unmistakably take roots in Osborne and Gaebler's book, with a mixture of market economics, privatization, and cultural and behavioral shifts of public management. A common theme is the call for moving away from a bureaucratic government toward an entrepreneurial government.

The problem with all this is that it undermines, and at times ignores, one critical fact, namely, that public administration operates within systems of law and according to a paradigm of management that accepts a partnership with the political system in setting policy and developing strategies. Replacing all this with notions without precise meanings, such as "reinventing" or "entrepreneurial," is not favorably accepted by many scholars of the field. Moreover, as Ronald Moe (1994, p. 116) argues, entrepreneurial management ultimately represents a decline in the capacity of the president and central management agencies to supervise and provide leadership for the executive branch. Other misgivings of fragmentation of management, dependency on consultants, and weakening of central role of the Office of Management and Budget are among the inevitable consequences of the new entrepreneurial management featured in the NPR's approach.

James D. Carroll (1995, p. 302) expresses different reservations about reform the NPR way. He points out that NPR's political theory is a paradigm based upon a paradox. The paradigm is administration empowered to satisfy the needs of the people free of politics, red tape, and hierarchy. The paradox is that this new paradigm for the information age resurrects the old paradigm of the progressive era, the much criticized politics-administration dichotomy. For Carroll, the NPR fails to reconcile traditions of constitutional governance and legal accountability with the search for flexibility, innovation, and improved productivity in addressing managerial issues.

A centerpiece among proposals for reform in the NPR studies (and positions promoted by the reinvention consultants) is downsizing government. The idea of downsizing is not a creation of the reinvention movement, although it has been enthusiastically supported by the movement. In fact, in the November 1990 elections, promises of downsizing government and justifying its revenue policies dominated debates of gubernatorial candidates in Florida, California, and Massachusetts. "Smaller and smarter" state government was the promise of the elected Democratic governor of Florida. "Downsizing," on a second thought, became "right-sizing," but the debate on a "smaller and smarter" government continued, focusing on three major issues: reduce the size of government in order to reduce cost; discover and eliminate waste, duplication, and dishonesty; and improve productivity and overall performance by investing in better techniques of output evaluation and measurement, so that taxpayers may receive greater returns on public dollars spent.

In a way, downsizing seems to be an extension of earlier ideas of retrenchment and cutbacks after shortfalls of public revenues and citizens' vocal opposition to higher taxes in California and elsewhere (Levine 1980; Holzer 1985). Realistically, downsizing initiatives include more than cutback management. In addition to shrinking government functions, downsizing is a search for alternatives, rationalizing existing systems of revenue, effecting greater equity in sharing the cost of public services, and sustaining economic development.

Accustomed to growth and expansion of services over the past decades, public organizations became hard-pressed to cope with the new climate of decline and retrenchment. In practice, public organizations rarely experience decline; as Robert Golembiewski (1990, p. 108) points out, they "have more or less explicit biases toward growth, toward how to do better while getting bigger." Thus, the challenge introduced by new exigency requires professional skill for developing a plan of action that grasps political realities.

Clearly, the corporate sector, which operates according to economic and subjective benchmarks of decline or expansion, has more substantive experiences with processes of growth or decline than governments. Mary Guy (1989, p. 3) relates corporate financial loss to economic benchmarks, such as a decline in sales, market share, profitability, or resources. Other benchmarks of organizational decline that she considers to be subjective include loss of prestige or reputation, a pessimistic shade to corporate culture, service level inadequacy, unclear priorities, and loss of leadership and direction. The process of decline in U.S. corporations is familiar, and restructuring for a variety of objective and subjective reasons is continuous.

In contrast, public organizations are less familiar with techniques and processes of downsizing. Intervention of public management is often a consequence of compelling conditions that dictate cutback. Because public managers often persist in the denial of new political and economic conditions surrounding them, the inevitable adjustments become more painful and unpleasant. Admitting to the need for downsizing by public managers, without accepting defeat or developing a sense of failure and despair, is a crucial mental and behavioral adjustment.

Downsizing of public service always generates its own serious predicaments, not the least of which is the negative emotions among employees, particularly those threatened by the process. Seniority and job security — prime incentives of public employment over the years — have been eroded by a steady elimination of positions and fewer opportunities for advancements up the ladder of public employment. Moreover, shortfalls of revenue and a sluggish economy inevitably result in low salary raises or, sometimes, no raises at all. Public managers, therefore, are faced with the difficult situation of how employees can be motivated when there are fewer and fewer incentives. Indeed, under conditions of steadily reduced financial benefits and promotion opportunities, a major challenge to management is how to keep competent middle managers and young supervisory level personnel in government, where pay is far below market levels.

Some techniques may soften the impact of decline. Early detection of the momentum of the downward spiral allows the public manager to subject the situation to realistic analysis of cause and effect and, accordingly, initiate appropriate responses. Timely recognition of the downward pressure requires development of a workable strategy, including mobilization of resources and the essential support for implementing the strategy. The next phase is monitoring progress to determine the need for intervention to adjust the rate of action and to take whatever measures are necessary to ensure adherence to the basic plan.

The downsizing strategy, and its derivative plan, usually reflects an agreement on goals, process, and timeframe. To enhance chances of success, credibility of motive is crucial; the whole process must be above reproach. For minimizing the pain of downsizing, job enrichment is a management tool worthy of application. With fewer opportunities for promotion and annual raises, jobs are made more substantive and more meaningful by offering middle managers more responsibilities and more support. Similarly, lateral movement in the organization to create more challenging situations and opportunities for staff development may contribute to such an objective. However, honest implementation that excludes political maneuvering, favoritism, and exceptions in making decisions remains indispensable.

Internal politics of the organization is rarely featured in literature on organization management. This politics is an informal exercise of power outside the defined lines of authority and often is engaged in by those who seek to get their way in the organization. Actually, organizational politics can serve negative or positive purposes and can employ legitimate or illegitimate methods. Negative politics denotes what Wendell French and Cecil Bell (1995, p. 307) characterize as extreme pursuit of self-interest, unsocialized needs to dominate others, a tendency to view most situations in win-lose terms, and a predominant use of tactics such as secrecy, surprise, holding hidden agendas, and deceiving. Balanced politics, on the other hand, is the pursuit of self-interest and the welfare of others. Those who practice positive politics engage in open problem solving and initiate actions that lead and influence. Negative internal politics are a pervasive influence, albeit subtle, surreptitious, and infrequently talked about openly. The rationalistic slant in management tends to overlook important segments of what takes place within the organization. Indeed, a significant opinion, particularly among practitioners, is that "what is taking place is far more personal, far more subjective, and far more power-oriented and political than most popular theories lead one to expect" (Cubbert & McDonough 1985, p. 2).

The problem is not limited to legitimate power that comes with formal authority, such as the power of a manager or supervisor over subordinates. This power (authority), for example, allows managers and supervisors to reward or punish employees according to established procedures. As John French and Bertram Raven (1958, pp. 150–167) have indicated, leaders or managers can buttress their legitimate powers with personal powers of expertise and referent if they happen to be in possession of such qualities and skills. Comparatively, these powers, too, are not difficult to trace, observe, and analyze. The type of power that is problematic is the one that develops behind the scenes, informally, through alliances and cliques, and generally for self-serving objectives. Individuals who have personal friendships with direct access to top leaders in the organization are able to enhance their informal powers in the organization. Individuals and groups with similar motives join ranks to divert the outcomes of decisions in their favor and to foster a system of cronyism and personal aggrandizement.

Students, after studying various concepts and techniques of rational decision-making processes in the literature, invariably react with disapproval: "but it is all politics." Whether the discussion is over budgetary decisions, personnel promotion policies, hiring practices at the senior level, or granting salary raises, the ideal always sharply contrasts with the reality. Internal politics is the final explanation.

In terms of downsizing public organizations, perhaps fear of internal politics is the main reason most employees would resist change. The general feeling is that only individuals lacking political power will suffer the consequences of the financial cutbacks or downsizing. For managers to underscore professional management, professional values and ethics may inspire some trust in the decisions of downsizing. Assuring staff that management is committed to fairness, equity, and collective interest may alleviate some of the anxiety over unfair practices.

In the final analysis, resource allocation must serve and be connected to organizational performance. Effective use of scarce resources includes connecting awards to performance. Salary raises, travel money, and symbolic recognitions are offered to the most productive and most valuable people in terms of the organization's mission. Also, whenever fewer people are able to do the same or more work, they should share in the benefits.

Threats and anxieties caused by reductions must be counterbalanced by positive programs that directly benefit the employees, such as enhancement of programs of personnel development and training. Related is the effort to maintain open channels of communication and to build trust and a sense of collective interest, instead of adversarial relations, with employee organizations. In dealing with ambiguity created by the change, greater managerial efforts could be invested to improve processes of goal setting in the organization and to define directions. Finally, a strategy based on practicing a proactive managerial stance in fostering full participation by members of the organization is the best mechanism to soften the blow and to minimize the damage to the remaining programs and activities of the organization.

In summary, eliminating unnecessary programs in government is not the issue; excesses and partisan use of the process are. In the private sector, however, economists and corporate managers seem to accept the rationale for layoffs and downsizing as self-evident, but the process has received less than a unified support. Indeed, the whole strategy of corporate downsizing is being questioned and its effects are being challenged. *Business Week* reports about a prevailing sense in the business world that "the pure efficiency approach did very little to generate distinctive competitive advantages" (Bryne 1996, p. 46). The news from the corporate world unmistakably indicate that best-managed companies do not "shrink themselves to greatness" but rather grow into it. In an update on downsizing, *Business Week* reports the results of a survey by the American Management Association that indicates that job elimination among companies has diminished and two-thirds of companies cutting jobs also added positions in other areas (Koretz 1996, p. 30). "Downsizing has become something of a misnomer," the magazine quotes the

American Management Association director of management studies (p. 30).

The lesson to public organizations has more than one dimension. First, downsizing is not the only alternative for facing shortfall of revenues or for balancing public budgets. Second, downsizing was in full swing, ironically, after the end of the second Reagan administration. In 1985, federal outlays as a percentage of gross domestic product reached the second highest level in two decades (23.9 percent). The number of federal employees per 1,000 population was 12.6, compared with 14.9 in 1970. However, in 1995, estimates put the federal outlays at 22.3 percent of gross domestic product and number of employees per 1,000 population at 10.7 (Carroll 1995, p. 305). Thus, number of employees per 1,000 population has declined about 30 percent since 1970, despite an overall increase in population. Third, ruthless downsizing is a poor strategy for managing human resources. Few organizations recover from such trauma in the short run. Finally, as James Savara (1996, p. 400) notes, "reformers over the decades . . . have manifested faith in government but sought to improve it." The problem with some reformers is that they "do not believe that government can be an instrument to achieve collectively chosen ends." Thus, we differentiate reforming government from dismantling it.

MAKING SENSE OF THE TANGLE

Traditional approaches emphasizing control and command processes generate rigidities and dysfunctions that prevent them from adopting many of the new managerial concepts and practices. Unless there is an emergence of organizational management with appropriate professional competence, the evolution will be slow. To implement "new" managerial processes with greater attention to results, quality, problem-solving capacity, and ability to adapt, organizational management must address issues of employees' skills, incentives, and creation of a more receptive climate to innovation and change.

The pressures for management reform are almost universal. In nearly all countries today, public management faces massive budget cutbacks, shortfalls of revenues, budget deficits, and public resistance to higher taxes. Consequently, the management of a public organization within this new reality, inescapably, has to do more with less and, frequently, has to account for what it does in measurable terms. In fact, academics and practitioners have been tinkering with promising managerial approaches much before the reinventing movement or the recent popularity of TQM. Such approaches range from team building and quality circles to MBO and cost-benefit analysis. With less uniformity, downsizing and productivity measurement also have been attempted.

The fact remains that comprehensive reform that involves people, organization, process, and relations with the environment is unavoidable. It is a high priority for governments worldwide. The challenges ahead, however, are:

How can managers build competence among people in the organization, assuming that these managers have done well and made the right choices in recruitment? Competence building requires training and personal development, as well as learning on the job. Training must have a defined purpose, values, and content. No doubt, performance is enhanced as an increasing sense of mastery is developed and ever-new horizons are opened to the employee. Evidence of the relation of relevant training to improvement of performance is undisputable. There also is the issue of motivation — how to motivate employees when there are fewer incentives, such as pay raises or promotions.

The new climate of decline and retrenchment in the public sector is a reversal of the usual mode of growth. Public organizations are less familiar with techniques and processes of downsizing. Admitting the need for downsizing by public managers, without accepting defeat or developing a sense of failure and despair, is a crucial mental and behavioral adjustment.

Resource allocation has to serve and be connected to organizational performance. Effective use of scarce resources necessitates linking awards to performance. Competent management cannot avoid offering salary raises, travel money, and symbolic recognitions to the people most productive and most valuable to the organization's mission. Definitely, whenever fewer people are able to do the same or more work, they should share in the benefits.

The demand for effective leaders in a fast-changing organizational reality remains largely unmet. Such leaders face the challenge and assume the responsibility for revitalizing the organization: they define the need for change, create new visions, mobilize commitment to those visions, and ultimately transform the organization.

Positively, such transformation of the organization requires new visions and new frames for thinking about strategy, structure, and people. Although some entrepreneurs can start with a clean slate, transformational leaders must begin with what is already in place. They are like architects who must redesign outmoded factories for a new use. Systems can be designed to create operational efficiency, but it is leadership that enables an organization to serve its mission and attain its vision. The leader for whom modern organizations search, is one who is able to transcend his or her own self-interest for the sake of the team, the organization, or the society.

In conclusion, important elements shape internal dynamics of public organizations and professionalize their management. Still, performance is the focus. Improving performance is the challenge. Developing indicators and methods of measurement to determine the level of goal attainment of the organization is an ongoing endeavor.

However, in all these tasks, people in the organization are the key to quantitative and qualitative improvements of performance. All processes of team building, quality circles, TQM, and others are serious efforts to mobilize human efforts and energies to face up to demands on public organizations. No doubt, significant progress has been made. In many associated managerial functions, improvements are substantive and noticeable: clarifying questions of accountability, improving connections between resources and outcomes, empowering employees, developing new perspectives on service that vitalize the notion of public service. Also, public management increasingly is applying performance audit, utilizing better reporting techniques, and enforcing provisions of higher ethical and professional standards of public management. This new context does not diminish the role of management and organizational leadership but, instead, stresses its significance.

NOTE

1. During the past few years, students in the author's seminars researched applications of TQM reforms in various Florida state and local agencies. Invariably, they reported no success stories, that it was too early to tell, or that improvements were attained but that they were not certain of the cause.

REFERENCES

Bowman, James S. 1994. At Last, an Alternative to Performance Appraisal: Total Quality Management. *Public Administration Review*, 54, 2 (March-April).
Bryne, John A. August 26, 1996. Strategic Planning. *Business Week*.
Carroll, James D. 1995. The Rhetoric of Reform and Political Reality in the National Performance Review. *Public Administration Review*, 55, 3 (May-June).
Cohen, Steven and Ronald Brand. 1993. *Total Quality Management in Government*. San Francisco, CA: Jossey-Bass.

Cubbert, Simile and John J. McDonough. 1985. *Radical Management, Power Politics, and the Pursuit of Trust*. New York: Free Press.

Denhardt, Robert B. and Barry R. Hammond. 1992. *Public Administration in Action: Readings, Profiles and Cases*. Pacific Grove, CA: Brooks/Cole Publishing.

Frederickson, H. George. 1996. Comparing the Reinventing Government Movement with the New Public Administration. *Public Administration Review*, 56, 3 (May-June).

French, John and Bertram Raven. 1958. The Bases of Social Power. In *Studies of Social Power*, edited by Dorwin Cartwright. Ann Arbor, MI: Institute of Social Research.

French, Wendell L. and Cecil H. Bell, Jr. 1995. *Organization Development*, 5th ed. Englewood Cliffs, NJ: Prentice-Hall.

Golembiewski, Robert T. 1990. The Boom in the Decline Literature. *Public Administration Review*, 50, 1 (January-February).

Guy, Mary E. 1989. *From Organizational Decline to Organizational Renewal*. New York: Quorum Books.

Hatry, Harry and John Greiner. 1984. *How Can Police Departments Better Apply Management-by-Objectives and Quality Circle Programs?* Washington, DC: Urban Institute.

Holzer, Mark. 1985. Productivity and Fiscal Pressure. *International Journal of Public Administration*, 7, 4.

Jreisat, Jamil E. 1992. *Managing Public Organizations: A Developmental Perspective on Theory and Practice*. New York: Paragon House.

Koretz, Gene. November 25, 1996. Economic Trends. *Business Week*.

Levine, Charles, ed. 1980. *Managing Fiscal Stress: The Crisis in the Public Sector*. Chatham, NJ: Chatham House.

Locke, Edwin and Gary Latham. 1984. *Goal Setting: A Motivational Technique that Works*. Englewood Cliffs, NJ: Prentice-Hall.

Mani, Bonnie G. 1995. Old Wine in New Bottles Tastes Better: A Case Study of TQM Implementation in IRS. *Public Administration Review*, 55 (March-April).

Moe, Ronald C. 1994. The "Reinventing Government" Exercise: Misinterpreting the Problem, Misjudging the Consequences. *Public Administration Review*, 54, 2 (March-April).

Nathan, Richard P. 1995. Reinventing Government: What Does It Mean?" *Public Administration Review*, 55, 2 (March-April).

Osborne, David and Ted Gaebler. 1992. *Reinventing Government: How the Entrepreneurial Spirit Is Transforming the Public Sector from Schoolhouse to State House, City Hall to Pentagon*. Reading, MA: Addison-Wesley.

Port, Otis. October 25, 1991. W. Edward Deming and J. M. Juran: Dueling Pioneers. *Business Week*.

Rago, William V. 1996. Struggle in Transformation: A Study in TQM,

Leadership, and Organizational Culture in a Government Agency. *Public Administration Review*, 56, 3 (May-June).

Savara, James H. 1996. Reforming or Dismantling Government? *Public Administration Review*, 56, 4 (July-August).

Schachter, Hindy L. 1995. Reinventing Government or Reinventing Ourselves: Two Models for Improving Government Performance. *Public Administration Review*, 55, 6 (November-December).

Swiss, James E. 1992. Adapting Total Quality Management (TQM) to Government. *Public Administration Review*, 52, 4 (July-August).

12

Organizational Performance

Organizational performance is broadly perceived to include more than quantity and quality of the output. It encompasses various additional ingredients ranging from employees' professional fulfillment to satisfaction of citizens, whether taxpayers or recipients of services. Improving performance is the reason most organizations undertake complex activities such as restructuring and strategic planning as well as adoption of programs, such as personnel training, quality circles, and team building. The final outcome of any substantive reform measures, however, is largely determined by the proficiency of implementation.

The processes of monitoring and evaluation of organizational performance remain empirical matters; they require measurement and application of criteria that incorporate external and internal organizational factors. How does one judge management capacity, and what indicators inform such judgment? Corporations, for example, have measurable benchmarks of good performance, such as improved profitability, increased return on investment, or increased market share. No such measures exist for the public organization, although it is still possible to underline vital signs of well-managed public organizations.

Yet, at all levels of government, public managers are intensely attempting to satisfy inquiries related to their performance and accountability. Some of the crucial questions are: What specific outcomes would indicate accomplishment of a manager's mission? What objective measures are being used to quantify success? Is the operation subjected from time to time to a critical, independent outside review or assessment? How do managers distinguish their performance from that of other managers or departments? What data about performance are needed, how much of them, how often to collect them? What technical know-how is needed by employees, and how can one develop such skills among employees? What incentives are built into the system to do performance measurement and appraisal well? Public organizations in general are seeking to understand the importance of such performance evaluation and how it leads to improvements in productivity, efficiency, and citizens' satisfaction.

It is commonly known, for example, that effective management requires the use of virtually all productive resources of the organization in a defined and coordinated plan of activities. Specific programs and operations that constitute the plan all combine in the effort to achieve the determined goals. Despite difficulties of establishing an agreement on permanent and universal prescriptions for effective management, some key elements are crucial for monitoring public organizations and their capacities for meeting their purposes. Besides the traditional methods, such as hierarchical control and inspection, effective monitoring essentially includes setting goals, measuring outputs, auditing performance, regular feedback, and management willingness to change and to adapt.

GOAL SETTING

Performance deals with results and their impacts. Results are measured against established goals of a public organization. The process of setting these goals must begin with identifying legitimate primary objectives (overall policies) that each public organization has, mostly in its enabling law (mandate). Next is the task of converting primary objectives into operational and specific goals or tasks to be accomplished. Difficulties are compounded, however, in transforming legitimate primary objectives into defined goals or tasks under conditions of limited or fragmented authority to operate and inadequate funding. Overall, a mandate or a policy may state only what must be done (or not done) in general terms. It is not possible for such mandates to delineate or express what management really needs or wants to do. Organizational management also may face attempts to subvert the process of delineating goals by interest groups favoring different policies and objectives. Such groups may exist within the organization — employees with different goals and priorities — or outside the organization — as in the case of special-interest groups.

When the organization is established deliberately to implement certain policies and programs, attainment of those purposes is the most reliable indicator of performance. The assumption that goal attainment is the real justification of the organization's existence also implies that the organization is a deliberate and rational entity; therefore, successful goal accomplishment becomes an appropriate measure of effectiveness. However, the emphasis on goal attainment as a measure of organizational performance, as Stephen Robbins (1990, pp. 53–54) points out, requires the presence of the following conditions:

Goals must be derived from a legitimate public policy.

Goals must be identified and clearly defined.

Goals must be few enough to be manageable.

Goals must represent consensus or general agreement within and without the public organization.

Progress toward these goals must be measurable with a reliable method.

Usually, setting of organizational goals is most effective when carried out in the context of a strategic plan, which anticipates future needs and prepares to take actions to meet them. Mature management relies on strategic planning for identifying long-range needs and trends, defining specific goals to serve such needs, estimating required resources, and directing significant parts of the managerial processes to accomplish the plan. Effective strategic planning focuses on fundamental questions facing the organization while setting the parameters that govern day-to-day activities (Bryson 1995). Evidence from the business sector indicates that formal strategic planning leads to superior performance (Stahl & Grigsby 1992, p. 8). It is instructive here to relate the experience of the private sector, which seems to indicate that corporations engage in strategic decision making for the purpose of enhancing their effectiveness and improving their chances of reaching their goals. In essence, strategic planning is the organization's response to three imperatives: first, how to deal with uncertainty and how to limit its potential negative consequences on the organization's performance; second, what desirable future state, or vision, is management pursuing, the rationale for it, and the resources necessary for achieving it; and third, how to maintain focus on the fundamentals of the organization, particularly its mandate, while pursuing its operational goals.

Finally, to reiterate a truism, individual goals are not the same as organizational goals. The assumption, however, is that, when employees achieve their collective assignments, the organization reaches its goals as well. In reality, this is an empirical question; individual goals are not always consistent with organizational goals, and conflicts between the two sets of values are more common than generally assumed. After organizational goals are set, the challenge is to gauge the progress made in achieving them.

PERFORMANCE MEASUREMENT

Performance measurement is the most reliable medium for monitoring progress toward accomplishing organizational goals. Public organizations are required more and more to carry out such a process in order to explain their financial needs and to verify their public mandates. The task of measurement has been made easier; "technological developments (reflected in the widespread use of computers), refinements in managerial skills, increase in the public's demand for service, and management's desire to rationalize its actions under the pressure of shrinking resources have all propelled the subject of measurement to the forefront of managerial concerns" (Jreisat 1987, p. 5).

Proponents of productivity measurement in government point out many possibilities of management improvements resulting from it. One is that measurement helps agencies to generate germane information about public programs for timely and more suitable decisions. Another advantage is that performance measurement promises to pattern internal standards of performance and, thus, contribute to a more meaningful process of oversight by elected officials, as well as by citizens at large. Additionally, perhaps one of the most important consequences of measurement is the potential improvements in the operations of the organization as a result of discovering performance problems and bottlenecks, their causes, and how to solve them.

Whether performance measurement realizes expectations is difficult to say. Many behavioral, technical, and organizational problems must be solved before a final assessment is possible of the real contributions of productivity measurement in the public sector. Although performance measurement still is not very high on the agenda of public managers (Jreisat 1990, p. 320), and regular funding of measurement efforts has been scarce, new laws are changing the picture altogether. For example, the Government Performance and Results Act of 1993 calls for a vigorous implementation of performance measurement across federal agencies by 1999 (Kravchuck & Schack 1996, p. 348). State and local governments, to various degrees, also have espoused the objective of gauging performance of programs and services within their jurisdictions.

Development of Indicators

One of the critical steps in designing a performance measurement system is devising realistic performance indicators for data gathering and comparisons across organizations and over time. Government services have utilized various indicators of performance such as cost, benefits, work loads, effectiveness, efficiency, productivity, outcomes, and impact. A unit of government would rarely utilize all of these indicators together. Perhaps only cost measurement is universal, because organizations have to prepare their budget estimates. The other measures are used sporadically and inconsistently. The process of measurement is made more complicated by the fact that governmental work is mostly services, which are not easily quantifiable. Moreover, suspicion of elected officials and mass media of public management generates fear of misuse of information in situations of productivity decline to serve political agendas. Hence, managers at all levels of government have been approaching the subject with undue caution and conservatism. Actually, this "potential for abuse encourages the politically astute manager either to reveal productivity data selectively or to suppress their collection entirely" (Downs & Larkey 1986, p. 63).

Developing and using outcome information, at all levels of government, is the mainstay of the increasingly important performance management systems. Measures will be employed for both strategic management and evaluation of results: planning and scorekeeping (Kravchuck & Schack 1996, p. 348). Municipal and state governments are increasingly requiring some forms of performance measurement from their management. The core of a performance-measurement design involves these principles (Jreisat 1992; Kravchuck & Schack 1996) but is not limited to them.

Formulate a clear and coherent mission based on clear understanding of the policy objectives of a program. This is a continuous activity.

Develop an explicit measurement strategy. The strategy emanates from the defined mission and provides the blueprint for the design and development of categories for measurement; data needed; data collection, storage, access, and reporting; and the technology required.

Allow participation by key users of the system in the design and development, including related policymakers and affected citizens.

Develop indicators (measures) in multiple sets for multiple users, as necessary. Not all people need the same information.

Ensure the development of realistic performance indicators for data gathering and comparisons (across organizations and over time).

As indicated, a central process in a performance management system is setting operational goals as well as reliance on criteria of efficiency and effectiveness. Other aspects of such a management system are performance audit and performance budgeting, which have been successfully implemented by numerous public organizations at all levels of government. Each of these processes is continually experiencing adjustments and adaptation to the needs of the particular organization. To institutionalize and sustain the use of these managerial techniques, particularly those aimed at monitoring and measuring performance, certain preconditions must exist, including a firm commitment of top managers to the success of these processes; inclusion of positive incentives for participants in order to accept new methods, identify with them, and help solve technical problems when they arise; training of employees at all levels to understand the process and master its operational technology; and a pervasive sense of professionalism among employees at all levels of the organization, which means greater commitment to excellence as well as a deeper sense of ethics and pride in public service.

As in similar governmental programs, implementing an effective measurement system requires continuous efforts for finding the most efficient and effective method of enforcement. Thus, adaptation and refinements are crucial for the process to achieve its purposes. Also, including citizens' ideas on the service they receive and on the quality of the service is a significant highlight of the current emphases in public management. In brief, public organizations are in the process of discovery and innovation through trial and error. The search is for appropriate organizational forms and managerial processes that satisfy current conditions and needs.

An organization that produces desired outcomes or achieves its determined goals is an effective one. When management is able to produce the required outcomes at reduced costs or increase the outcomes at the estimated cost or below, then the management is more efficient. Concentration on effectiveness and efficiency in public administration literature has been derided, particularly in traditional political science literature and some "humanist" organizational perspectives. One concern of the critics has been the claim that, under the guise of effectiveness and efficiency, bureaucracies tend to substitute political goals with bureaucratic goals. The general understanding is that, in a democratic system, political goals represent the people's preferences expressed through voting and elections; hence, these goals are inherently legitimate and moral. In contrast, goals established by appointed administrators lack such justification. The humanists assume that the first obligation of the organization is to its employees and their well-being. Claims of efficiency and effectiveness, according to this perspective, tend to mechanize the system and, thus, undermine employees' interests and the quality of employees' life at work. Some of the criticisms of managerial efficiency and effectiveness tend to narrowly define their considerations and to exaggerate their negative consequences.

The most frequently used techniques for evaluating managerial efficiency are cost-benefit and cost-effectiveness analyses. This efficiency is less abstract than economic efficiency and is more susceptible to fairly accurate calculations. Managerial efficiency is essentially a relationship between input (cost) and output (results and impact) of organizational functioning. Economic efficiency, in contrast to managerial efficiency, has broader and more abstract concerns that include organizational elements as well as decisions on allocation and distribution effects. George Downs and Patrick Larkey (1986, p. 7) point out that the criterion of efficiency that is widely preferred by economists is the Pareto criterion, that is, an economic policy or decision is economically efficient if it is not possible to change the policy and have someone better off and no one worse off. Two problems must be faced in applying this principle of economic efficiency: the reality that coming up with new policies that do not make someone worse off is extremely difficult and that accurate forecasts and measurement of the potential effects of a new policy require consideration of numerous variables and contingencies that often become unmanageable and unrealistic.

Effectiveness deals with attainment of goals according to established standards of quality. Thus, effectiveness measures output against planned goals over a period of time. At the risk of oversimplification, an example may illustrate the concept. If the organizational goal is to build 100 miles of new roads with certain specifications over the coming year, then building 80 miles of these new roads means the organization is 80 percent effective. If the organization was able to build the roads with less money per mile than was estimated or delivered in the past, then the organization is more efficient. Thus, efficiency and effectiveness do not move in the same direction all the time. Frequently, organizations do achieve their planned goals but at a higher cost, indeed, sometimes with ridiculous overruns.

One must guard against the potential for distortive reductionism when effectiveness is defined strictly in terms of goal attainment. In fact, goals are not always so easily determined, and overall effectiveness may be influenced by numerous other managerial factors. As Robbins (1990, p. 51) points out, there is almost unanimous agreement in the literature today that organizational effectiveness requires multiple criteria. Different organizational functions require different methods of evaluation. Goal attainment may hide problems of low quality of output, high accident rate, employee dissatisfaction, low morale, disagreement on goals, and a host of other negative characteristics.

More evaluation of efficiency and effectiveness of performance is carried out in the public sector than is generally recognized. Annually, public organizations submit budgetary requests in which they estimate the costs of operations. Sound budgetary practices usually provide information about goal attainment for the past year and articulate goals expected to be accomplished in the coming year or several years. In addition to setting operational goals, successful managers establish performance standards of quality, estimate cost of programs, evaluate managerial capacities to achieve these goals, and so forth. Performance budgeting, for example, enhances the managerial aspects of the budget process by providing a focus on operational efficiency through identifying work units (programs), defining their goals, measuring the cost of each unit, and providing data about them. Thus, a variety of evaluative activities is conducted in public organizations, but these activities remain fragmented, episodic, expensive, and often less than reliable.

Performance Audit

Performance audit is a valuable management tool for monitoring organizational performance. This audit is concerned primarily with information about program accomplishments and the system of measurement and reporting employed. Performance audit began in the United States during the 1950s, as an expansion of the scope of financial auditing, but gained considerable momentum in the 1970s along with performance budgeting and cost-benefit analysis (Brown & Pyers 1988, p. 737).

The General Accounting Office (GAO) accords performance audit high priority throughout the federal government. The Governmental Accounting Standards Board, which establishes accounting principles for state and local governments, has been bringing greater pressure on governments to set standards of performance and to develop performance measurement systems. Among the expected benefits are achieving true accountability in government and helping public managers make more-informed decisions. Particularly significant for public managers and management analysts is the growing concern with questions of impact as well as effectiveness and efficiency of decisions. Impact analysis primarily deals with the effects of the decision and the actual realization of its intended purposes. Such concerns are not exclusive and always extend to cost, compliance with rules, and sustaining organizational vitality (Jreisat 1997).

In 1974, the U.S. comptroller general issued a statement concerning standards of audit of public organizations, suggesting consideration of three types of audit: financial and compliance, economy and efficiency, and program results or effectiveness. These three types of audit are now considered essential guidelines for all levels of government (Herbert, Killough, & Steiss 1984, p. 264). Performance audit and managerial accounting have been providing valuable information to benefit internal management, particularly for planning purposes, decision making, and control. Objectives of performance audit include more than compliance with laws and regulations; they cover programs, functions, impediments, alternative actions, and the why and how of management. Indeed, public managers themselves use performance audit as a method of validating managerial practices or introducing operational changes to the organization.

Clearly, a new role for performance audit of public operations has been in the making for several years. This role is different from the traditional view of auditors as bean counters. Today's performance audit is more positive and more understanding of substantive managerial concerns than those of traditional, more familiar financial audits. Consequently, performance audit is not geared to embarrass or criticize public agencies but to assist management in discovering hidden costs, estimating impact of operations, devising better methods of managing, or making the finance function more vital in the total management processes. In particular, effective performance audit:

offers detached, independent, external evaluation of operations and proposes ideas for improvement. (Positive influence on management is the desired result, not the mere counting of errors, cataloging of failures, or meting out of punishment.)

generates essential information about the management of programs and the consistency of such programs with overall policy as well as with established goals.

confirms sound managerial practices as it identifies inefficient ones, helps in the
   development of indicators of good performance, and supports prudent
   management in purging cumbersome organizational structures and stultify-
   ing procedural requirements.

   To accomplish such tasks, performance auditors observe operations,
review procedures in use, and examine financial records and reports.
Auditors seek to ascertain costs and benefits and to analyze variations
between actual and established or expected standards of performance.
Pertinent issues and problems are discussed candidly with management
and employees. Performance audit also extends to personnel policies of
training and development, as well as job analysis and job classification
and their effects on operations.
   When properly conducted and appropriately received by agencies, a
performance audit should always result in managerial improvements and
enhanced effectiveness of the organization. A broad definition of "performance audit," as we use the term here, may overlap with some notions of
program evaluation. This should not be a significant problem at the
conceptual or the practical level. We prefer performance audit because it
lends itself to standardization and regularity. It benefits from the use of
tried and tested techniques of examination and measurement, as in the
Generally Accepted Accounting Principles, without being mired by philosophical debates of social science research procedures. This is not to deny
that certain technical and behavioral obstacles in the path of successful
performance auditing have to be overcome. As Richard Brown and James
Pyers (1988, p. 742) point out, the design of training, education, and
incentive systems to alter the environment may be the greater challenge.
   Development of performance audit is not isolated from the general
change in political and administrative values and approaches since the
1970s. Revenue shortfalls and huge budget deficits prompted the need for
fiscal constraint. Continuing fiscal stress, management cutbacks, competition for decreasing resources, and citizens' growing expectations of
accountability in government have fostered and expanded the demand for
finding "better ways" to manage government policies and programs.
Citizens and elected officials exerted and continue to exert pressures on
public administrators to "stretch tax dollars" by increasing efficiency and
effectiveness of public management. Consequently, monitoring, evaluating, and auditing performance have become significant responses to the
heightened emphasis on outcomes.
   Although concerns with performance of public programs and activities
are universal, performance audit remains mainly a U.S. invention. In its

short history, performance audit itself has undergone dramatic changes in format, content, and importance. Moreover, performance budgeting and the constant strive to measure and improve organizational outputs and program results have become global pursuits. It is no wonder that performance audit in the 1990s is one of the most promising management concepts. In essence, performance audit is a reformulation of conventional concepts and techniques that combine practices of organization and methods and economy and efficiency drives with more recent techniques of efficiency scrutinies and program evaluation.

The emphasis on economy and efficiency of programs usually includes whether the entity is acquiring, protecting, and using its resources (personnel, property, and space) economically and efficiently; the causes of inefficiencies and wasteful practices; and whether the entity is complying with laws and regulations on matters of economy and efficiency. The basic premise here is that organizations have objectives that they seek to attain through activities or programs. Management essentially is responsible for selecting such activities and programs that provide the most efficient and effective results. By selecting a program or designating a certain activity from among several competing alternatives, management is obligated, by this selection, to relate cost to benefit (input to output). Mainly, this is accomplished through the budgetary process, but it is not limited to it. Concern with the relationship between the cost of a program and its results also is reflected in other managerial processes, such as the accounting system in use, financial reporting, mechanisms of financial control, and performance measurements.

Traditional budgetary decisions have been preoccupied with the input side of the equation, in which managers habitually emphasize financial needs (costs) of programs more than their outputs. Today, the performance of a program is crucial. In developing programs, more and more expectations are that management spells out performance standards by which it determines when the objectives have or have not been met. It is assumed that standards to be met include measurable quality and quantity of performance.

The process of an audit is a course of several interrelated steps and events that unfold over a period of time to achieve a defined purpose or goal. Such a process is not mechanical in the sense of being a sequence of exact procedures; rather, it is a progression of steps that outlines how an audit is carried out in a flexible and adaptive form. As a dynamic activity, a well-conceived audit is a unique design of how to proceed in order to accomplish what is to be done.

The initial phase of a performance audit requires setting forth a broad framework for planning the audit and agreeing on its purpose and procedures. Because of a range of possible approaches, initiators of the audit must decide what the audit should accomplish before the process is activated. They may examine any aspect of the organization or the program that relates to performance, such as procurement practices, resources used, cost, duplication of employees' efforts, overstaffing, operating procedures, and so forth. Typically, a program audit attempts to identify bottlenecks, waste, conflicts, and factors that inhibit or reduce efficiency and effectiveness of operations.

An important rule is that careful implementation requires evaluating evidence before formulating final opinions. Such evidence involves written or verbal confirmation of the presence and effective functioning of internal controls and records. The task of auditors is simplified with the availability of authoritative and valid documents in support of recorded transactions. Verification of information usually entails physical examination, visual observation, or oral testimony by parties inside or outside the organization being audited. Whatever the form or the method, it is imperative that auditors evaluate sufficient competent evidence as a condition for maintaining fairness.

A professionally managed audit also seeks to obtain and evaluate evidence from management in order to ascertain the degree of correspondence between what is claimed and what is carried out. Effective auditors exhibit cooperative and supportive attitudes toward management in their search for common grounds, with the goal of bringing about improvements. Turning the process into a policing act creates conditions conducive to distortion and misrepresentation. Negative audits drive the staff into being concerned with surviving the ordeal rather than learning from it. Mutual trust and confidence between auditors and managers improve the definition of problems and enhance opportunities for solving them.

Thus, discussions between auditors and management of the agency under review, through two-way communication and give-and-take sessions, greatly strengthen auditors' effectiveness and increase the value of their recommendations. Customarily, before a report is published, which is the primary product of a performance audit, it is made available to the agency concerned for comments and reactions. This could be decisive for improving the chances of implementing the report's recommendations.

Moreover, seeking the agency's reaction often results in rectifying any factual errors and removing an agency's pretext for criticizing the report on grounds of inaccuracy. Frequently, an audit is concluded with a seminar at the agency's premises in which a dialogue and constructive interaction may produce deeper understanding of the issues. Certainly, convincing management to accept auditors' conclusions, or at least minimizing the force of initial resistance, is a worthy objective.

The auditors' final report, containing findings and recommendations, is presented in clear and straightforward language, with financial and numerical data employed only to illustrate the analysis and recommendations. Reports of performance audit represent the independent judgment of the auditors and, thus, have a considerable normative stance.

Unlike program evaluation, which grew out of the social sciences, performance auditing is an extension of accounting and financial audits. The usual distinctions between performance audit and program evaluation, however, are rapidly disappearing. The contention that program evaluation measures a wide range of social concerns, rather than the narrow managerial efficiency focus of the performance audit, is a superfluous argument in light of the comprehensive coverage of current performance audits. Similarly, the derivative notion that performance audit is of utility only to line managers is false.

Actually, performance audit and program evaluation share the same ultimate objective, that of improving the performance of a program or a whole organization. As practiced over the past several years, performance audit has extended its purview far beyond the concerns of traditional accounting and budget analysis, which have failed to offer policymakers and managers the help they need, namely, how do we develop responsive and efficient management of public service agencies in an environment of financial stress? This question includes the administrative commitment to improving the chances of implementation of legislatively mandated programs.

At least one primary difference between performance audit and program evaluation is worth noting. Performance audit, unlike an evaluation, never can be regarded as complete upon the mere statement of disclosed or unveiled problems. Usually, its presentations are accompanied by proposals for solutions to specific problems or improvements in overall effectiveness.

Far from being a narrow accounting tool, performance audit in its most comprehensive content encompasses analysis of policy, monitoring of programs, measuring results, and developing alternative processes to deliver public services. Within this expansive mode, performance audit also may be regarded as a catalyst for organizational change, functioning as a vehicle for implementing Total Quality Management in public agencies.

This means that performance audit must succeed where other approaches have failed, namely, in attaining a radical shift in management philosophy and operations by developing a permanent commitment to quality improvements in all processes and at all levels of public organizations.

The continual extension of coverage and inclusion of functions, however, do not always mark vitality or confirm strength of performance audits. It is a serious concern whether performance audit is becoming an umbrella concept organized around the public inquiry: "What are we getting for our money." A potential consequence of this view is that performance audit, by becoming anything its conductors want, risks being nothing in particular. Worse, such dispersion carries the seeds of disintegration over time.

In a global context, deficit spending and the heavy burden of public debt in most countries have prompted a variety of remedial proposals. The most frequently recommended solution is building the administrative capacities of the state in order to improve the performance of public service agencies. From this perspective, improving performance has been globally touted as an obligation of modern management. The success of private organizations that transformed themselves into flexible, lean operations through the adaptation of innovative management concepts provides a powerful impetus for public sector programs.

IMPEDIMENTS

At all levels of government, political considerations are paramount, often outweighing the desire for economy and efficiency. Interest in program costs is often of greater concern to managers than to politicians. Elected officials primarily are interested in their reelection and in what they consider to be the will of their constituents. Although performance audits are of most value when the long-term effects of measurement are considered, it is always difficult for elected officials to make long-range decisions based largely on financial considerations.

Generally, public administrators are less than enthusiastic about having their departments or agencies undergo the scrutiny of either elected officials or the public. This sort of oversight by elected officials might result in a perceived micromanagement of agencies by legislators. Similarly, public knowledge of performance measurement of individual departments without the benefit of a thorough understanding of the department's goals and objectives might encourage public managers to consider misrepresenting financial matters in order to manage public opinion.

Judgments made by the public and by elected officials as a result of performance measurements become troublesome when comparisons are made between departments. The value of comparisons between the performance measurement of the Department of Interior and the Department of Defense is unclear; yet, such comparisons must be made when considering the effective use of public funds. Both the public and elected officials need to realize that performance measurements cannot be the only factors considered in determining an organization's value.

Conversely, to set these types of examinations and evaluations aside is to suggest that effectiveness of organizations cannot be evaluated, but performance measurements and evaluation have developed under the presumption that effectiveness can be monitored and periodically assessed. Measurement is the key to a performance improvement process and an essential means for controlling quality and quantity of output, despite the fact that many related questions of measurement have not been satisfactorily answered. Also, performance budgeting has not mastered the need for stronger connection between performance and revenue allocations. What can or may be measured in government operations? Who conducts measurement? What interpretation can be made from the raw data? How can these data be correlated with budgeted dollars so that the public may readily understand service agency performance? Notwithstanding progress achieved in measuring outputs of public programs in the past few years, these and similar questions remain troublesome.

Interest in measurement is not to deny the valid claim that the most important aspect of performance auditing of public service agencies lies not in quantitative analytical methods but, rather, in the internal and external politics effecting service improvement — the ultimate goal. At the same time, it seems that the public will be observing and evaluating public service agencies in terms of performance versus tax dollars as well as the quality of service delivered.

Among the results of recent changes in performance auditing are a growing interest in public policy and an increasing orientation toward a problem-solving approach. Such a trend has not received universal support or acceptance, however. Debates over the role of the GAO in 1994 illustrate the political sensitivity of legislators toward an independent, professional analysis of public policies. Lawmakers continually cite the accounting office's findings in deciding whether to create, abolish, cut, or revise programs. Yet, lawmakers of both parties have expressed concern that the GAO sometimes seemed more eager to make policy pronouncements than simply provide information (Pear 1994, p. A1).

The GAO produces reports on many volatile issues, including health care, defense-related procurement, immigration, and trade. It alerted Congress to problems in the savings and loan industry long before most people were aware of them. It has documented problems in dozens of weapons programs. Federal agencies accept three-fourths of its recommendations, and Congress follows more than half of its suggestions for legislative action (Pear 1994, p. A1). A study by a panel of experts from the National Academy of Public Administration, a nonprofit organization chartered by Congress to increase the effectiveness of federal, state, and local government, describes the GAO as an invaluable institution and found "no evidence of deliberate partisan bias" in its work. However, the study said that the GAO "seems to be exceeding its appropriate role" by venturing into the analysis and development of public policy (p. A12).

Clearly, role definition is vital for any organization involved in performance audit. Until performance audit is universally accepted and practiced, such a task will face criticism, if not hostility, from political as well as administrative sources. Perhaps the most widely acknowledged apprehension regarding the practicality of performance monitoring is the public's concern with expenditures. The benefits of professional monitoring eventually will outweigh all costs associated with its implementation, which initially will be great. Considering the current financial condition of both federal and local governments in the United States and most other governments of the world, it is imperative that such programs be presented in a manner that ensures political acceptance of the required additional expenditures.

For developing countries, the crucial factor is to build capacities of public agencies and to develop employees' knowledge and skills to be able to conduct performance audits. These systems are facing a dearth of professional neutral competence among staffs, essential for exerting the authority of expert knowledge and professional ethics in monitoring, proposing, and ushering in new ideas and improvements. So far, senior public managers have not developed sufficient appreciation of the positive role of audits and their potential contributions to achieving overall improvements or better accountability.

Although there is no simple formula for realizing such necessary changes in developing countries, faithful execution of performance audits is not likely without them. Thus, a sort of managerial vicious cycle continues to keep in check all potential disruptions of the status quo. To carry out a performance audit plan effectively in these developing systems, therefore, presence of certain preconditions is vital.

Unwavering support of the political leadership is essential. Corrupt and uninspired leadership constitutes the single greatest discouragement of efforts to study and analyze government practices. Such leaders may praise popular activities that claim to reform existing conditions but bury them at the implementation and monitoring phases. The political order is the context that envelops and influences management in numerous ways. Political leadership is able to induce or stifle professional management and, thus, is a contributor to existing managerial culture, tradition, and level of integrity and ethics applied in the conduct of government functions at large.

There must be greater recognition and appreciation of the vital role of accounting standards and performance measurement practices in public programs. This entails enriching the accountancy profession with new talents and according it high priority in public policies. Government accounting in developing countries is completely overshadowed by the budget function, which is emphasized and granted preeminence. Budget people frequently maintain their own separate accounting records, which are more accurate, timely, and useful than those of accounting offices. Government accounting is poor in quality, inadequate in content, and late in presenting data that are easily ignored (Wesberry 1990, p. 345). Typically, accounting in developing countries has been limited primarily to serving the legal purpose of documenting and summarizing receipts and expenditures in a formal report that is presented several years after the execution of the transactions reported. When financial records do not provide an accurate snapshot of government activities or financial status, determining accountability becomes a daunting quest.

Empowerment of employees at the operational levels through substantive decentralization of decision making is essential. Unquestionably, existing staffs in most developing countries are not qualified or equipped to carry out responsibilities of auditing the performance of public programs. Consequently, improving their professional standards is a fundamental step, not only in terms of obtaining and evaluating evidence but also in demonstrating independence, reliability, and ethical conduct. In highly centralized systems, professional considerations easily give way to hierarchical restrictions. Particularly in organizational environments that emphasize conformance and obedience, it is not customary for employees to readily reveal corruption or waste by people of high authority.

There must be transparency of financial transactions so that accounting processes lend themselves to measures of validation of correct operations or verification of the accuracy of financial information. Issues of accountability and good government usually are strengthened when an administrative unit actually develops the ability to monitor its operations, diagnose its problems, and recommend solutions for them — all in the public eye and with democratic means.

Currently, operating accounting systems in developing countries rarely introduce change or propose dramatic conclusions in their audits. This is not to say that their actions have not resulted in some prevention of fraud and waste. Many Asian and Latin American countries have been attempting to reform their financial managements through a variety of approaches. In the two decades after World War II, the Philippines, India, Indonesia, Malaysia, Singapore, and others have attempted to apply performance-oriented financial administrative systems. Performance and program budgeting also have been on the agenda of most Asian and Latin American countries.

So far these efforts have resulted only in modest accomplishments. Success of management audits may be important for the evolution of any good government; achieving it, however, proved to be illusive for most governments. Consequently, this discussion is concerned with defining the particulars that contribute to effective auditing as well as the contextual preconditions that facilitate its competent discharge. Despite the obvious advantages to conducting performance auditing, it is sometimes disparaged for perceived deficiencies: lacking clear criteria, second-guessing management, and placing auditors in judgment roles. Moreover, despite progress made in setting standards and defining processes, performance audit continues to carry an element of subjectivity and personal judgment.

REFERENCES

Brown, Richard E. and James B. Pyers. 1988. Putting Teeth into the Efficiency and Effectiveness of Public Service. *Public Administration Review*, 48, 3 (May-June).

Bryson, John M. 1995. *Strategic Planning for Public and Nonprofit Organizations*, 2d ed. San Francisco, CA: Jossey-Bass.

Downs, George and Patrick Larkey. 1986. *The Search for Government Efficiency*. New York: Random House.

Herbert, Leo, Larry Killough, and Alan Steiss. 1984. *Governmental Accounting and Control.* Monterey, CA: Brooks/Cole.

Jreisat, Jamil E. 1997. Performance Audit. In *International Encyclopedia on Public Policy and Administration*, edited by Jay M. Shafritz. New York: Henry Holt.

____. 1992. *Managing Public Organizations: A Developmental Perspective on Theory and Practice*. New York: Paragon House.

____. 1990. Productivity Measurement and Finance Officers in Florida. *Public Productivity and Management Review*, 13, 4 (September).

____. 1987. Productivity Measurement: Trial and Error in St. Petersburg. *Public Productivity Review*, 44 (Winter).

Kravchuck, Robert and Ronald Schack. 1996. Designing Effective Performance-Measurement Systems Under the Government Performance and Results Act of 1993. *Public Administration Review*, 56, 4 (July-August).

Pear, Robert. October 17, 1994. Report Criticizes the Objectivity of the Federal Watchdog Agency. *New York Times*.

Robbins, Stephen P. 1990. *Organization Theory: Structure, Design, and Applications*, 3rd ed. Englewood Cliffs, NJ: Prentice-Hall.

Stahl, Michael J. and David W. Grigsby. 1992. *Strategic Management for Decision Making*. Boston, MA: PWS-Kent.

Wesberry, James, Jr. 1990. Government Accounting and Financial Management in Latin American Countries. In *Government Financial Management: Issues and Country Studies*. Washington, DC: International Monetary Fund.

13

Conclusions

In this book, we reject the notion that organization theory is fortified with few certitudes and beset with many assumptions. Upon deeper examination of organization management theory and practice, the reader hopefully realizes that there is a long tradition of conceptualization and a wealth of insightful organizational and managerial knowledge. As in other fields of social science, this knowledge also varies in levels of reliability and relevance as it encompasses many unconfirmed postulates accumulated over decades of application.

Public organization theory and process, as they evolved over time, demonstrate a developmental sequence that can be described in definable stages or viewed as sustained theoretical thrust. The shifts of conceptual development seldom result in a completely new theory, let alone nullifying or replacing existing ones. New concepts, instead, often become additions and modifications, enriching existing thinking. The diversity of sources contributing to the advancement of administrative knowledge — research, teaching, and practice — as well as multiple disciplinary interests common to modern organizations may explain the slow progress of theoretical consolidation and displacement. To be sure, many organizational concepts, even if not empirically disproved and discarded, have been devalued or reduced to oddities of historical significance only.

The developmental perspective displays leaps in organization theory and process that may not always constitute a definite pattern but indicate a steady attention to key administrative issues over time and space. Organizational analysis also indicates constant attention to basic features such as goals, leadership, performance, and how best to utilize resources. Understanding of these features is essential for producing worthwhile examination, comparison, and evaluation of managerial concepts and practices.

To appreciate the depth and comprehensiveness attained by studying organization management developmentally, consider the emergence of the human relations approach. This perspective will not be adequately explained in isolation from its forerunner, rational-classic approaches. Similarly, the importance of modifications of perspectives on decision making, leadership, communication, and other managerial functions cannot be realized fully without understanding the developmental process that shaped each of these functions in theory and in application. David Rosenbloom's (1991, p. 95) question is pertinent: "How do we know what we know and how can we extend what we know?" and, indeed, is shaped "by what we have learned from those who preceded us." He concludes that reliance on recent scholarship only and analyses for authority diminishes public administration intellectual heritage and erodes its knowledge base.

Ultimately, disparity among organizational perspectives may elevate integrationist tendencies and achieve higher levels of synthesis. Until we reach this phase, public administration must continue to broaden its horizon and encourage an inclusionary, rather than exclusionary, discernment and appraisal of administrative information. At the present, the urgent need for scholars and practitioners is to stimulate theoretical convergence of reliable skills and practices in order to improve organizational performance.

At the methodological front, certainly public administration is ripe for significant change in various practical means, such as empirical verification, practical assessments, normative judgments, and techniques of forging professional consensus. Theoretical advancements, however, will come only in meaningful additions to existing organization theory and, as in the past, through middle-range theoretical developments rather than at the grand level. Middle-range theory elevates analytical frameworks above casually generated working hypotheses and provides these frameworks with more focus than is possible under grandiose attempts to explain all social behavior with a given systematic set of assumptions (Merton 1968). Because middle-range theories differ from grand theories and from summary statements of empirically observed relationships, they are efficient tools for applying evidence to a few organizational aspects at a time, for linking concepts to each other, and for providing a balance between the abstract and the concrete in the formulation of hypotheses (Moore, Johns, & Pinder 1980, p. 1).

Recognizing the advantages of middle-range theoretical constructs does not mean complete acceptance of tendencies to associate the development of administrative theory with one type of research methods — empirical or quantitative. Devaluation of the qualitative studies, critics charge, produces narrow, positivistic, and inherently biased scholarship (Box 1992, p. 62; Bailey 1992, p. 47; Thayer 1984, p. 553). "If research leads to reducing the field to numbers, it risks losing the substance of public administration and reinforcing the barriers between academicians and practitioners" (Bailey 1992, p. 53). At the heart of these concerns is the issue of whether public administration is a discipline or a profession. As a discipline, administrative questions, and methods for researching them, are determined as in other disciplines, say, political science. As a profession, the field proceeds with a constant eye on the practitioners and the issues and problems they encounter, just as in medicine, business, or engineering. In this case, problem solving rather than methodological orthodoxy is the primary test of research value.

Consequently, organization theory is constantly being formulated and reformulated as a result of knowledge gained through various means such as individual experiences, case studies, consensus of the management profession, logical deduction, critical observation, and quantitative verification of hypotheses. Opting for one method over another must be based solely on the inquiry being conducted. Confirmation of a hypothesis via statistical exercises is important to raise the level of confidence in the concepts, but, for the long-range view of the field, the formulation of the hypothesis, not merely its testing, determines its utility and contribution to knowledge. Although testing of a hypothesis can be reduced to a simple statistical exercise, formulating a meaningful hypothesis (worth testing) requires understanding organizations and the ability to differentiate their critical elements. Certainly, the evolution of administrative knowledge defines many of the critical organizational elements and processes interacting with the larger environment. Whatever organizational perspective is applied, one cannot avoid the multidimensional qualities of organization theory and process, as these critical elements illustrate:

Structure specifies roles and responsibilities, relationships, centers of power, patterns of communication and coordination, and so on.

People (human resources) are mobilized in order to achieve cooperation and to fulfill their roles through complex and mutually influencing techniques of motivation, communication, decision making, team building, professional training, and performance evaluation.

Organizational culture covers significant symbolic, normative, and perceptual aspects of the processes dealing with human resources of the organization. This includes employees' needs for meaningful involvement, cultural cohesion, and a sense of equity and fairness in the reward system. As James Wilson (1989, p. 27) points out, organizational culture is "a distinctive way of viewing and reacting to the bureaucratic world" that shapes whatever discretionary authority the operators may have.

Managerial leadership provides the bond that ties organizational functions and structures, skills that focus on the fundamental mission of the organization, the wide range of information about activities throughout the organization, and use of information to make more effective decisions. Repeatedly, we face the need for public managers who can foster a culture of excellence, innovation, cooperation, and quality of performance in contemporary public organizations.

Organizations do not exist in a vacuum; their environments have critical effects on every aspect of their performance. The environmental modifiers often are assumed instead of analyzed and evaluated. The political, legal, economic, and cultural elements of society exert a variety of pressures and influences on the management of public organizations.

The political context, however, is most important, because the political process legislates the main goals, appropriates the essential resources, and maintains numerous constraints on public organizations. Similarly, because public organizations are engaged primarily in delivering services to the public, they can influence the political process without appearing obtrusive. Tension exists, however, because public administration is concerned with the administrative side of government, and what government does is mainly politically determined. Although administrators are able to improve the performance of government through effective enforcement of its policies, administrative discretion is always circumscribed by political and legal considerations. When society is experiencing turbulent changes, such as earlier developments in eastern Europe or the republics of the former Soviet Union, administrative difficulties are compounded. These cases prove that the overall performance of public organizations is inextricably tied to the overall performance of the political system. Finally, the globalization of politics and the interdependence of world economies have gradually extended their effects to public administration concepts and practices. New trends have been set in motion. In the United States, the impact of the collapse of the Soviet empire and the growing burden of public debt owed by other nations are among the major factors leading to far-reaching alignments of government priorities in allocation of budget resources. The traditional balance of military and social spending has been altered by events outside U.S. boundaries more than by any other domestic consideration.

Thus, fundamental change is not always generated within the confines of the organization but often is dictated by external developments. In fact, there is consistency in the literature on this point. The variation and the turbulence are almost always in the changing environment, which produces needs and demands requiring fundamental organizational adjustments.

In a review of "great books" in public administration, Frank Sherwood (1990, p. 260) concludes with a call to view the larger picture. He writes: "The contemplation of future status and needs for literature in public administration must inevitably be in the context of the larger society and the events that will define the character of the twenty-first century." Sherwood points out that the Japanese achieved their world status in ways unique in history. Guns and imperialistic exploitation have not been parts of their strategy. On the other hand, he sees the demise of the Soviet Union in terms of the persistence of its command system, which provided little opportunity for initiative, was inflexible, and provided few incentives to use resources well. The lesson is not hidden for U.S. bureaucracies that exhibit many of the same characteristics at the same time that their human resources are declining (Sherwood 1990, p. 261).

Although the role of public administration in modern society is unique, if not complicated, expectations are contradictory. Managerial values of efficiency and effectiveness, for example, do not always ensure, and may undermine, obligations of equity, representation, social responsibility, and responsiveness. These concerns necessitate that public administration conform to societal norms and preferences, as translated into public laws. The efficiency and effectiveness drive also signifies the importance of intrinsic qualities such as expertise, independent judgment, continuity, and professionalism. Dynamic tensions join these two potentially incompatible pressures when applied to the operations of public organizations, but to perceive that a choice exists of one influence or the other is inappropriate. Both aspects are essential in order to represent the whole of public administration, and neither by itself is a complete constitution of its total reality. This is why public administration theory and practice are continually being changed and adapted, hence administrative reform is so central in balancing the professional and the technical concerns.

Most countries today are pursuing administrative reform concurrently (or claiming to do so), while attempting to redefine the role of the state. A constant objective of public administration reform strategies has been strengthening the accountability of public decisions. The means invariably entail improvement of outcomes (results) of public spending and the definition of consequences (impacts) of such spending, preferably in measurable terms. Not surprising, proposed solutions are invariably compatible.

Pressures for reform are driving public management to come up with imaginative new ways of doing things that ensure improved quality and reduced cost of public service. Contemporary public management operates against a backdrop of immense ideological momentum, incorporating many popular but simplistic notions about society and government. Thus, government reformers are continuously fending off slogans derived from this negative ideology, such as government is not the solution to the problem; government is the problem.

Nevertheless, ideas of reform, which generally produce positive results for government, tend to cluster around few main strategies for change: privatization (often associated with programs of restructuring, downsizing, or contracting out); decentralization and the derivatives of devolution, deconcentration, and delegation; technology, including reliance on new machines and equipment (most prominent among them computers and their versatile, increasing capacity); performance measurement and improvement (promised in such measures as performance-based budgeting, performance audit, benchmarking, and so forth); and civil service reforms that involve specific techniques of employee training and development, incentives, empowerment, participation, and team building.

Less pronounced, however, in these administrative reform endeavors is the ongoing search for more effective links between public functions and citizens' needs and expectations. Similarly, the essential rendering of paths of future change and the designation of those responsible for it is implied or assumed more than declared.

To deal with internal and external uncertainties, managers must improve their use of the processes of communication, promote environmental support, and convey a sense of responsiveness without neglecting other crucial managerial functions. The irony is that public managers in modern public organizations are hamstrung by ineffective incentive systems and lack of motivational instruments that encourage employees to save, innovate, improve, and increase output. The views of public managers, on the front line of application of administrative knowledge, are central for defining problems and tendencies. Thus, I asked a total of

140 current and future public managers who enrolled in my seminars on public administration theory and practice (between 1992 and 1996) to identify the most critical issues challenging public managers at the present. Their opinions are descriptive and illustrative feedback and also are a testimony to the current concerns and aspirations of professional management. Employees desire greater creativity in the management of their agencies; they are alarmed by persistent problems of revenue shortfalls, diminishing work incentives, and continuing political deals by elected leaders. They emphasize the importance of enhancing commitment of public organizations to values of equity, representativeness, and employee involvement in organizational management more than has been attempted. To this group, the most compelling issues of public management today are:

Public management needs to demonstrate high levels of professionalism and to show a sense of pride in what they do and the manner in which they do it. A participant explained that professionalism means "adherence to recognized standards of performance" and a "sense of obligation to discharge one's duties with diligence and integrity." Another respondent noted that elements of professionalism include responsiveness to public needs and making sure that programs and functions of public organizations truly meet those needs, particularly in times of shrinking resources and limited revenue bases.

Ethics and ethical standards are high on the scale of priorities for public managers. Developing standards of ethical behavior requires educating individuals on the proper implementation of these standards, communicating codes of ethics, establishing mechanisms for monitoring implementation, and defining suitable behavior whenever ambiguity appears.

Public organizations are searching for new and creative thinking on how to deal with the economic, social, and environmental problems facing society. Administrative problems are increasingly complex and do not lend themselves to technological solutions. Public managers today, therefore, need to be more informed, better educated, more skilled in the use of new tools and equipment, and more willing to accept new approaches to managing their units. Some of the results of the search for new and innovative ideas are illustrated by the use of privatization, contracting out, user's fees, and volunteerism to accomplish goals of public policy.

Issues of equity and representativeness of public decisions are gaining enormous attention and receiving uncompromising support from employees and from citizens at large. Public organizations are in the midst of an immense transformation in the way they operate. One participant described this as "putting the public back into public administration." Public managers are expected to observe the value of treating all citizens fairly and equally and to represent public interest first and foremost.

Employee participation takes different modes but is not an entirely new notion. After the reinvention of government and the quality drive, empowerment of employees is a core concept in most of the suggestions being offered by the new thinking. Too often, one respondent points out, public managers surround themselves with "yes men," thereby depriving the organization of differing values and opinions. Public managers need to understand that participatory management does not mean that the manager abandons his or her responsibilities. Reliance on hierarchy and legal power have been excessive in public organizations. Employee empowerment is a genuine effort of devolution of authority in the organization; it means allowing those who do the work and know most about it to make decisions pertaining to it.

Indisputably, significant progress has been made in associated managerial functions such as better definition of accountability, improving the connection between funding and outcomes, empowering people, developing new perspectives on public service, and overall improvements in professional management. However, most of the progress could be in jeopardy if shrinking budget deficits and pandering political decision making continue to denigrate public employment through elimination of annual raises, threats to job security, and weakening of the incentive system of public service. Consequently, the leadership role in public organizations is tested under different conditions. The new reality requires organizational leaders to be more effective in representing public employment. Leaders have to negotiate more proficiently with the political context in order to protect the integrity of public programs essential for the welfare of the community at large.

In public organizations, performance through people has not been explored and implemented sufficiently. Political leadership often fosters centralization, leading to control through budgetary and other legislative approaches. Thus, public organizations have been deprived of the full use of capabilities of all their employees, particularly those closer to the service delivery level. Finally, all our efforts to study public organizations share the ultimate goal of searching to heighten their rationality, reduce their waste, improve their responsiveness to citizens, and minimize wasteful internal conflicts. The search continues, and organizations of the future will be better for it.

REFERENCES

Bailey, Mary Timney. 1992. Do Physicists Use Case Studies? Thoughts on Public Administration Research. *Public Administration Review*, 52, 1

(January-February).

Box, Richard C. 1992. An Examination of the Debate Over Research in Public Administration. *Public Administration Review*, 52, 1 (January-February).

Merton, Robert K. 1968. *Social Theory of Social Structure*. New York: Free Press.

Moore, Larry, Gary Johns, and Craig Pinder. 1980. Toward Middle Range Theory. In *Middle Range Theory and Study of Organizations*, edited by C. Pinder and L. Moore. Boston, MA: Martinus Nijhoff Publishing.

Rosenbloom, David H. 1991. How Do We Know What We Know and How Can We Extend What We Know? *Public Administration Review*, 51, 2(March-April).

Sherwood, Frank P. 1990. The Half-Century's "Great Books" in Public Administration. *Public Administration Review*, 50, 2 (March-April).

Thayer, Frederick C. 1984. Understanding Research. *Public Administration Review*, 44, 6 (November-December).

Wilson, James Q. 1989. *Bureaucracy*. New York: Basic Books.

Selected Bibliography

Adair, John. 1983. *Effective Leadership*. London: Pan.

Adler, Nancy, Robert Doktor, and Gordon Redding. 1986. From the Atlantic to the Pacific Century: Cross-Cultural Management Reviewed. *Journal of Management*, 12, 2.

Allen, Richard K. 1977. *Organizational Management Through Communication*. New York: Harper & Row.

Allison, Graham T., Jr. 1992. Public and Private Management: Are They Fundamentally Alike in All Unimportant Respects? In *Classics of Public Administration*, 3rd ed., edited by Jay M. Shafritz and Albert C. Hyde. Pacific Grove, CA: Brooks/Cole.

Argyris, Chris. 1957. *Personality and Organization*. New York: Harper & Row.

Argyris, Chris and Donald A. Schon. 1978. *Organizational Learning: A Theory of Action Perspective*. Reading, MA: Addison-Wesley.

Bailey, Mary Timney. 1992. Do Physicists Use Case Studies? Thoughts on Public Administration Research. *Public Administration Review*, 52, 1 (January-February).

Barnard, Chester I. 1962. *The Functions of the Executive*. Cambridge, MA: Harvard University Press.

Bass, B. M. 1981. *Stogdill's Handbook of Leadership*. New York: Free Press.

Bazerman, Max A. 1986. *Judgment in Managerial Decision-Making*. New York: John Wiley.

Beer, Michael. 1980. *Organization Change and Development*. Santa Monica, CA: Goodyear Publishing.

Behn, Robert D. 1995. The Big Questions of Public Administration. *Public Administration Review*, 55, 4 (July-August).

Behn, Robert D. and J. W. Vaupel. 1982. *Quick Analysis for Busy Decision Makers*. New York: Basic Books.

Belasco, James A. and Ralph C. Stayer. 1993. *Flight of the Buffalo: Soaring to Excellence, Learning to Let Employees Lead*. New York: Warner Books.

Bell, Robert. 1985. *The Culture of Policy Deliberation*. New Brunswick, NJ: Rutgers University Press.

Bennis, Warren and Burt Nanus. 1985. *Leaders*. New York: Harper & Row.

Bergquist, William. 1996. Postmodern Thought in a Nutshell: Where Art and Science Come Together. In *Classics of Organization Theory*, 4th ed., edited by Jay M. Shafritz and J. Steve Ott. New York: Wadsworth.

Box, Richard C. 1992. An Examination of the Debate Over Research in Public Administration. *Public Administration Review*, 52, 1 (January-February).

Bozeman, Barry. 1987. *All Organizations Are Public*. San Francisco, CA: Jossey-Bass.

Bryman, Alan. 1996. Leadership in Organizations. In *Handbook of Organization Studies*, edited by Stewart Clegg, Cynthia Hardy, and Walter Nord. Thousand Oaks, CA: Sage.

____. 1986. *Leadership and Organization*. London: Routledge & Kegan Paul.

Bryson, John M. 1995. *Strategic Planning for Public and Nonprofit Organizations*, 2d ed. San Francisco, CA: Jossey-Bass.

Burke, W. Warner. 1994. *Organization Development: A Process of Learning and Changing*, 2d ed. Reading, MA: Addison-Wesley Publishing.

Burns, James MacGregor. 1978. *Leadership*. New York: Harper & Row.

Clegg, Stewart, Cynthia Hardy, and Walter Nord, eds. 1996. *Handbook of Organization Studies*. Thousand Oaks, CA: Sage.

Crozier, Michel. 1964. *The Bureaucratic Phenomenon*. Chicago, IL: University of Chicago Press.

Cubbert, Simile and John J. McDonough. 1985. *Radical Management, Power Politics, and the Pursuit of Trust*. New York: Free Press.

DeHoog, Ruth Hoogland. 1984. *Contracting Out for Human Services*. Albany: State University of New York.

Denhardt, Robert B. 1993. *Theories of Public Organization*. Belmont, CA: Wadsworth.

Doig, James W. 1983. "If I See a Murderous Fellow Sharpening a Knife Cleverly . . .": The Wilsonian Dichotomy and the Public Authority Tradition. *Public Administration Review*, 43, 4 (July-August).

Downs, Anthony. 1967. *Inside Bureaucracy*. Boston, MA: Little, Brown.

Downs, George and Patrick Larkey. 1986. *The Search for Government Efficiency*. New York: Random House.

Dubin, Robert. 1978. *Theory Building*, rev. ed. New York: Free Press.

Eddy, William B. 1981. *Public Organization Behavior and Development*. Cambridge, MA: Winthrop.

Esman, Milton J. 1991. *Management Dimensions of Development: Perspectives and Strategies*. West Hartford, CT: Kumarian Press.

Fiedler, Fred E. and Martin M. Chemers. 1974. *Leadership and Effective Management*. Glenview, IL: Scott, Foresman.

Frederickson, H. George. 1990. Public Administration and Social Equity. *Public Administration Review*, 50, 2 (March-April).

____. 1980. *New Public Administration*. University: University of Alabama Press.

Frost, Peter J., L. F. Moore, M. R. Louis, C. C. Lundberg, and J. Martin. 1985. *Organizational Culture*. Beverly Hills, CA: Sage.

Fry, Brian R. 1989. *Mastering Public Administration: From Max Weber to Dwight Waldo*. Chatham, NJ: Chatham House.

Gardner, John W. 1989. *On Leadership*. New York: Free Press.

Gellhorn, Ernest and Ronald M. Levin. 1990. *Administrative Law and Process*, 3rd ed. St. Paul, MN: West Publishing.

Gerth, H. H. and C. Wright Mills. 1946. *From Max Weber: Essays in Sociology*. New York: Oxford University Press.

Gladden, E. N. 1972. *A History of Public Administration*, vol. II. London: Frank Cass.

Golembiewski, Robert T. 1990. The Boom in the Decline Literature. *Public Administration Review*, 50, 1 (January-February).

____. 1990. *Ironies in Organizational Development*. New Brunswick, NJ: Transaction Publishers.

Goodsell, Charles T. 1983. *The Case for Bureaucracy*. 3rd ed. Chatham, NJ: Chatham House.

Gortner, Harold, J. Mahler, and J. B. Nicholson. 1987. *Organization Theory: A Public Perspective*. Chicago, IL: Dorsey Press.

Greiner, John M., Harry Hatry, Margo Koss, Annie Millar, and Jane Woodward. 1981. *Productivity and Motivation*. Washington, DC: Urban Institute Press.

Gulick, Luther. 1937. Notes on the Theory of Organization. In *Papers on the Science of Administration*, edited by L. Gulick and L. Urwick. New York: Institute of Public Administration.

Gvishiani, D. 1972. *Organization and Management*. Moscow: Progress Publishers.

Harmon, Michael M. 1981. *Action Theory for Public Administration*. New York: Longman.

Harmon, Michael M. and Richard T. Mayer. 1986. *Organization Theory for Public Administration*. Boston, MA: Little, Brown.

Harris, Philip R. and Robert T. Moran. 1987. *Managing Cultural Differences*. Houston, TX: Gulf Publishing.

Hatry, Harry and John Greiner. 1984. *How Can Police Departments Better Apply Management-by-Objectives and Quality Circle Programs?* Washington, DC: Urban Institute.

Heady, Ferrel. 1996. *Public Administration: A Comparative Perspective*, 5th ed. New York: Marcel Dekker.

Heffron, Florence and Neil McFeeley. 1983. *The Administrative Regulatory Process*. New York: Longman.

Hofstede, Geert. 1993. Cultural Constraints in Management Theories. *Academy of Management Executive*, 7, 1.

Hunt, James G. and Lars L. Larson, eds. 1974. *Contingency Approaches to Leadership*. Carbondale: Southern Illinois University Press.

Huse, Edgar F. 1975. *Organization Development and Change*. New York: West Publishing.

Johansen, Bruce E. 1990. Native American Societies and the Evolution of Democracy in America, 1600–1800. *Ethnohistory*, 37, 3 (Summer).

Jreisat, Jamil E. 1992. *Managing Public Organizations: A Developmental Perspective on Theory and Practice*. New York: Paragon House.

____. 1991. Bureaucratization of the Arab World. In *Handbook of Comparative and Development Public Administration*, edited by A. Farazmand. New York: Marcel Dekker.

____. 1991. The Organizational Perspective in Comparative and Development Administration. In *Handbook of Comparative and Development Public Administration*, edited by A. Farazmand. New York: Marcel Dekker.

____. 1990. Productivity Measurement and Finance Officers in Florida. *Public Productivity and Management Review*, 13, 4 (September).

____. 1975. Synthesis and Relevance in Comparative Public Administration. *Public Administration Review*, 35, 6 (November-December).

Kaplan, Abraham. 1964. *The Conduct of Inquiry*. San Francisco, CA: Chandler.

Katz, Daniel and Robert Kahn. 1982. *The Social Psychology of Organizations*, 3rd ed. New York: John Wiley.

Kaufman, Herbert. 1976. *Are Government Organizations Immortal?* Washington, DC: Brookings Institution.

Kellerman, Barbara. 1984. *Leadership: Multidisciplinary Perspectives*. Englewood Cliffs, NJ: Prentice-Hall.

Kennedy, Paul. 1987. *The Rise and Fall of the Great Powers*. New York: Random House.

Kouzes, James M. and Barry Z. Posner. 1990. *The Leadership Challenge*. San Francisco, CA: Jossey-Bass.

Kravchuck, Robert and Ronald Schack. 1996. Designing Effective Performance-Measurement Systems Under the Government Performance and Results Act of 1993. *Public Administration Review*, 56, 4 (July-August).

Lee, Robert D., Jr. and Ronald W. Johnson. 1983. *Public Budgeting System*, 3rd ed. Baltimore, MD: University Park Press.

Likert, Rensis. 1981. System 4: A Resource for Improving Public Administration. *Public Administration Review*, 41, 6 (November-December).

____. 1961. *New Patterns of Management*. New York: McGraw-Hill.

Lindblom, Charles E. 1980. *The Policymaking Process*, 2d ed. Englewood Cliffs, NJ: Prentice-Hall.

____. 1959. The Science of "Muddling Through." *Public Administration Review*, 19 (Spring).

Lipsky, Michael. 1980. *Street-Level Bureaucracy*. New York: Russell Sage Foundation.

Locke, Edwin and Gary Latham. 1984. *Goal Setting: A Motivational Technique that Works*. Englewood Cliffs, NJ: Prentice-Hall.

Lynn, Laurence E. 1987. *Managing Public Policy*. Boston, MA: Little, Brown.

March, James G. and Herbert A. Simon. 1958. *Organizations*. New York: John Wiley.

Marini, Frank, ed. 1971. *Toward a New Public Administration: The Minnowbrook Perspective*. Scranton, PA: Chandler Publishing.

Mayer, Lawrence C. 1972. *Comparative Political Inquiry*. Homewood, IL: Dorsey Press.

McGregor, Douglas. 1960. *The Human Side of Enterprise*. New York: McGraw-Hill.

Merton, Robert K. 1968. *Social Theory of Social Structure*. New York: Free Press.

Meyer, Alan. 1981. How Ideologies Supplant Formal Structures and Shape Responses of Environments. *Journal of Management Studies*, 19.

Moe, Ronald C. 1994. The "Reinventing Government" Exercise: Misinterpreting the Problem, Misjudging the Consequences. *Public Administration Review*, 54, 2 (March-April).

Moore, Larry, Gary Johns, and Craig Pinder. 1980. Toward Middle Range Theory. In *Middle Range Theory and Study of Organizations*, edited by C. Pinder and L. Moore. Boston, MA: Martinus Nijhoff Publishing.

Morgan, Gareth. 1986. *Images of Organization*. Beverly Hills, CA: Sage.

Mosher, Frederick C. 1968. *Democracy and Public Service*. New York: Oxford University Press.

Mosher, Frederick C., ed. 1981. *Basic Literature of American Public Administration (1787–1950)*. New York: Holmes & Meier.

____. 1975. *American Public Administration: Past, Present, Future*. University: University of Alabama Press.

Nanus, Burt. 1989. *The Leader's Edge*. Chicago, IL: Contemporary Books.

Nath, Raghu, ed. 1988. *Comparative Management*. New York: Ballinger.

Nathan, Richard P. 1995. Reinventing Government: What Does It Mean? *Public Administration Review*, 55, 2 (March-April).

Neumann, Francis, Jr. 1996. What Makes Public Administration a Science, Or, Are Its "Big Questions" Really Big? *Public Administration Review*, 56, 5 (September-October).

Nigro, Felix A. and Lloyd G. Nigro. 1980. *Modern Public Administration*, 5th ed. New York: Harper & Row.

Novick, David, ed. 1965. *Program Budgeting*. Cambridge, MA: Harvard University Press.

O'Brien, Sharon. 1989. *American Indian Tribal Governments*. Norman: University of Oklahoma Press.

Osborne, David and Ted Gaebler. 1992. *Reinventing Government: How the Entrepreneurial Spirit Is Transforming the Public Sector from Schoolhouse to State House, City Hall to Pentagon*. Reading, MA: Addison-Wesley.

Ostrom, Vincent. 1973. *The Intellectual Crisis in American Public Administration*. University: University of Alabama Press.

Ouchi, William G. 1981. *Theory Z: How American Business Can Meet the Japanese Challenge*. Reading, MA: Addison-Wesley.

Ouchi, William G. and Alan L. Wilkins. 1985. Organizational Culture. *Annual Review of Sociology*, 11.

Perrow, Charles. 1979. *Complex Organizations: A Critical Essay*, 2d ed. Glenview, IL: Scott, Foresman.

Peters, Thomas J. and R. H. Waterman. 1982. *In Search of Excellence*. New York: Harper & Row.

Peters, Tom. 1995. *Thriving on Chaos*. New York: Wings Books.

Rago, William V. 1996. Struggle in Transformation: A Study in TQM, Leadership, and Organizational Culture in a Government Agency. *Public Administration Review*, 56, 3 (May-June).

Rainey, Hal G. 1991. *Understanding and Managing Public Organizations*. San Francisco, CA: Jossey-Bass.

Redford, Emmette S., David Truman, Andrew Hacker, Alan Westin, and Robert Wood. 1968. *Politics and Government in the United States*, 2d ed. New York: Harcourt, Brace.

Reed, Michael. 1996. Organizational Theorizing: A History Contested Terrain. In *Handbook of Organization Studies*, edited by Stewart Clegg, Cynthia Hardy, and Walter Nord. Thousand Oaks, CA: Sage.

Riggs, Fred W. 1991. Public Administration: A Comparativist Framework. *Public Administration Review*, 51, 6 (November-December).

____. 1964. *Administration in Developing Countries*. Boston, MA: Houghton Mifflin.

____. 1961. *The Ecology of Public Administration*. New York: Asia Publishing House.

Ripley, Randall B. and Grace A. Franklin. 1984. *Congress, the Bureaucracy, and Public Policy*, 3rd ed. Homewood, IL: Dorsey Press.

Robbins, Stephen P. 1990. *Organization Theory: Structure, Design, and Applications*, 3rd ed. Englewood Cliffs, NJ: Prentice-Hall.

____. 1981. *The Administrative Process*. Englewood Cliffs, NJ: Prentice-Hall.

Rohr, John A. 1986. *To Run a Constitution: The Legitimacy of the Administrative State*. Lawrence: University Press of Kansas.

Rosenbloom, David H. 1986. *Public Administration: Understanding Management, Politics, and Law in the Public Sector.* New York: Random House.

____. 1983. Public Administration Theory and the Separation of Powers. *Public Administration Review*, 43 (May-June).

Rourke, Francis E. 1984. *Bureaucracy, Politics, and Public Policy*, 3rd ed. Boston, MA: Little, Brown.

Savara, James H. 1995. Dichotomy and Duality: Reconceptualizing Relationship between Policy and Administration. In *Ideal & Practice in Council-Manager Government*, edited by H. G. Frederickson. Washington, DC: International City Managers Association.

Schachter, Hindy L. 1995. Reinventing Government or Reinventing Ourselves: Two Models for Improving Government Performance. *Public Administration Review*, 55, 6 (November-December).

Schachter, Hindy Lauer. 1989. *Frederick Taylor and the Public Administration Community: A Reevaluation.* Albany: State University of New York Press.

Schein, Edgar H. 1985. *Organizational Culture and Leadership.* San Francisco, CA: Jossey-Bass.

Schick, Allen. 1990. Budgeting for Results: Recent Developments in Five Industrialized Countries. *Public Administration Review*, 50, 1 (January-February).

Schneider, Benjamin, ed. 1990. *Organizational Climate and Culture.* San Francisco, CA: Jossey-Bass.

Scott, William G., T. R. Michell, and P. H. Birnbaum. 1981. *Organization Theory*, 4th ed. Homewood, IL: Richard D. Irwin.

Selznick, Philip. 1957. *Leadership and Administration.* New York: Harper & Row.

Sherwood, Frank P. 1990. The Half-Century's "Great Books" in Public Administration. *Public Administration Review*, 50, 2 (March-April).

Simon, Herbert A. 1979. *Models of Thought.* New Haven, CT: Yale University Press.

____. 1961. *Administrative Behavior*, 2d ed. New York: Macmillan.

____. 1960. *The New Science of Management Decision.* New York: Harper & Row.

Sims, Henry P., Jr. and Peter Lorenzi. 1992. *The New Leadership Paradigm.* Newbury Park, CA: Sage.

Smircich, Linda. 1983. Concepts of Culture and Organizational Analysis. *Administrative Science Quarterly*, 28 (September).

Smith, Michael P. 1984. Barriers to Organizational Democracy in Public Administration. In *Critical Studies in Organization and Bureaucracy*, edited by F. Rischer and C. Sirianni. Philadelphia, PA: Temple University Press.

Stahl, Michael J. and David W. Grigsby. 1992. *Strategic Management for Decision Making.* Boston, MA: PWS-Kent.

Stahl, O. Glenn. 1983. *Public Personnel Administration*, 8th ed. New York: Harper & Row.

Stillman, Richard J. II. 1996. *The American Bureaucracy*, 2d ed. Chicago, IL: Nelson-Hall.

____. 1990. The Peculiar "Stateless" Origins of American Public Administration and the Consequences of Government Today. *Public Administration Review*, 50, 2 (March-April).

Stogdill, R. M. 1948. Personal Factors Associated with Leadership: A Survey of the Literature. *Journal of Psychology*, 25.

Stone, Alice B. and Donald C. Stone. 1975. Early Development of Education in Public Administration. In *American Public Administration: Past, Present, Future*, edited by Frederick C. Mosher. University: University of Alabama Press.

Stupak, Ronald J. and Jerry E. Moore. 1987. The Practice of Managing Organization Development in Public Sector Organizations. *International Journal of Public Administration*, 10, 2.

Swiss, James E. 1992. Adapting Total Quality Management (TQM) to Government. *Public Administration Review*, 52, 4 (July-August).

Szilagyi, A. D., Jr. and M. J. Wallace, Jr. 1983. *Organizational Behavior and Performance*, 3rd ed. Glenview, IL.: Scott, Foresman.

Thayer, Frederick C. 1981. *An End to Hierarchy and Competition*, 2d ed. New York: New Viewpoints.

Tichy, N. M. and M. A. Devanna. 1986. *The Transformational Leader*. New York: Wiley and Sons.

Van Riper, Paul P. 1987. The American Administrative State: Wilson and the Founders. In *A Centennial History of the American Administrative State*, edited by R. C. Chandler. New York: Free Press.

Waldo, Dwight. 1980. *The Enterprise of Public Administration*. Novato, CA: Chandler and Sharp.

____. 1948. *The Administrative State*. New York: Ronald Press.

Walker, Wallace E. 1986. *Changing Organizational Culture*. Knoxville: University of Tennessee Press.

Walters, Jonathan. 1996. Management Fad Mad. *Governing*, 9 (September).

Wamsley, Gary and M. N. Zald. 1973. The Political Economy of Public Organizations. *Public Administration Review*, (January-February).

Warwick, Donald P. 1975. *A Theory of Public Bureaucracy*. Cambridge, MA: Harvard University Press.

Wesberry, James, Jr. 1990. Government Accounting and Financial Management in Latin American Countries. In *Government Financial Management: Issues and Country Studies*, edited by A. Premchand. Washington, DC: International Monetary Fund.

Wilson, James Q. 1989. *Bureaucracy*. New York: Basic Books.

Wilson, Woodrow. 1887. The Study of Administration. *Political Science Quarterly*, 2, 1 (June). Reproduced in Jay M. Shafritz and Albert C. Hyde, eds. 1992. *Classics of Public Administration*, 3rd ed. Pacific Grove, CA: Brooks/Cole.

Woll, Peter. 1977. *American Bureaucracy*, 2d ed. New York: W. W. Norton.

Wren, Daniel A. 1979. *The Evolution of Management Thought*, 2d ed. New York: Wiley.

Yukl, Gary A. 1989. *Leadership in Organizations*. Englewood Cliffs, NJ: Prentice-Hall.

Zaleznick, Abraham. 1989. *The Managerial Mystique: Restoring Leadership in Business*. New York: Harper & Row.

Index

ABOUT THE AUTHOR

Jamil E. Jreisat is Professor of Public Administration and Political Science at the University of South Florida. He is the author of several books, chapters, and articles in the area of public administration theory and practice, budgeting, and comparative/development administration.

ISBN 1-56720-121-0

9 781567 201215

90000>

HARDCOVER BAR CODE